second edition

LANGUAGE AND ITS STRUCTURE

some fundamental linguistic concepts

second edition

LANGUAGE AND ITS STRUCTURE

some fundamental linguistic concepts

RONALD W. LANGACKER

university of california at san diego

 harcourt brace jovanovich, inc.

new york   chicago   san francisco   atlanta

ISBN: 0-15-549192-X

Library of Congress Catalog Card Number: 73–2180

Printed in the United States of America

preface

I was naturally very pleased at the warm reception that was accorded the first edition of *Language and Its Structure*. In preparing the present edition, I have tried to make needed revisions without altering the basic character of the book. The most obvious change has been the addition of suggestions for study and discussion to accompany each chapter. These are not routine questions to test reading and comprehension of the text—any instructor can devise questions to serve that purpose. Instead, they are intended to stimulate original thought on the part of the student, to suggest readings and research projects to complement the subject matter of the book, and to provide illustrative language data for analysis. Most of the textual alterations have been relatively minor. However, Chapter Five has been almost completely rewritten, and substantial changes have been made in Chapters Two and Nine.

Part One is introductory. Chapter One points out the reasons why language is worthy of study and concludes with a thumbnail history of language study. Chapter Two, which touches on a number of different topics, lays the groundwork for the more detailed discussion of language structure in Part Two. Chapter Three deals with dialect geography, social attitudes toward language, and writing.

Part Two is a non-historical examination of language structure. Lexical items are discussed in Chapter Four, as well as the ways in which the components of a language are organized to pair meanings and sound sequences. Chapters Five and Six are devoted to syntax and phonology respectively, emphasizing the English language in the interest of clarity and coherence.

Part Three concerns the relationships between linguistic systems. In Chapter Seven, the historical relationships between earlier and later stages of a single language are discussed. Chapter Eight treats genetic relationships, while Chapter Nine examines the sense in which all languages can be said to be related, namely in their surprisingly extensive structural similarities.

The various people who have contributed to this book in one way or another are by now too numerous to mention individually. Let me thank them collectively for their information, criticism, advice, corrections, typing, editing, indexing, and encouragement.

R. W. L.

contents

PART

basic concepts

CHAPTER 1 by way of introduction

the importance of understanding language

Language is everywhere. It permeates our thoughts, mediates our relations with others, and even creeps into our dreams. Most human knowledge and culture is stored and transmitted in language, which is so ubiquitous that we take it for granted. Without it, however, society as we now know it would be impossible.

Despite its undeniable importance in human affairs, language is poorly understood. Misconceptions about it are legion, even among well-educated people, and not even professional linguists can claim to understand it fully. It is a radical mistake to assume that the nature of language is self-evident or that we know all about a language just because we speak it. Gradually, however, linguists and other scholars are gaining a better understanding of this remarkable instrument of human communication. The purpose of this book is to summarize a significant portion of what is known about language for the benefit of those with little or no previous training in linguistics.

An accurate appreciation of language is worth acquiring for several reasons. *First,* many serious problems in today's world involve language in an essential way. To what extent are language differences barriers to understanding? Is a universal language feasible or desirable? Should a massive reform of English spelling be undertaken? How should children be taught to read? Should the writers of dictionaries bow to popular usage? Is it worthwhile for the government of a multilingual nation (like India) to try to impose one language on all speakers as an official national language? If so, which one? At what level should foreign languages be taught in our schools? To what extent are the members of minority groups and the lower classes handicapped in their social and economic advancement by their speech? It is not our concern here to provide answers to these very difficult questions, but anyone interested in finding valid answers to them should not set out without at least a minimal understanding of language.

Second, insights about language are of immense intellectual significance, with direct and indirect relevance to other disciplines. Philosophers, for example, are greatly concerned with language. It is important for our view of man that we know whether language is entirely learned or largely innate. Language, in other words, could be one of the grounds on which to settle a long-standing debate between rationalists and empiricists. The rationalist claim is that people are born with innate ideas, that much of an individual's psychological organization is "wired in" and genetically transmitted. Empiricists, on the other hand, claim that a person is born as a blank slate, psychologically speaking, and that psychological organization is determined almost entirely by experience, not by genetic inheritance. Both rationalists and empiricists have turned to language to find support for their views on this important question, which we will examine in more detail in Chapter Nine. Philosophers are also concerned with language as an instrument of philosophical analysis. Are human languages viable as the media of philosophical inquiry and theory? Can philosophical errors be attributed to the misuse of language? What is the relationship between language and logic?

Language is also relevant to psychology in a number of ways. In fact, since language is largely a mental phenomenon, its study may be considered a branch of psychology. Any adequate theory of human psychology must give some account of thought processes; language is of central importance here because so many of our thoughts assume linguistic form. The relationship between language and concept formation is of great interest to psychologists, since many, if not most, of our concepts are given verbal labels of some sort. Language also provides a significant test for theories of psychological organization. Languages are highly structured, and we have learned to identify and describe their structures in considerable detail; any theory of psychological organization, therefore, must adequately accommodate the kinds of structures we know to be characteristic of human languages.

The concepts and techniques of linguistic analysis have also influenced the other social sciences to some degree, anthropology in particular. Since language is more obviously structured than other facets of human psychology, such as systems of belief or networks of social organization, social scientists interested in these other domains may learn something of value from the analysis of language.

Third, an introduction to the nature of language is important to anyone interested in the practical applications deriving from linguistic research. Fundamental insights about language should certainly prove valuable to anyone studying or teaching a language (even the native language of the student or teacher). Accurate machine translation, if it can be accomplished at all (and this appears quite doubtful at present), can hardly be programed without a reasonably sophisticated knowledge of language on the part of the programer. Anthropologists must know the language of a people for their investigation of its culture to be most fruitful. Missionary work in uncivilized areas requires a great deal of practical and theoretical knowledge about language; the language of the natives must be learned quickly and well, and considerable understanding is needed to devise and teach an adequate writing system for the native tongue.

Fourth and finally, an accurate appreciation of language is valuable if only because no one can be considered truly well educated if he remains ignorant about the instrument of so much of his instruction. Since language permeates virtually all human affairs and is central to so many of them, an appreciation of language can hardly be considered peripheral. An introduction to language really needs no other justification. Anyone who wishes to know and understand himself must come to understand in some measure the character of the linguistic system that plays such a fundamental role in his mental and social life. In short, language should be understood "because it is there."

linguistics

Linguistics is the study of human language. A linguist who becomes interested in a particular language attempts to take it apart to see how it works, just as a mechanic may, purely out of curiosity, take apart an unfamiliar motor. A mechanic who has taken a motor apart will probably put it back together again; since a linguist takes a language apart only figuratively, his subsequent task is not one of reassembly, but rather one of description. A linguistic description of some language is called a **grammar** of that language. A grammar, then, is a set of statements saying how a language works. It includes, for example, a description of the principles for combining words to form grammatical sentences.

The linguistic description of languages is often undertaken with no ultimate practical goal in mind. **Descriptive linguistics**, in other words, is akin to pure science. A physicist is likely to investigate some aspect of the physical world that interests him with no intention whatsoever of turning the results of his research to practical application; he investigates it because it intrigues him, because he wishes to contribute to human knowledge. Similarly, linguists are interested in one particular aspect of psychological reality, namely the psychological phenomenon we call language. The desire to know more about this phenomenon is ample justification for investigating it.

Descriptive linguistics involves the description of a language at one point in time. **Historical linguistics**, on the other hand, is the study of language history. Historical linguists study the changes that occur in a language through time (and all living languages change through time, however imperceptibly), seeking to reconstruct earlier stages of it where written records are not available and to determine precisely what changes have taken place in the course of its historical development. Other branches of linguistics include **anthropological linguistics**, the investigation of languages as part of the investigation of their associated cultures; **psycholinguistics**, the study of language acquisition and linguistic behavior, as well as the psychological mechanisms responsible for them; **sociolinguistics**, which is concerned with the functioning of language in society; **phonetics**, the analysis of speech sounds with respect to their articulation, acoustic properties, and perception; and **applied linguistics**, the attempt to put the insights resulting from linguistic research to practical uses, particularly in the area of language teaching.

a thumbnail history of language study

The study of language has a long history, although linguistics as we now know it has come into being mainly in the past century and a half. Man has probably wondered about language for as long as he has had it. Cultures reflect man's natural concern with language in many ways. In some cultures, knowing the real name of a person or spirit is believed to give the possessor of this knowledge a certain power over that person or spirit. In some Australian tribes, a word similar to the name of a person must be suppressed in favor of a substitute when that person dies. The language of religious rituals is quite commonly considered sacred; any change in the words themselves or even in their pronunciation is felt to threaten the efficacy of the ceremony.

Our own culture is no exception. The Old Testament contains explanations for the origin of language and its diversity: Adam was called upon to name every living creature, and linguistic diversification is related in the story of the Tower of Babel. More recently, many Roman Catholics opposed the decision to allow the Mass to be conducted in the vernacular rather than in Latin. Other modern forms of "word magic" are found in the world of marketing, where considerable emphasis is laid on finding a suitable name for a new product, and in the realm of standards of conduct, where a person with dark skin, long hair, or unpopular beliefs may be arrested for using a four-letter word.

A significant linguistic tradition developed in India long ago, but it was not known in the Western world until the nineteenth century. The religious hymns of the Hindus were composed in Sanskrit around 1200–800 B.C. Over the centuries, Sanskrit of course changed. Like religious leaders in other cultures, however, the Hindu priests believed that the efficacy of their religious practices could not be assured unless their renditions of the ritual hymns were completely faithful to the original with respect to both text and pronunciation. Hindu grammar consequently developed as an attempt to preserve the religious language in full detail. The classic work of this tradition, dated around 400 B.C., is attributed to a grammarian named Pāṇini. To this day, Pāṇini's grammar has not been surpassed as a concise and insightful description of Sanskrit. It has dominated Indian grammar throughout the centuries.

Western grammatical tradition can be traced to the ancient Greeks, who raised the question of whether there is something essential in the relation between a word and the thing to which it refers or whether the relation is an arbitrary one. For example, is there some way in which the word *fish* is specially (or uniquely) suited to the creatures we angle for with hook, line, and sinker, or is the fact that we call these creatures *fish* just an accident of linguistic history? To the Greeks we trace the notion that the elements of a language can be classified into "parts of speech," such as nouns, verbs, and conjunctions. We can also find in their work the idea of case.

The grammatical practice of the Romans was based squarely on that of the Greeks. Throughout the medieval period, Latin occupied a central position in the world of education and scholarship. When one studied grammar, one usually studied Latin grammar. Even in modern times, Latin grammar has often been used as a model for the description of other languages. As a result, there is an essentially unbroken grammatical tradition stretching from the twentieth century all the way back to ancient Greece. Children are still being taught about parts of speech.

Modern linguists have often tended to slight what they call **traditional grammar** and to underestimate the insights of medieval and early modern students of language. Traditional grammarians have been charged with confusing speech and writing, with slavishly copying the dogmas that previous grammarians have expounded, with trying to force all languages into the Latin mold, and with trying erroneously to equate language and logic. There is more than just a grain of truth in these accusations. Many of us can remember learning in school to conjugate English verbs according to a paradigmatic scheme suited to Latin but not to English:

I praise	*we praise*
you praise	*you praise*
he, she, it praises	*they praise*

There is no point in learning to parrot six present-tense verb forms for English *praise*, because there are actually only two:

I, you, we, they praise
he, she, it praises

To find out why a six-form display was adopted for English, one has only to look at Latin, where a six-form display is proper:

laudō	'I praise'	*laudāmus*	'we praise'
laudās	'you praise'	*laudātis*	'you praise'
laudat	'he, she, it praises'	*laudant*	'they praise'

Nevertheless, the insights of traditional grammar are deeper, and its contributions greater, than its critics tend to realize. It is much easier to make sweeping criticisms than to evaluate, with care and understanding, many centuries of work. As our theories of language structure become more sophisticated, we become more conscious of the fact that traditional grammarians were not so far off the track. There is indeed some close (though not fully understood) relation between language and logic. Linguistic elements do fall into classes, like nouns and verbs, although there are many more such classes than traditional grammarians realized. Linguists have come to the conclusion that all human languages are similarly designed, but many traditional grammarians anticipated them long ago by engaging in the investigation of **universal grammar**. Traditional grammar books are not really wrong, but they do share with all other attempts to describe languages, including the most advanced, the inevitable fault of being incomplete.

Our understanding of language took some long strides during the nineteenth century. Most importantly, scholars came to appreciate what it means for one language to be **related** to another. They established that most of the languages of Europe and northern India are related as members of a single language **family**, which is known as the Indo-European family. It has been claimed, and not without reason, that the discovery of the relationship and historical development of these languages is to be classed with the truly great products of human intelligence. These philological advances, it is interesting to note, can be attributed in part to the influence of the linguistic tradition of ancient India. Previously unknown in the West, this tradition came to the attention of philologists when they realized that Sanskrit was related to the major European languages. The analytic techniques that had long ago been applied in the description of Sanskrit have been a significant factor in the evolution of modern linguistics.

In addition to their view of linguistic relationship, the nineteenth-century philologists contributed other insights. They discovered that changes in the sound system of a language are regular, in a special sense we will examine later, and not idiosyncratic, as one might suspect. They recognized the extent and importance of the **borrowing** of linguistic traits from one language into another. The advances they made constituted a beginning, not a routine culmination of any antecedent tradition of historical linguistics. Their techniques are now being applied to language families around the world, and the avenues of research that they opened up are far from being exhausted. In Chapters Seven and Eight we will examine language change and relatedness more fully.

A language is a complicated system that changes slowly through the centuries. To understand the changes that occur in such a system, the linguist must first have some knowledge of the structure of the system at one or more points in time. Descriptive linguistics, then, is logically prior to historical linguistics, though it emerged as a distinct and self-conscious discipline only in the twentieth century.

For several decades, descriptive linguists laid the heaviest emphasis on the sound systems of languages, paying relatively little attention to meaning or to **syntax** (the principles for combining words to form grammatical sentences). There were several reasons for this emphasis. The preceding tradition of historical linguistics relied most heavily on the sound systems of languages; descriptive linguists inherited this tendency, along with the inclination to look for regularities in sound systems. At the same time, interest was growing in the description of the unknown and poorly known languages of the world, particularly the languages of the American Indians. In studying an unknown language, one of the first things a linguist has to do is master its sounds and devise a notation for transcribing utterances. In addition, the strong but unfortunate influence of behaviorism in psychology left its mark. The pseudoscientific doctrine that only overt, externally observable behavior is valid evidence in psychological investigation reinforced the tendency of linguists to concentrate on sound systems and to ignore the more abstract domains of meaning and syntax.

In recent years, linguists have recognized that meaning and syntax are crucial to an understanding of language. (Traditional grammarians recognized this centuries ago and in fact anticipated many modern "discoveries" in these areas.) They have also recognized that language is basically a psychological phenomenon, one that cannot be studied fruitfully just by observing linguistic behavior. The resulting approach to the investigation of language, a movement known as **generative grammar**, provides the basic orientation of this book. Generative grammar is very much in keeping with contemporary views on the philosophy of science and also, as we have just seen, with the ideas of traditional grammarians. It represents both a revolution in grammatical thinking and a reaffirmation of the validity of structural insights about language that have been accumulating for many centuries.

Our purpose here, however, is not to examine the intricacies of competing linguistic theories or to show how they differ. Rather than wander through theoretical disputes and terminological thickets, we will examine, simply and directly, what language is and how it is put together. Because we want to understand ourselves, it is important that we try to understand this psychological entity which permeates our mental and social life. To the extent that linguistics sheds some light on the nature and structure of language, it is a subject of interest to all of us.

suggestions for study and discussion

1. Examples are given in the text of "word magic," the attitude that words have intrinsic power beyond their basic communicative or expressive function.

Can you find other instances of word magic in our society, cases where the choice of words used to say something is considered more important than what is actually said?

2. For a detailed critique of the methods of traditional grammar and their relation to modern grammatical thinking, consult Palmer's short book *Grammar* (see the Selected Readings at the back of this book). The history of language study is described much more fully in Robins, *A Short History of Linguistics*, and in the other works cited in the section on the history of linguistics. The Selected Readings also cite works in linguistic subdisciplines (such as anthropological linguistics, psycholinguistics, sociolinguistics, and applied linguistics) that this book does not cover in detail.

3. After you have finished reading this book, examine a traditional grammar book, such as Alonzo Reed and Brainerd Kellogg, *Graded Lessons in English: An Elementary English Grammar* (New York: Clark & Maynard, 1887); R. W. Zandvoort, *A Handbook of English Grammar*, 3rd edition (Englewood Cliffs, N. J.: Prentice-Hall, 1966); Frederic M. Wheelock, *Latin: An Introductory Course Based on Ancient Authors*, 3rd edition (New York: Barnes & Noble, 1963); or J. E. Mansion, *French Reference Grammar for Schools and Colleges*, new edition (Boston: D. C. Heath and Co.). Compare and contrast its approach to grammar with that described in this book, particularly in Chapter Five. You might consider questions such as these: Are the objectives of the two approaches the same or comparable? What is the nature of their data? How do they compare with respect to explicitness and completeness of coverage? What, if any, is the counterpart in traditional grammars to the various kinds of syntactic rules discussed in Chapter Five? What do traditional grammars say about constituent structure? About underlying representations?

4. When you have completed this book, read a number of representative entries in any large dictionary of English. What kinds of linguistic information does the dictionary give? What principles does it follow for arranging the alternate meanings of lexical items so as to show their relationship to one another? To what extent does it take cognizance of the notion of the morpheme and the other lexical concepts discussed in Chapter Four? How does the syntactic and phonological information given in the dictionary entries compare to the linguistic notions of the syntactic and phonological representations of lexical items as discussed in Part Two?

5. In its strictest form, the doctrine of behaviorism would require that linguistic investigators confine their attention to the stimuli that impinge on the human organism and to the overt, externally observable linguistic responses the organism emits. In particular, any appeal to introspection or to the intuitive judgments of native speakers is proscribed. Are these limitations reasonable or necessary? How would scrupulous adherence to these restrictions affect the study of language? Do traditional grammars adhere to them? (These matters are discussed extensively in B. F. Skinner, *Verbal Behavior* [New York: Appleton-Century-Crofts, 1957], and in Noam Chomsky's review of Skinner's volume, reprinted in Fodor and Katz, *The Structure of Language*, pp. 547–78.)

CHAPTER 2 · an initial look at language

language acquisition

Children display an amazing ability to become fluent speakers of any language consistently spoken around them. Every normal human child who is not reared in virtual isolation from language use soon comes to speak one or more languages natively.

The child's acquisition of his native language is not known to be dependent on any special tutoring. Some parents may try to "reinforce" their child's verbal behavior with smiles or other rewards, or to bridge the gap between their mature linguistic competence and the child's incipient one by means of "baby talk." But there is no particular reason to believe that such activity bears on the child's ultimate success in becoming a native speaker of his parents' language; children can pick up a language just as well by playing with other children who happen to speak it as they can through the concentrated efforts of doting parents. Little is known about the specific environmental factors that make it possible for language acquisition to occur, but the primary ingredient would appear to be merely sufficient exposure to language use in a social context.

This capacity for acquiring language is remarkable for a number of reasons. It is remarkable first because of its uniformity throughout the human race. There simply are no cases of normal human children who, given the chance, fail to acquire a native language. By way of comparison, it is not at all unusual for a child to fail to master arithmetic, reading, swimming, or gymnastics despite a considerable amount of instruction. Language acquisition, in other words, is species uniform. It is also species specific. Many animals can communicate, and chimpanzees have even been taught to express rather complex thoughts by combining gestures or other visual symbols to form sentence-like messages. However, even the most elaborate nonhuman communication systems are strikingly rudimentary alongside the great intricacy and complexity of human language. The symbolic ability of the higher primates (or of whales and dolphins) may conceivably turn out to be much more extensive than we realize, but for the moment it seems reasonable to claim that no other species can acquire anything even distantly comparable to human language, although some animals can learn to solve problems, use tools, and so on. Language acquisition thus appears to be different in kind from acquisition of the other skills mentioned.

The process of acquiring language is further remarkable for its comparative speed and perfection. When we actually attempt to take a language apart to see how it works, we find that it is extraordinarily complex and that it involves highly abstract organizational principles. Yet, within the first few years of his life, every human child has succeeded in mastering at least one such system. Furthermore, the linguistic system that the child masters is for all practical purposes identical to the one employed by the people around him; the differences are very slight when measured against the magnitude of the accomplishment. If the child is regularly exposed to two languages, he will very probably learn both; moreover, he will by and large succeed in not confusing the two linguistic systems, which is a considerable achievement in itself.

It has often been observed that adults are not capable of learning a language in the natural, spontaneous way that children are. For the adult, learning a foreign language usually involves great effort and seldom results in perfect mastery of the new idiom. An American child of six who moves to Japan with his parents will be at home in Japanese fairly quickly; his parents, however, may have to depend on the child as an interpreter. The differences between language learning in the child and in the adult may have been exaggerated, but the onset of adolescence does seem to constitute some sort of dividing line in the ability to master a new linguistic system. For example, a person past adolescence is not likely to learn to speak a foreign language without a noticeable accent, however slight.

Some interesting questions are raised by the observation that every normal human child learns one or more languages unless he is reared in linguistic isolation. What constitutes normality in this context? What happens when a child is not exposed to language during his early years?

With regard to language acquisition, normality can be interpreted very broadly. In fact, language learning is possible despite severe physical or psychological deficiencies. Neither the inability to hear nor the inability to vocalize nor even mental retardation will necessarily prevent a child from mastering a linguistic system.

In the case of deaf children, some special training is of course required, since the deaf obviously cannot learn a language by hearing it. Nevertheless, deaf children can acquire a very good grasp of a language through various visual devices. Language learning is even possible when deafness is accompanied by blindness, as was shown most dramatically by the accomplishments of Helen Keller. Although deaf children can sometimes make significant progress toward normal pronunciation, particularly when deafness sets in some time after birth, it is chiefly in the domain of vocal articulation that they experience the greatest difficulty, as might be expected. However, vocal articulation is only one facet of linguistic competence, and the ability of totally deaf children to master meaning, grammar, and lexicon is remarkable indeed.

Children who are unable to use their vocal organs to produce speech sounds also can learn a language with no particular difficulty. They are able to understand language perfectly and can learn to communicate through writing as well as anyone else can. The acquisition of language is thus in no crucial way dependent on verbalization.

Native language acquisition is much less likely to be affected by mental retardation than is the acquisition of other intellectual skills. A child who is mentally deficient to the extent that he cannot be taught arithmetic can still acquire language. Only in the most severe cases, in the lower range of idiocy, is language completely absent. Here is another indication that language learning is different in kind, in some essential way, from the attainment of many other intellectual abilities.

Children can be quite inventive in regard to language. "Secret languages" like pig latin provide good illustrations of the linguistic flexibility and creativeness of children. According to specific principles of transposition, the speaker of pig latin transforms ordinary English utterances into sound sequences that prove quite baffling to the uninitiated listener: *Is-thay entence-say, or-fay example-ay, is-ay itten-wray in-ay ig-pay atin-lay*. Such languages, usually based on a standard language in a straightforward way, are not at all uncommon. Children can easily become fluent in such a language and, since adults are usually slower in these matters, can use it as a secret code to prevent adults from monitoring their conversations.

However, there is at present no evidence to suggest that children can invent a language from scratch, with no prior exposure to human speech. Direct evidence on this point is hard to obtain, for decency and child abuse laws prevent experimenters from isolating children from all language use during their formative years to see whether language would develop spontaneously. Occasionally children abandoned in the wilderness are raised by wolves or other animals as extra cubs, and in one reported instance two sisters were raised together in this fashion. In no instance had a feral child developed any kind of language when found, but it is difficult to evaluate the significance of these cases because of complicating factors such as possible deafness, mental retardation, and general ill health. The evidence is no more conclusive in cases of children raised in human society but in linguistic isolation (for instance, raised by a deaf-mute or shut off from the world except for feeding). When language has arisen in circumstances such as these, the linguistic isolation of the children involved has not been total, and their language has clearly been based on adult speech. Once a linguistically isolated child is discovered and brought into a normal environment, he may eventually achieve something approaching full language proficiency, provided he is found at an early enough age and is not deficient in hearing or intelligence. These facts suggest that exposure to language during a certain maturational period is a minimum requirement for language acquisition, but it is difficult to draw any more definite conclusions.

As we noted in Chapter One, the business of linguistics is to arrive at an understanding of language. Central to this concern is an understanding of the capacity for language acquisition, which we have seen to be noteworthy for a number of reasons. An adequate account of language acquisition is still very far from our grasp, but this goal provides a great deal of motivation for investigating the structure of languages. One reason why linguistics is worth doing, in other words, is that it can ultimately be expected to shed some light on the nature of this rather remarkable aspect of the psychological development of the human child.

on origin and species

We observed in the preceding section that language acquisition is species uniform and species specific. All human beings learn a language, but no other animals, not even the most intelligent ones, attain to anything comparable. These remarks deserve some amplification, since misconceptions related to this point are quite common.

The diversity of human language has led, through the ages, to many speculations about the source of this diversity and the factors that determine the variety of speech that will develop in a given locale among a given group of speakers. Racial, cultural, and even geographical-climatic differences have been invoked to "explain" linguistic differences. In regard to the notion that geographical or climatic factors may influence the form of language, let us simply say that no specific claims along these lines have ever been advanced that will withstand even minimal scrutiny. Racial and cultural determinants do not fare much better, but they warrant more careful discussion.

Language is a social phenomenon whose form is in large measure determined by biological factors. It is hardly controversial that man's anatomical and neuro-physiological structure constrains the nature of human language (as an obvious example, languages will not employ sounds that are physically impossible to articulate). To the extent that the form of language is biologically determined, therefore, it is reasonable to ask whether linguistic differences are in any way controlled by racial differences, but the answer appears to be negative. As we have noted, one of the central facts of language acquisition is its species uniformity—any human child is capable of becoming a native speaker of any human language. Which language a child learns depends entirely on his models, those from whom he learns to speak. Note, for instance, that children of American immigrants of all races and nationalities grow up speaking perfect American English. To be sure, racial and linguistic differences are often correlated, as witnessed by the distinctiveness of black American English, but the correlation must be attributed to social rather than biological factors. (Notice that the speech of many blacks is indistinguishable from that of the white population.) No more significance is to be attached to the special character of black English than, say, to the special character of the English spoken in New England. These race-correlated dialect differences are perpetuated because black children usually learn to talk from other blacks.

Just as there is no inherent relation between language and race, there is none between language and culture. The Athabaskan family of American Indian languages embraces speakers of several distinct cultures. Conversely, languages of two unrelated families, Keresan and Tanoan, are represented in the Rio Grande Pueblo culture. Such examples demonstrate that neither language nor culture dictates the form the other will assume. Nevertheless, language and culture are tightly intertwined. The most obvious example of this interdependence is literature, oral and written: principles of literary style, prosody, and so on that are developed in terms of one language cannot always find satisfactory equivalents in a second. Words designating concepts specific to a given culture are likely to present a serious translation problem. The adoption of a new language is often accompanied by the gradual adoption of a new culture. Language and culture are closely associated in practice, therefore, but there is no reason to believe that any particular type of linguistic structure is specially suited to any particular type of culture.

It has sometimes been maintained that primitive peoples speak primitive languages. In fact, however, there is no correlation between degree of cultural advancement and complexity of linguistic structure. The languages of primitive peoples can be every bit as complex and rich in expressive power as any European language. Anything that can be said in one language can be said in any other, though perhaps more clumsily. Claims that "primitive" languages have very small vocabularies, that they have no grammar, that most of their words are onomatopoetic, that they cannot express abstract ideas, and so on are just plain false. The Luiseño Indians have words for specific kinds of baskets but no generic, more abstract term (like our *basket*) that embraces all varieties. This does not mean that they are incapable of abstract thought or that their language is impoverished; it simply means that baskets are more important to them than to us, so that their linguistic categorization in this area of experience is more detailed than ours.

Just as there are no primitive languages, there are no "corrupt" languages. Languages change, but they do not decay. On no rational basis is it correct to lament that language X, at some distant point in the past, was a pure and perfect vehicle to express our thoughts but that it has declined steadily to its present state of decadence. This is so much puristic nonsense. The English of today and the English of a thousand years ago are very different; by the same token, however, the English of a thousand years ago was radically different from its antecedent of a still earlier period. At any stage, a language is fully adequate to its purpose. It is the product of change and, if it continues to be spoken, will continue to undergo changes. The idea of a "pure" language is illusory.

The question of how language arose in the human species has intrigued scholars for centuries, but we really know nothing about the origin of language. As far back as we can trace any language historically, it looks like the same kind of entity as any contemporary language. The languages of two or three thousand years ago do not seem to be any simpler or any more primitive than the languages of today, or any different in kind. There must have been a time in the history of mankind when language was not fully developed, when men used some primitive forerunner of the complex linguistic systems used today. From all indications, however, this time must be so far in the past that we cannot hope to find any record of these earlier stages. With respect to the origin of human language, it is quite possible that we will always be limited to speculation.

The only thing we can presently say with any assurance about the origin and development of language is that it involved major evolutionary changes in man's neuro-psychological structure. Theories which do not posit neural evolution as a significant factor are clearly inadequate in important respects. Some people have speculated that language stems from primitive man's imitation of animal cries. Others have suggested that instinctive cries of pain or emotion, or the grunts and rhythmic chants that accompany great physical exertion, were the original source of speech. But such vocalizations are so untypical of human language that it is hard to see why they should be postulated as the source of all language. A more fundamental inadequacy of these theories is that they misconstrue the nature of the problem. They presuppose that what needs explaining is how primitive man was first induced to vocalize. The real problem, however, is to explain how language in all its present complexity and abstractness could ever develop from the very modest beginnings it must have had. Without positing neural evolution as a major factor, there is no apparent way to explain how the intricate and highly complex grammatical and phonological systems of human language could have arisen in accordance with reasonable psychological principles. Man must have acquired language as the result of evolutionary changes in the structure of his mind. It was not a matter of someone "getting the idea" and the others "catching on," which is almost equivalent to the notion that a group of primitive men sat down around a conference table and voted to invent language.

We learn nothing conclusive about the origin of language by examining the various ways in which animals communicate. Some animal communication takes place via fixed systems of signals, but this similarity to human language is such a vague and general one that it can hardly be taken as indicating any special relationship to language. Indeed, the organization of natural animal communication systems is radically different from that of human language.

Systems of animal communication reflect one of two basic organizational schemes. Under one scheme, signals vary continuously along one or a small number of dimensions. For instance, some scholars believe that bees are able to communicate fairly precisely the location of a food source by means of a dance done in the hive. The distance of the source from the hive is indicated by the frequency with which the dancing bee makes turns: the greater the distance, the less frequent the turns. The direction of the source, with respect to the position of the sun, is indicated by the angle of the straight portion of the bee's dance. Bees can therefore transmit an unlimited number of messages. However, they are unlimited in a rather trivial sense, for every message is a variant of the single message schema "There is nectar at distance X from here in direction Y." Human language has aspects similar to this, but they are rather peripheral. A parallel case would be the spectrum of our verbal responses to pain. According to the intensity of the pain, the response varies along a continuum from a mild "Ouch!" all the way up to an agonized scream.

In the second type of organizational scheme, the animal controls a small, finite number of discrete signals, each of which conveys a specific message. Higher primates, such as gibbons and chimpanzees, are credited with having such a system. One type of cry may indicate impending danger, another the desire for food, and so on, up to maybe a couple of dozen separate signals. With this type of scheme there is a strict numerical limitation on possible messages, a limitation that is lacking in human language. If you try to write down all the sentences of English, or of any other human language, you will quickly come to realize the futility of the task. You could go on writing forever without exhausting the supply of well-formed sentences, each of which has its own particular meaning.

Human language is thus crucially different from both varieties of animal communication. A human speaker controls an unlimited set of discrete signals; animal communication systems involve either a limited set of discrete signals or a continuum of nondiscrete signals. This difference alone would appear to be much more impressive than the sole similarity we have noted (namely that, like human language, some animal communication relies on fixed systems of signals), and it casts doubt on the notion that human and animal communication might be directly related. Recently it has been suggested that normal language change, together with the tremendous intellectual growth that has marked the evolution of the human species, is sufficient to explain the development of human language from a primitive communication system of the kind displayed by the other higher primates. However, no evidence has been adduced that such a development actually took place; nor has it been demonstrated that change and conceptual growth alone are sufficient to account for the great structural sophistication of language as we know it. For the time being, this view must be regarded as a conjecture whose validity and even plausibility has yet to be established.

We may observe a number of other differences between language and natural systems of animal communication. One of these is the vastly greater structural complexity of the signals of a human language. A bee's dance or a chimpanzee's cry has virtually no internal structure other than that involved in the actual physical production of the signal. Every sentence of a human language, however, displays structure on at least two other levels. First, it consists of a linear string of words, each of which has a more or less definite individual meaning and each of which consists of a sequence of sounds drawn from the small inventory of sounds used systematically in the language. Second, every sentence has a complex grammatical structure. (We will examine grammatical structures in Chapter Five.) There is no counterpart to either of these levels of structure in systems of animal communication.

Another difference is that learning is much more important as a factor in human language than in animal communication. Human languages have very much in common, but they differ from one another on many specific points. When a person learns German, he must learn at least all those details that distinguish German from Burmese and every other possible human language. Regardless of how much of human language is innate, the learning task is considerable. Just mastering the collection of words to be found in a small German dictionary is a sizable task. The communicative dance of bees, by way of contrast, must be innately specified virtually in its entirety, and there is nothing to suggest that the situation is radically different with respect to other systems of animal communication.

Finally, we may observe that animal communication systems are closed, whereas human languages are open-ended. As long as bees communicate, they will only be able to exchange variants of the same message —in what direction the nectar is and how far away. Apes cannot communicate freely about anything for which they do not have a specific signal, and even in these cases the possibilities are extremely restricted. People, on the other hand, can talk about anything they can observe or imagine. Moreover, what they can say on any given topic is almost unlimited. This greater flexibility stems in large part from the complex grammatical structure of human languages. Furthermore, new items are constantly being added to the lexicon of a language. Words and fixed phrases are continually being coined and borrowed from other languages to meet the changing communicative needs of speakers. There is no counterpart to this in natural animal communication.

Our conclusions regarding the relation between language and animal communication are not appreciably altered when we turn from natural animal communication systems to artificial systems devised by man. In recent years investigators have had noteworthy success in teaching chimpanzees to communicate with man in the visual medium, through sign language or with plastic symbols of different shapes and colors. They have found that chimpanzees can be trained to associate a large number of distinct concepts with different visual signs and to use these signs appropriately with fairly high reliability. Some of the concepts chimps have been taught to symbolize are highly abstract ones, such as 'if . . . then' and the notion of questioning. Moreover, they are able to string together a number of separate symbols to convey rather complex notions, such as 'You me go out hurry' or 'Sorry sorry please good out.'

These results are impressive and show that we must be careful not to underestimate the cognitive abilities of other species. However, they do not in themselves answer the question of how human language originated or call into serious doubt the claim that evolutionary changes in man's neuro-psychological structure must be posited. These visual communication systems of course have no analog of the phonological systems of human language. The syntactic abilities of apes have not yet been fully assessed, but they are certainly very rudimentary when compared to those of man. Nor is it known as yet whether apes can be made to use these systems to communicate spontaneously with one another, or whether such a system could be transmitted from one generation of apes to the next. Although it is important that we keep an open mind on such matters, there would seem to be no imminent danger that a chimpanzee will master English or Chinese and thereby destroy our illusion that man is unique.

sound and meaning

If the difference between language and natural animal communication systems had to be summarized in one word, a good choice for that word would be **novelty**.

Every time a bee communicates the location of a supply of nectar, it is repeating a variant of one basic message that has already been transmitted among bees countless times. When an animal gives a call warning others of its kind that danger is imminent, it does not make up a new one; the call is one that these animals have used many times before. There is no novelty here, only a repetition of past communicative events.

This is decidedly not the case with respect to human language. One outstanding characteristic of language use is its creativity, its freedom from control by the past linguistic activity of the user. A great many sentences that occur are novel ones and have never occurred before. (If you are not convinced of this, you might try to find in other books duplicates of every sentence on this page.) Of course, popular expressions and very short sentences are often repeated—for example, **Come in!** or **Supper is ready**—and we must also allow for instances of intentional quotation, but the point is still a valid one. A human speaker has the ability to create and understand an unlimited number of completely novel sentences. If a sentence duplicates one that has occurred previously, chances are that it was created anew the second time and the repetition was purely coincidental. Talking does not consist of parroting sentences that have been heard and memorized.

Our ability to create and understand novel sentences cannot be accounted for by any appeal to the human capacity for analogizing. Some people have maintained that novel sentences are constructed by analogy from sentences previously experienced. Suppose, for example, that someone has heard and remembered the sentences **Peter will help with the dishes, Peter will help with the laundry**, and **Barbara will help with the dishes**. By analogizing from these three, by solving the proportion, he creates the sentence **Barbara will help with the laundry**. The last sentence has never before occurred in his experience, but he is able to create it by analogy with the other three. This explanation of linguistic novelty is untenable. If only analogy were involved, there would be no way to account for our ability to distinguish between correct analogies, like the one cited above, and incorrect analogies, such as the derivation of the ungrammatical **Snow are white** from the previously experienced sentences **I like kittens, I like snow**, and **Kittens are white**. True and false analogies can be distinguished only by invoking a set of grammatical rules of the kind discussed in Chapter Five, but the postulation of such rules will itself account for linguistic creativity and hence render the analogy theory vacuous. We do not go around collecting sentences to hold in memory for future use in speaking and understanding. Nor do we have to search through our personal linguistic archives and carry out the steps of solving a proportion whenever we want to say something. We create and understand sentences quite spontaneously.

Equally inadequate to account for the novel character of our linguistic creations is the view that a language is a set of verbal habits. We will not attempt to document why this view is untenable; it is so deeply embedded in the tradition of behaviorist psychology that a careful exposition of the concepts involved would take us far beyond the scope of this book. Suffice it to say that no version of the stimulus–response model of psychological organization can even begin to account for the complex structure of human language (to be examined in Part Two) and that the mechanisms of conditioning and reinforcement by themselves are in principle inadequate to explain language acquisition.

By the time a child reaches the age of five or six, he has mastered the fundamentals of his native language. He has achieved the ability to create and understand, spontaneously and effortlessly, an unlimited number of sentences that are completely novel to his experience. If we wish to understand language and language acquisition (to the extent that we can at present), we must first have some idea about the nature of the competence that is acquired when someone learns to talk. Bearing linguistic creativity in mind, let us therefore address ourselves to this question: What sort of thing is a language?

To start out in very broad terms, we may say that a language is an instrument of communication. When person A has some idea he wishes to convey to person B, he performs certain physical actions with his articulatory organs (for example, his lips, tongue, and vocal cords). These actions create sound waves which travel through the air to B. B hears the sounds and, if all goes well, B gets the message. This characterization is basically valid, even though a language may sometimes be used without communicative intent. If A stubs his toe and lets fly a volley of profanity, for instance, his verbalization is probably quite devoid of any desire to communicate.

Any given attempt to communicate by way of a language is of course subject to partial or complete failure. Speaker A may try to get an idea across to B and simply fail. Perhaps B does not speak the language A is using. Perhaps B cannot hear the utterance clearly and mistakes one word for another. Perhaps A makes a slip of the tongue and says exactly the opposite of what he wants to say. For the most part, however, our communicative attempts are reasonably successful. The idea B gets is usually the idea A wants to convey. Although there are many possible sources of error, and despite the fact that communication is never perfect, we are usually successful enough with speech to continue using it without having to worry very much about its effectiveness.

When A wishes to convey an idea to B, the signal that A produces to do so is a sequence of sounds. B cannot observe A's idea directly; he can only observe the sounds A emits. From them, he somehow deduces what he believes A's thought to be. A and B use a language to communicate, but the language is neither the sounds passing through the air nor the thought they represent. The language is the device that allows A and B to pair the two. It is some set of principles that make it possible for A to translate the idea he wants to express into an overt signal and that enable

B to reconstruct this idea from that signal. A language is a device that establishes sound–meaning correlations, pairing meanings with signals to enable people to exchange ideas through observable sequences of sounds.

Take a concrete example. A is looking out the window and sees a strange sight. To let B in on what is going on, A utters the sentence *The cat just chased a dog up a tree!* B gets the message; he understands the sentence and is now in possession of information about the essential aspects of the situation that A is reporting. A has used English to translate this information into a sound sequence, and B has used English to deduce the same or comparable information from the sound sequence. English is a device which, among other things, establishes a correlation between the sound sequence *The cat just chased a dog up a tree!* and a meaning. Part Two of this book is devoted to a detailed examination of the internal structure of a language. For the moment we will limit ourselves to a few preliminary but important observations about this structure.

It is apparent that the sentence *The cat just chased a dog up a tree!* has meaning only because the individual words of the sentence have meanings. The meaning of a sentence is determined in some way by the meanings of the words from which it is constructed. It is of course not true that the meaning of a sentence is the simple sum of the meanings of the words it contains; *The cat just chased a dog up a tree!* and *The dog just chased a cat up a tree!* contain the same words, but their meanings differ. The relationship between the meaning of a sentence and the meanings of its parts is thus more abstract than a simple additive one. It will be examined more carefully in Chapter Four.

The relation between a word and its meaning is in general quite arbitrary; it is a matter of convention. There is no inherent reason why felines should be designated by the word *cat* instead of by some other word. That the word *cat* is used in this way by English speakers is merely an accident of linguistic history. In other languages, other strings of sounds are used to designate those furry creatures with sharp claws. Moreover, we would expect a similarly pronounced word in some other language to mean something else entirely. There is no mysterious sense in which a word and the concept with which it is paired are specially suited to each other. A language would function just as well if its word–concept pairings were entirely different.

As we look at various languages, we do in fact find that they differ from one another in their word–meaning pairings (except, of course, for words that are borrowed from one language into another and for cognate forms in related languages; these will be discussed in Part Three). Occasionally there are similarities. For example, the Aztec word *huel*, pronounced like the English adverb *well*, has a similar meaning. Such similarities, however, are sporadic and stand out clearly as exceptions to the general rule. Looking beyond this isolated case, we find, for instance, that the English and Aztec forms for something that is eaten are quite different; *food* and *tlaqual* are not at all similar. Conversely, similar forms normally differ in meaning. The English word *ma* means 'mother.' There happens to be a form *ma* in Aztec, but it means 'hand,' not 'mother.' The few similar pairings that do crop up can safely be attributed to chance.

It is a generally valid principle, therefore, that the relation between a word and its meaning is arbitrary. A word designates some concept, but there is no inherent connection between the two. That they are paired is an accident of linguistic history.

One must admit a number of partial exceptions to this generally valid principle. Their importance is hard to assess with any precision, but it is certainly not major. The principle requires only qualification, not drastic amendment.

Many words are clearly **onomatopoetic**, that is, imitative of non-linguistic sounds. For these words, of course, there is a special relationship between meaning and pronunciation. The English words *bow-wow* and *moo*, for example, resemble to some degree the sounds made by dogs and cows respectively. This is not an accident, for these words were most certainly coined with imitative intent, as were many other names for animal noises. *Meow* does sound something like the noise made by a cat; *baa* is a fair imitation of the sound of a sheep; and so on. Onomatopoetic forms are not limited to this semantic domain, although the imitative character of forms cited from other semantic domains is not always so obvious. In English, a bell goes *ding-dong*; a clock goes *tick-tock*; we speak of a metallic *clang*; a bomb explodes with a *boom*; and so forth.

It is interesting to observe that even imitative words such as these are to a large degree conventionalized. The corresponding imitative words are different in different languages, despite their similarity to one another and to the sound they designate. To take some classic examples, the crowing of a rooster is represented as *cock-a-doodle-doo* in English, as *kikeriki* in German, and as *coquerico* in French. The sound of whispering is imitated to a certain degree in English *whisper*, German *flüstern*, French *chuchoter*, and Spanish *susurar*, but these imitative attempts are somewhat different from one another; a speaker must learn the correct imitation for his language, and to this extent the forms are conventional. French sheep go *bê* instead of *baa*, and bells go *bim-bam* when they ring in German.

A second qualification of the principle is often proposed, the validity of which is much harder to assess. Words, generally speaking, have meaning, but the individual sounds that make them up do not. *Ma*, for instance, means something, but the vowel of *ma*, which is symbolized

[a], by itself means nothing. (Linguists use square brackets to enclose phonetic symbols designating sounds; they are to be distinguished from the representations of these sounds in ordinary spelling.) It is often maintained, however, that some sounds are associated with particular ideas or give certain impressions. For example, the vowel sound of *heat*, symbolized [i], is said to be connected with the notion of lightness, brightness, or lack of substance, at least when contrasted with [a]. The latter, in relative terms, tends to give the impression of size and power. These claims cannot be dismissed entirely, but it would be easy and tempting to overestimate their importance. We will examine two more examples but reserve final judgment.

The vowel sound of *hut*, symbolized [ʌ], often occurs in English words that denote concepts involving heaviness, dullness, or filth. Among others, we find: *dull, blunder, bungle, clumsy, tub, stub, slug, plug, rut, gutter, gull, gully, gullet, gullible, bug, jug, humdrum, dumb, humbug, slum, slush, muck, mud, muddle, mug, numb, numskull, slut, mumble, grumble, grunt, disgruntled, mumps, gummy, sullen, mull, bum, plumbing, stun, slumber, flunk, bump, lump, club, rubble, rumble, hulk, rump, pudgy, sulk, pump, clump, bulk, cudgel, thump, hump, bulge, junk.* It would be easy to add more. On the basis of this list, the sound [ʌ] seems to have negative connotations for English speakers.

The vowel sound of *hit*, symbolized [ɪ], often occurs in English words whose meanings involve rapid or repetitive motion, lack of intensity, or smallness: *flip, twitter, swish, flit, titter, giggle, limp, little, fiddle, rip, tip, flimsy, sip, pimple, dimple, zip, whip, slip, pin, flicker, strip, primp, fickle, tickle, nimble, nipple, film, thimble, lick, tingle, jingle, gimmick, tint, lint, hint, slit, twig, twinkle, twinge, twit, sizzle, skim, whim, kid, wrinkle, click, fizzle, fidget, filch, pilfer, ripple, cricket, crimp, crick, crinkle, frill, fringe, pinch, nibble, whisper.* It would not be entirely unreasonable, therefore, to argue that the sound [ɪ] gives the impression of rapidity or insignificance.

We should be careful not to overestimate the importance of this kind of **sound symbolism**. It is all too easy to abuse the concept and read symbolism into all sorts of cases where it is not operative. Sound symbolism is not imaginary, but neither is it very powerful; there are many exceptions to seeming correspondences between sounds and components of meaning. While [ʌ] is often associated in English with heaviness, dullness, or filth, *cut* and *sun* are hardly characterized by these notions. Conversely, neither *heavy* nor *filth* contains the vowel [ʌ]. In any event, sound symbolism merely qualifies the arbitrary character of word–meaning pairings and in no sense prevails over it. Given the negative connotations of the sound [ʌ], it is still an almost wholly arbitrary, unpredictable fact about

English that insects are designated by the word *bug*. The symbolism in no way renders nonarbitrary the choice of *bug* to designate them, out of the many possible words containing [ʌ].

Nursery words constitute another partial exception to the principle that the relation between a word and its meaning is arbitrary. Perhaps because of their ease of articulation, certain sounds are consistently among the first that a child learns to produce deliberately. These include the vowels [a] and [æ] (as in *bra* and *hat*) and consonants like [m n b d p t] (which are pronounced the way you think they are). It turns out that the words children use for 'father' and 'mother,' in languages all over the world, are very often composed of sounds drawn from this list. In English, for example, we have the words *mama, papa, mom, mommy, dada, daddy, dad, ma, pa,* and *pop*. Compare the words for 'father' in a number of other languages: Spanish *papá*, Russian *papa*, German **Papa**, Swahili *baba*, Turkish *baba*, Hungarian *apa*, Takelma *ma*, Aztec *ta*, and Diegueño *ntat*. (Takelma, Aztec, and Diegueño are three unrelated American Indian languages.) Forms designating the mother include French *maman*, Russian *mama*, Swahili *mama*, Turkish *ana*, Hungarian *anya*, Takelma *ni*, Aztec *nan*, Diegueño *ntal*, and Chinese *ma*. These similarities are not too surprising, since most of the sounds in these words are among those acquired early and since the child's parents are virtually the first entities he has occasion to name. Another contributing factor, no doubt, is the eagerness of the parents to recognize references to themselves in the child's vocalizations.

To summarize, a language can be viewed as an instrument of communication. It serves to establish sound–meaning correlations, so that messages can be sent by the exchange of overt acoustic signals. The meaning of a sentence is determined by the meanings of the words from which it is constructed, and the basis for the sound–meaning correlations established by a language is thus to be found in the relations between individual words and their meanings. The bond between a word and its meaning is for the most part arbitrary, or conventional, with only marginal qualifications.

linguistic subsystems

As speakers of a language, we are capable of stringing words together to form novel sentences that express our thoughts. In learning a language, then, one thing that we have to learn is a set of words, each of which pairs a meaning and a pronunciation. In addition, we must learn some set of principles that tell us how individual words may be combined to form sentences. For purposes of discussion, we can therefore isolate three aspects of linguistic structure; to describe a language, we have to talk about the meanings of words, about the sound sequences that are paired with these meanings, and about the ways in which words combine with one another to form sentences. Accordingly, we will speak of a language as involving a **semantic system**, a **phonological system**, and a **syntactic system**.

In speaking of the semantic system of a language, we are referring not only to the fact that the words of the language have meanings but also to the way in which they divide the range of our conceptual experience into categories. In English, for example, we make a linguistic distinction between the colors designated by the words *blue* and *green*. There is no psychological necessity to this distinction; in many languages, a single term covers the entire portion of the color spectrum that includes blue and green. In Hopi (an American Indian language), different words are used for water in its free states and water held in a container. There is no corresponding lexical distinction in English, since we use *water* for both. No two languages match exactly with respect to how experience is categorized.

Although the choice of a sound sequence to designate a given concept is essentially arbitrary, the sequence that is chosen must fall within certain limits imposed by the structure of the language. A language is characterized by a phonological system, and every native word of the language is represented by a sound sequence that meets the restrictions of this system. Compare someone speaking English with someone speaking, say, French. The auditory effect is very different; English and French just do not sound alike. They have different phonological systems, different sets of principles determining the pronunciation of sentences. Phonological systems will be discussed more fully in Chapter Six, so we will confine ourselves here to some general observations. At least three main facets of phonological structure can be discerned: inventories of sound types, effects of neighboring sounds on one another, and permissible sound sequences. The fact that languages invariably differ from one another in these three areas accounts in large part for their different auditory effects.

A language is characterized by an inventory of sound types, and every native word of the language is composed of a sequence of sounds drawn from this inventory. Among the sounds characteristic of English, we have already used [a æ i ɪ ʌ m n b d p t] in examples, and there are quite a few more. Other languages use other sounds. English has the sounds [č ǰ] (the initial sounds of *char* and *jar*), but French has neither; German has the sound [x] (the last sound of **Bach**), but neither English nor French has; and so on. Moreover, sounds that we would be inclined to call "the same" in two languages are not necessarily identical in phonetic detail. Both English and French have a [t] sound, but the two sounds differ noticeably in their phonetic properties, at least to a trained observer.

Neighboring sounds in an utterance tend to affect one another, in ways that differ somewhat from language to language. A sound may be pronounced in one way when uttered in isolation but in a slightly different way when placed in a given phonological environment. For instance, the [n] of *ten* is pronounced with the front part of the tongue touching the ridge just behind the upper teeth. However, if the *-th* suffix is added to *ten* to form the word *tenth*, the [n] sound is pronounced differently, with the tongue touching the teeth. This phonological alternation is not peculiar to the word *ten*. The same alternation can be observed by pronouncing *eleven* and *eleventh*, or by comparing the articulation of *ant* and *anthem*.

The phonological system of a language imposes restrictions on the combinations of sounds permitted in words. Taking English as an example, we find that some sound sequences are possible English forms and others are not. *Slim* is an English word. *Slin* is not an English word, but it could be. English words may begin with [slɪ] (*slim*); end with [m] (*tin*); have [m] after [l] (*lint*); or have [sl] before [ɪ] (*slit*). The fact that *slin* is not an English word is not due to any constraint on sound sequences imposed by the phonological system of English; it is just an accident of linguistic history. On the other hand, *slih* is not an English word and could not be one. No English word can end in [h], the initial sound of *hat*. (Here, of course, we are speaking of sounds, not of orthography. Many English words, for instance *English*, are spelled with a final *h*, but none ends with the sound [h].) No English word can begin with [tl]. No English word consists entirely of consonants, or has fourteen consecutive vowels, and so on. These constraints hold across the board for all English words. They specify a range of phonological possibilities within which any form must fall for it to be a word of our language. *Stug* is a possible English word that does not happen to occur; *bnug* could not occur as an English form.

Just as there are constraints on the ways in which sounds can be combined to form words, so there are constraints on the ways in which words can be combined to form sentences. Not every string of English words constitutes a grammatical English sentence. The string *Helen picked a flower yesterday* does, but the strings *Snow are white* and *Tree cat dog chased just a up a the* do not. As part of the process of learning a language, a person must master some set of principles that allow him to string words together to form acceptable sentences and to avoid forming unacceptable ones. The syntactic system, or syntax, of a language consists of these principles.

Consider the set of all English words in use today. This set contains many elements, many thousands of elements in fact, but it is clearly finite. An exhaustive list of them can be drawn up, as in an unabridged dictionary. It is true that new words are being added to the English lexicon all the time, with others falling into oblivion, and the compilers of dictionaries no doubt overlook some words. Nevertheless, the point remains valid. If one were to list all the words familiar to the members of a speech community, the list could in principle be finite and exhaustive. Things are quite different with regard to sentences. The number of sentences that would be considered perfectly acceptable by members of a speech community is astronomically large, and it is impossible in principle to list all the grammatical sentences of a language. A simple observation is enough to establish this: There is no sentence to which we can point and say, "Aha! This is the longest sentence of the language." Given any sentence of English (or any other language), it is easy to find a longer sentence, no matter how long the original is. If *S* is a declarative sentence of English, *I know that S* is also an English sentence. Therefore, since *Booze is expensive* is a grammatical sentence of English, so is *I know that booze is expensive*. Since the latter is, so is the still longer string *I know that I know that booze is expensive*. This entails that *I know that I know that I know that booze is expensive* is also a grammatical sentence. Obviously, we could continue without limit and construct a well-formed sentence of any desired length.

The example is a trivial one, but the point is not. The set of well-formed sentences of English is infinite, and the same is true of every other language. Just as there is no greatest number, so there is no longest sentence of a language. It is in principle impossible to list all the sentences of a language, just as it is in principle impossible to list all the natural numbers. When a person learns a language, he obtains some grasp of an infinite set of sentences. He cannot learn these sentences as a list; rather, he must master some finite set of principles in accordance with which words can be combined to form sentences. These principles are such that they allow for the construction of any one of an unbounded set of possible sentences. Some analogies may prove helpful to illustrate the point.

Learning to count involves mastering a small, finite set of principles. We can conceive of these principles as a set of instructions a person learns to carry out. They are such that he can give you the immediate successor of any positive integer you may present him with. Presented with the integer 3749, he can give back 3750. Starting from 1 and applying these principles, a person who has learned to count can continue to count indefinitely. From 1, he arrives at 2; from 2, he arrives at 3; and so on. At no point does he reach a number to which the instructions fail to assign an immediate successor. There is no upper bound beyond which the instructions fail to apply. Clearly, learning to count does not involve simply memorizing pairs of numbers, the second of which is the immediate successor of the first. For one thing, the burden placed on memory would be prohibitive. Moreover, a person who has learned to count can correctly give the successor of a number that he has never before encountered. If someone presents you with the number 459,768,312, you have no particular difficulty arriving at its successor, 459,768,313, and you do not do so by consulting your memory and asking yourself, "Let's see, what number was 459,768,312 paired with?"

Similarly, what a person does when he learns to multiply is master some finite set of principles that are applicable to an unbounded set of pairs of numbers and that yield the correct product for each pair. Once learned, these principles enable him to multiply any two numbers, even if he has never encountered either previously. By mastering a finite set of principles, or instructions, for multiplying, a person obtains a grasp of infinitely many sets of numbers x-y-z such that x times y equals z. In some sense, he "knows" that 13,479 times 231,641 equals 3,122,289,039; he has probably never reflected on this particular fact, but it is within his competence to discover or verify it should he have occasion to. His competence is finite (it must be, since a person has neither the time nor the mental capacity to learn an infinite list of instructions), but it projects to an infinity of cases.

In just this sense the fluent speaker of a language controls an unbounded set of grammatical sentences. He has mastered a finite set of principles specifying how words can be combined to form sentences, and these principles project to an infinite set of grammatical sentences of the language. Most of these sentences will never actually occur in his linguistic experience, yet they fall within the range of syntactic possibilities specified by the structural principles he has mastered. By mastering them, he has in effect learned the distinction between strings of words that constitute grammatical sentences and strings of words that do not. If English is the language he has mastered, he has learned the distinction between grammatical strings like **Snow is white** and **The cat just chased a dog up a tree** on the one hand, and on the other hand ungrammatical strings such as **Snow are white** and **Tree cat dog chased just a up a the**. The principles of sentence construction that he has internalized yield all of the former but fail to specify any of the latter. We will discuss syntactic systems more extensively in Chapter Five.

grammaticalness

A few words are perhaps in order about the notion "grammatical sentence," since this notion has played an important role in our discussion. The linguist's use of the grammatical-ungrammatical distinction has generated a great deal of animosity, most of it based on simple misunderstanding. Let us make clear from the start just what is meant.

It is the task of linguists to describe languages, but it is not their task or prerogative to prescribe. Linguists want to say what languages are like, but they have no right to say what languages should be like or to dictate how people should talk. It is sometimes charged that linguists are violating this canon and being prescriptive when they distinguish between grammatical and ungrammatical sentences. But this is not the intent. What is being claimed by the linguist, when he distinguishes between well-formed sentences and ill-formed ones, is that the speaker whose language is being described makes such a distinction himself. The linguist is simply describing in a straightforward way what he finds; he is not imposing a false dichotomy on anyone.

Any fluent speaker of English can recognize that the sentence **Helen picked a flower yesterday** is well formed in a sense in which **Flower Helen yesterday a picked** is not. He can recognize that **Bill and Patricia kissed** is structurally correct in a sense in which **Kissed Patricia Bill and** is not. He may never have occasion to reflect on these differences, but at the same time he could hardly fail to perceive them should they be called to his attention. There are infinitely many sentences that are clearly well formed in English, without any doubt. Likewise, there are infinitely many sentences that can be excluded, without any doubt, from the class of grammatical English sentences. Linguists claim nothing more. There may be cases that are not so clear, sentences about which a given speaker might have difficulty making up his mind. No one denies this, but it is not a crucial point. The syntactic principles of a language may well be blurred around the edges. However, this in no way casts doubt on the existence of a set of principles of sentence construction that a person masters when he learns a language—principles that specify certain sequences of words as being grammatical sentences of the language and exclude others. To abandon the distinction because of some borderline cases would be to distort our picture of language far more than it is distorted by the idealizing assumption that a decision can be made for every sentence.

"Why so much emphasis on sentences?" it is sometimes asked. "People do not always use full sentences. In many situations, the production of a full sentence would be very much out of place. A word or a short phrase is often all that is necessary or expected." Very true—and no one denies it, including linguists who distinguish between grammatical and ungrammatical sentences.

Conversations abound with exclamations—*Heavens!, Damn!, Hell!*—and fragments of sentences—*Hardly, Can he really?, Could be, But Marvin does, True.* They belong to a language just as much as full sentences do, and therefore would have to be described in any full linguistic description; no one proposes to leave them out. There are a number of reasons, however, for placing a great deal of emphasis on full sentences and comparatively little emphasis on shorter expressions.

Exclamations such as *Heavens!* and *Damn!* are to be found in all languages; every speaker has an inventory of them that he draws upon when he has occasion to. This inventory, unlike the inventory of sentences of a language, is clearly finite and can be listed exhaustively. These exclamations are used over and over again and are anything but novel. There is really nothing more to say about them, so far as the structure of the language is concerned; writing down an exhaustive list of standard exclamations is only a matter of patience.

Sentence fragments are just what the name implies. They can be recognized as elliptical versions of more complete sentences, though it is not always obvious what particular sentence a given fragment abbreviates. *Can he really?* is to be understood as *Can he really do that?, Can he really be so cruel?,* or whatever other sentence happens to be appropriate for the occasion. Behind *True* lurk fuller sentences such as *What you say is true.* In these observations we find the reason for placing primary emphasis on full sentences and only secondary emphasis on sentence fragments: Sentence fragments can be understood and described in terms of full sentences, but the opposite does not hold true. By describing full sentences, we are going a long way toward the description of sentence fragments. If, on the other hand, we were to focus all our attention on fragmentary expressions like *True* and *Could be,* we would learn little or nothing about the syntactic principles that account for full sentences and hence for linguistic creativity. (Note, by the way, that sentence fragments are not necessarily ungrammatical. Fragments can be either grammatical or ungrammatical, just as full sentences can. **Could be**, for instance, is a grammatical fragment, but **Be could** is not.)

People frequently make errors when they talk. They put words in the wrong places, talk themselves into syntactic corners from which no grammatical escape is possible, neglect to make the verb agree with the subject, and commit all sorts of other syntactic sins. Are we therefore justified in claiming that people can recognize the difference between well-formed and ill-formed sentences?

The answer is that we are. In saying that a person has mastered a set of principles for constructing sentences, we in no way imply that he cannot make mistakes in applying these principles. Similarly, the claim that a person is capable of multiplying 13,479 and 231,641 does not mean that he will necessarily come out with the right answer on a given attempt. People can make mistakes even in working problems they are competent to solve, and talking is no different from other kinds of problem-solving in this respect. If anything, there are more possible sources of error in speaking than in other domains. A person may commit an error in uttering a sentence because he is too tired to pay attention to what he is saying, because something distracts him in the middle of it, because he changes his mind about what he wants to say while he is saying it, because he attempts to perform a sentence so long that near the end he forgets how he began, and so on. That he controls the boundless class of grammatical sentences of his language does not mean that he will always employ this linguistic competence flawlessly in speaking or hearing.

This point is a very important one. It is essential to distinguish between the structure of a language and the way in which this structure is used. With respect to a speaker, we may refer to the distinction between his linguistic **competence** and his linguistic **performance**.

As we have noted, a language is a set of principles establishing correlations between meanings and sound sequences. These principles underlie and make possible communication by means of overt verbal behavior, but they cannot be equated with this behavior. A language is a set of principles that a speaker masters; it is not anything a speaker does.

In short, a language is a kind of code, but the code itself must be distinguished from the act of encoding or decoding. The same kind of distinction can be made between a symphony and the performance of it. No matter how poorly it is performed, the symphony remains unaffected. It is an abstract musical system that underlies the activity of musicians but cannot be equated with their activity. In the same sense, a linguistic system underlies the verbal activity of its speakers. A language is an abstract set of psychological principles that constitute a person's competence as a speaker. These principles make available to him an unbounded class of sentences that he can draw upon in concrete situations. They are a crucial ingredient of linguistic creativity.

It is this abstract linguistic system—the linguistic code—that linguists seek to describe. They are at most secondarily concerned with actual verbal behavior, which is only an indirect manifestation of the psychological principles that make human language unique. The structure of a language is not affected when its speakers make mistakes in talking, any more than a symphony is affected when it is poorly performed. A speaker possesses a set of principles that specify some sentences as being well formed and exclude others, but this does not mean that every string of words he utters will be grammatical. Linguists intend no such claim when they distinguish between grammatical and ungrammatical sentences.

There is a related point that requires comment because it is so often misunderstood. When linguists describe the structure of a language, in no sense are they describing what people do when they create or understand sentences. The grammar of a language is not a recipe that can be followed in diagnosing the communicative needs of the situation, deciding what has to be said, selecting a sentence to say it, and translating this sentence into speech. Nor is it a recipe for the hearer to follow when he monitors an utterance and figures out what is being said. It is a description of the principles that specify what strings of words are well-formed sentences of the language, a description of the intrinsic structure of the linguistic system. How this structure is translated into verbal behavior is another question entirely.

The grammatical description of a language is like the written score of a symphony in this respect. The notes of the score do not describe step by step the precise motions that the conductor makes with his arms, nor do they say what the violinist does with his fingers to produce the right sounds on his instrument. Rather, they symbolize the intrinsic structure of the musical work. What physical motions the members of the orchestra must carry out in order to manifest this work in observable form are far beyond the domain of the score. The grammar of a language is a symbolic representation of the abstract linguistic system in the same way that the musical score represents the abstract musical system. In describing the structure of a language, the linguist does not aim to say what physical and mental motions speakers of a language perform when they produce sentences. He attempts to characterize the abstract linguistic system that speakers draw upon when they talk and understand but does not attempt to give a step-by-step account of verbal behavior. In other words, he attempts to describe linguistic competence rather than linguistic performance.

It is not that linguistic performance is devoid of interest. On the contrary, the linguist would like very much to learn just what people do, step by step, when they speak and listen. The reason for his concern with linguistic competence is, quite simply, that a description of linguistic competence is logically prior to a description of linguistic performance. The principles that specify the well-formed sentences of a language constitute one essential component of the psychological apparatus involved in speaking and understanding; we draw upon these principles when we produce and comprehend sentences. Any adequate account of linguistic performance therefore presupposes an adequate account of the abstract linguistic system, but the opposite is not true. We must know what sort of thing a language is before we can hope to understand how the speaker and the hearer use it in practice.

language and thought

The fact that language can be used to express our thoughts gives rise to some interesting questions. How are language and thought related? Can we think without language? Is our thinking molded by the structure of our language? These are very difficult questions, questions that we cannot hope to answer definitively without a much better understanding of human psychological structure than we presently have. Conflicting opinions have been advanced. The following observations carry no guarantee that all linguists or psychologists would agree with them.

If we define thought as conscious mental activity, we can observe first that thought, or at least certain kinds of thought, can take place completely independently of language. The simplest example is that of music. We have all had the experience of being absorbed in listening to an instrumental work or mentally running through a familiar tune. Language is simply not involved. (The existence of music with lyrics is of course beside the point.) Musical composition is in no way dependent on language, so far as the actual process of creation is concerned, and the same would seem to be true of various other forms of creative or problem-solving activity. The sculptor at work is in no significant sense guided by language. He may, of course, receive much of his instruction through language, talk about his creations, and even entertain himself with an internal verbal soliloquy as he chips away with hammer and chisel. But such verbalization does not appear to be instrumental in his creative activity. There may be many stretches of time during which he is so busy conceptualizing forms and techniques that words disappear entirely from his thoughts. Much the same is true of a person engrossed in solving a jigsaw puzzle. Suddenly perceiving that two independently completed sections belong together is in no way a linguistic accomplishment, although one may subsequently exclaim, "Aha! This must go over here!" It is thus hard to understand why some people have maintained that thought without language is impossible. They have probably been construing thought quite narrowly to mean something like propositional thought. If thought is construed too narrowly, the claim becomes a tautology; it is not very informative to learn that thought which involves language is impossible without language.

A further argument for the existence of thought without language is the common experience of wishing to express some idea but being unable to find a satisfactory way to put it into words. If thought were impossible without language, this problem would never arise.

Nevertheless, much of our thought clearly does involve language, some of it in an essential way. Some scholars have lamented the "tyranny" of language and claimed that the "world view" of a person or community is shaped by the language used. However, the problem of assessing the influence of language on thought deserves to be treated with great caution. Certainly people have sometimes been misled by a blind reliance on words, but we can recognize such cases and set the record straight; if language were all that tyrannical, we would be unable to perceive that it sometimes leads us into error when we are not being careful. Furthermore, we must entertain the possibility that when we think in words, our thought is not molded by language at all; there may be a more general human cognitive capacity at play, for which language merely serves as a medium, just as music serves as a medium for the composer's creative powers.

Scholars generally agree that words greatly facilitate certain kinds of thinking by serving as counters, or symbols, that can easily be manipulated. We all have a fairly good idea of what arithmetic is; we know how to add, subtract, multiply, and divide. We also know the word *arithmetic*, which serves as a label for this conceptual complex. When we think about arithmetic (how it fits into the rest of mathematics, how it is taught in our schools, whether our children are good at it, whether we like it, how hard it is), we can use the word *arithmetic* as a symbol in our thought processes. It is much easier to manipulate the word *arithmetic* in our thoughts than to operate with the entire conceptual complex that this word symbolizes. The use of verbal symbols thus makes thought easier in many cases. One might even argue that some kinds of thinking would be impossible without the existence of these convenient counters to operate with.

Verbal labels are particularly important in the realm of abstract ideas. *Justice, democracy, liberty, communism,* and *education* are familiar terms, yet it would be very hard to pin down their meanings precisely. *Justice* does not evoke a concrete image in the way *table* does. We can usually agree on whether or not something is a table, but how sure can we ever be about justice? When is something correctly labeled *obscene*? Does the word *liberty* have any real significance? We certainly have at least a vague idea of what is meant by these terms, but their meanings tend to be quite elusive and to vary considerably from person to person. These concepts probably would not exist at all if there were no words for them, serving to gather and hold together a number of vague, not very coherent notions. Because they are abstract, words like these are quite loosely tied to reality. In a sense, they are almost empty. If one is not careful, they can become emotionally charged labels functioning only to brand someone or something as good or bad. It is unfortunately very easy to call someone a *communist* or to do something *in the defense of liberty*, and it is very easy to be misled by the empty use of words.

What is the relation between our thought processes and the structure of our language? Is language a tyrannical master, relentlessly forcing our thinking to follow certain well-worn paths, blinding us to all other possibilities? Is our conception of the world crucially conditioned by the language we speak, as some people have claimed? These questions can be posed with respect both to words and to grammatical structures.

We have seen that a word can be helpful in forming, retaining, or operating with the concept it designates. We have also seen that no two languages match precisely in the way in which they break up conceptual space and assign the pieces to words as meanings: English distinguishes between *green* and *blue* while other languages use a single word to designate this entire range of the color spectrum; some languages have words for individual kinds of trees but lack a general term, analogous to English *tree*, to designate the entire class. Differences like these extend throughout the vocabulary and will be found no matter which two languages are compared. Our question, then, is to what extent these differences in the linguistic categorization of experience are responsible for corresponding differences in thought.

There is little doubt that lexical differences have some effect on thought, at least in the sense that it is easier to think about things we have words for. We are accustomed to labeling some colors with the term *red* and others with the term *blue*. When presented with a typically red or blue object, we can quickly name its color; the terms *red* and *blue* are readily available to us, for we have had lifelong experience in calling some things red and others blue. We will have little trouble remembering the color of a red or blue object. Suppose, however, that you are presented with an object that is an extremely dark shade of brown, so dark that it is almost black. There is no common term in English for this particular color. Most likely you will hesitate to call it either *brown* or *black*, because it is not typical of the colors usually called *brown* or *black*. Eventually you may resort to a phrase like *very dark brown* or *brownish black*, but such a phrase will probably not come to mind so quickly and readily as *red* or *blue*. We are not so accustomed to distinguishing shades of brown from one another as we are to distinguishing red from blue. It will prove harder to remember a particular shade of brown (as opposed to other shades of brown) than to remember the color of a typically red object. If our language, on the other hand, had a separate word for this very dark shade of brown and if we were accustomed to categorizing objects of this color by describing them with this word, there might not be such difficulties.

Our thinking is thus conditioned by the linguistic categorization of experience in that it is easier to operate with concepts coded by single words than with concepts for which no single term is available. The way in which one's language breaks up conceptual space thus has at least a minimal effect on thought. But there is absolutely no evidence to suggest that this influence is in any significant way a tyrannical or even a powerful one. We are perfectly capable of forming and mentally manipulating concepts for which no word is available. We can make up imaginary entities at will and, if we so choose, proceed to name them. For example, imagine a unicorn with a flower growing out of each nostril. No word exists for such an entity, but it is easy to think about it nevertheless. We could dream up a name for it, but we do not have to.

What about the grammatical structures of a language? Do they force our thinking into certain customary grooves to the exclusion of other possibilities? Do they determine our way of viewing the world, as many scholars have maintained?

Overtly, languages sometimes display very striking differences in grammatical structure. (We will see later, however, that upon deeper examination languages appear to be very similar to one another grammatically.) For example, what we express in English with adjectives is expressed in some other languages with the equivalent of intransitive verbs. The word-for-word translation of the sentence meaning 'The tree is tall' would thus be *The tree talls*. To say that the river is deep, one would say literally

The river deeps. Much more commonly, languages differ in the grammatical categories that are obligatorily represented in sentences. One such category is gender. In French, for instance, every noun is classified as either masculine or feminine, and in the singular the article meaning 'the' appears as *le* if its noun is masculine but as *la* if its noun is feminine. Whereas in English we say *the cheese* and *the meat,* in French one makes a distinction and says *le fromage* but *la viande.* In German, there is a three-way distinction. *Der Käse* 'the cheese' is masculine; *die Kartoffel* 'the potato' is feminine; and *das Fleisch* 'the meat' is neuter. In other languages, there are even more gender categories requiring agreement. (These distinctions, by the way, are grammatical ones; they have nothing very directly to do with sex.)

Gender is of course only one example. Number, case, tense, and aspect are other categories often found in familiar European languages. And many languages mark categories that seem more exotic to speakers of English. It is not unusual for the plural to be marked differently depending on whether the objects involved are close together or scattered about. Certain Navaho verbs of handling, meaning such things as 'drop' or 'pick up,' vary in form depending on the shape of the thing that is handled. Thus one form will be used if the object is round or amorphous in shape; another form will be used if it is long, slender, and rigid; and so on. Sentences in the Siouan languages contain markers indicating the speaker's estimation of the veracity of what is expressed.

No one denies that these overt grammatical differences exist. If two languages are different enough in structure, a literal, item-by-item translation of a sentence from one language into the other can seem most bizarre to speakers of the second language. It is quite another thing, however, to claim that these differences in grammatical structure entail significant differences in the thought processes of the speakers. No evidence has ever been presented to support this claim. Grandiose assumptions about one's world view being determined by the structure of one's language have never been shown to be anchored in fact. There is absolutely no reason to believe that the grammatical structure of our language holds our thoughts in a tyrannical, vise-like grip.

It is not really surprising that no such evidence has been found. The claims are based on really very superficial aspects of linguistic structure. If French nouns are divided into two gender classes while English nouns are not, so what? No valid psychological conclusions follow from this arbitrary, rather uninteresting grammatical fact. If, in your native language, you were brought up to say the equivalent of *The flower reds, The tree talls,* and *The river deeps,* it would not follow that you lived in an especially exciting mental world where colors were actions on the part of objects, where trees continually participated in the activity of tallness, where rivers stretched themselves vertically while flowing horizontally. These ways of expressing yourself, being customary, would not strike you as poetic, as they strike a speaker of English. You would live in the same world you live in now.

suggestions for study and discussion

1. List as many onomatopoetic words as you can to supplement the examples given in the text. Is there any clear division between imitative and nonimitative lexical items? Can imitative words be separated naturally into coherent groups the members of which are formed on a similar pattern? Can you find other examples of sounds or sound combinations in English, like [ɪ] and [ʌ], which appear to carry special connotations?

2. Languages invariably differ from one another in the way in which their lexical items impose a linguistic categorization on experience. There are many well-known examples, including the different ways in which languages divide the color spectrum, differences in kinship terminology (see Burling, *Man's Many Voices*), and alternative classifications of plants and animals. However, differences in the linguistic categorization of experience can be found in all areas of the vocabulary. If you are familiar with two or more languages, find some of the ways in which they differ in their lexical encoding of experience.

3. Give some additional examples of kinds of thought that are essentially independent of language. What kinds of thought depend on language in a crucial way? Try to think of some concepts that you possess for which no standard linguistic expression exists.

4. Language lends itself very well to false deductions. Consider the following fallacious argument, for instance:
John was looking for a unicorn.
If John was looking for a unicorn, there must be a unicorn which John was looking for.
Therefore at least one unicorn exists.
What is wrong with this argument? Give other examples of false deductions based on the misuse of language. What do such examples show about the relation between language and thought? Do they cast doubt on the viability of human language as the medium of philosophical inquiry?

5. Language is easy to misuse for propagandistic purposes. For example, a president who says *I don't question the loyalty of those who disagree with my*

policies in Vietnam is in fact calling the loyalty of the dissenters into question, for if their loyalty were really not in doubt, there would be no reason to comment on it one way or the other. A small sample of lexical items that tend to be used more for their emotional impact than for their intellectual content was cited in the text. Observe language in use and isolate some of the propagandistic linguistic devices it contains. Almost any sample of language will do: a political speech, commercials, newspaper editorials, or a boy trying to persuade a girl to go out with him on a date.

6. Record the sentence fragments found in a sample of speech, or construct a representative list on the basis of your own intuitions. What full sentences do the fragments abbreviate? Can you find regularities in the relation between fragments and full sentences and formulate rules to describe these regularities?

7. The analogy theory of grammar has been shown to be false, chiefly because of its vacuity—both grammatical and ungrammatical sentences can be constructed by analogy from grammatical ones, and the ability of a speaker to distinguish between them can be accounted for only by supplementing the analogical model with grammatical rules, rules that would render superfluous the analogical model itself. One false analogy was illustrated in the text; here is another: from the previously experienced, grammatical sentences *I believe John, I believe John to be incapable of murder,* and *It's Mary that John kissed,* a speaker could derive by analogy the ungrammatical sentence *It's Mary that John to be incapable of murder kissed.* Construct other examples of false analogies. What supplementary principles are needed to rule out these incorrect results? An interesting and instructive game would consist of making up some ungrammatical sentence and challenging another player to derive it, starting from grammatical sentences only, by means of a chain of analogies.

8. Some of the recent linguistic work with chimpanzees is summarized in Roger Brown, 'Teaching Sign Language to a Chimpanzee,' in Laird and Gorrell, eds., *Reading About Language,* pp. 38–46. One of the questions Brown considers is whether the signs in the chimpanzee "sentences" are merely separate signs strung together or whether they are grouped syntactically in any consistent way. On the basis of the data available to him, he concludes that the question is still an open one. Read Brown's article, examine the data he presents, study Chapter Five of this book, and judge for yourself. (You may also want to read an article by Ann James Premack and David Premack, who have conducted some of this research with chimps: 'Teaching Language to an Ape,' *Scientific American* 227:4 [October 1972], pp. 92–99.)

9. It is clear that the sentences of a language are infinite in number. It is also clear that the words of a language in common use are finite in number. It is not so obvious whether all the words of a language—both common ones and "potential" ones that are seldom if ever used—constitute a finite set or an infinite one.

Part of the difficulty lies in determining whether compounds (see Chapter Four) should be regarded as words. If compounds are regarded as words, it would be difficult to argue that the words of a language are necessarily finite in number, for there is no apparent upper limit to the possible complexity of compounds. For example, the compounds *vacuum cleaner* and *salesman* can be combined to form the larger compound *vacuum cleaner salesman*; one who trains such an individual could be referred to by means of the larger compound *vacuum cleaner salesman trainer*; a helper of such a person could be described as a *vacuum cleaner salesman trainer helper*; one who washes the latter could be characterized by the compound *vacuum cleaner salesman trainer helper washer*; and so on. Does the point ever come when compounds such as these cease, due to excessive complexity, to be well formed? Are such compounds to be considered part of the language, even if they have never occurred? Should they be considered words?

Derivational affixes pose a similar problem, though here it is clear that we are dealing with words and not word sequences. An adjective can be derived from a noun by the addition of the suffix *al*: *region + al = regional*; by adding *ize* to an adjective, we can derive a verb: *rational + ize = rationalize*; the suffix *ation* makes a verb into a noun: *relax + ation = relaxation*; an adjective plus *ist* constitutes a noun: *real + ist = realist*; and finally, we can form an adjective from a noun by suffixing *ic*: *photograph + ic = photographic*. Given these derivational principles, we can construct words of any desired degree of complexity: *nation, national, nationalize, nationalization, nationalizational, nationalizationalist, nationalizationalistic, nationalizationalisticalizationalistic,* and so on. Can we nonarbitrarily point to any stage in the process at which the addition of another suffix makes the resulting word ill formed? Are words like the last one cited meaningless, or are their meanings just so specialized that they are hard to grasp and almost impossible to use? Are these words to be considered part of the English language?

10. One behaviorist theory of language acquisition is the theory of operant conditioning. According to this theory, a child spontaneously vocalizes in essentially random fashion. The child's parents reinforce these vocalizations differentially in order to shape his linguistic behavior; if a verbal response resembles their language, they reinforce it positively with some reward, and if it does not, they reinforce it negatively by ignoring it or by punishing the child. Over a period of time, the child's vocalizations will be progressively shaped by this differential reinforcement in such a way that they resemble the parents' speech more and more closely. Thus we learn to talk, according to this theory. Are the facts of language acquisition, as presented in this chapter, compatible with this theory?

11. Given below is what is known as a finite-state diagram. It consists of a finite number of states, numbered from 1 to 7, and a finite number of transitions from one state to another, marked by arrows. This diagram can be interpreted as representing the operation of a sentence-producing automaton. The automaton starts in state number 1, and it changes from one state to another until it reaches the final state, number 7, where it shuts off. The only state-to-state transitions possible are those indicated by the arrows in the diagram. Each time a transition is made, the machine emits the word that labels the

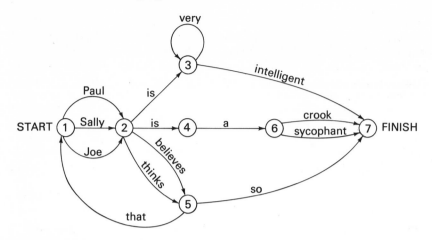

arrow symbolizing the transition. As the automaton progresses from state to state, it therefore emits strings of words—that is, sentences. This particular finite-state diagram will enable the automaton to produce any one of an infinite number of grammatical English sentences, and no ungrammatical sentences. Among the sentences it generates are the following: *Paul is intelligent; Sally is very intelligent; Joe is very very very intelligent; Sally is a sycophant; Paul is a crook; Joe believes so; Sally thinks so; Paul thinks that Joe believes that Sally thinks so; Joe believes that Sally thinks that Joe is very very very very intelligent; Sally thinks that Paul is a crook.*

Since a finite-state diagram describes a potentially infinite set of sentences, and since the grammar of a language must describe the sentences of the language, it is natural to ask whether the grammar of a language could consist simply of an elaborate finite-state diagram. The interest of this model is further enhanced in that it is quite similar in spirit and perhaps even in detail to the simple stimulus–response model of psychological structure. In fact, however, this model is known to be inadequate to characterize the syntactic structure of human language (see Chomsky, *Syntactic Structures*).

Make up other finite-state diagrams to account for different ranges of data, being sure that they do not permit the production of ungrammatical sentences along with the grammatical ones. What syntactic phenomena cannot be handled by such a model without great awkwardness and complexity? What phenomena cannot be handled at all? When you have read Chapter Five, consider how, if at all, a finite-state device can express the regularities described by the syntactic rules discussed there.

CHAPTER 3 language in society

linguistic diversity

It is believed that some three to five thousand languages are spoken in the world today. It is difficult to be precise about the number, however, for at least two reasons. For one thing, we do not have the voluminous, detailed information from all parts of the world that we need in order to make an accurate estimate. The second reason involves the very concept of a language. While we have a rough, intuitive idea of what we mean by the term **language**, the facts of language use are such that it is often extremely hard in practice to decide when this term is properly applied.

At first glance there might seem to be no problem. English is a language, as are French and Dutch. English is the language spoken in the United States, England, Canada, and a few other places; French is the language spoken in France, parts of Canada, and so on; Dutch is the language spoken in the Netherlands. But things are not really this simple. When we try to determine language boundaries, we find that they cannot be marked on a map in the straightforward way in which national boundaries can, at least not without gross oversimplification.

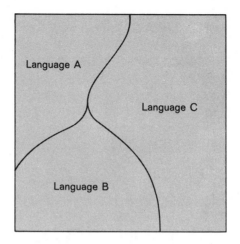

figure 3.1

To understand the problems, let us postulate a situation in which language areas could easily be marked on a map, just as countries are marked. Thus Figure 3.1 might be a linguistic map of some geographical area. A map such as this one has two implications. First, it implies that there is linguistic uniformity within each subarea marked off by the boundary lines. For instance, everyone living in the region marked "Language A" is said to speak the same language. Second, the map implies that there are clear enough linguistic differences between any two regions that one is justified in drawing a line between them. Thus, according to Figure 3.1, language B and language C are easily distinguished, so that a single line of demarcation can realistically be drawn between them.

In fact, however, neither of these implications holds true. In the first place, language areas in general display a surprising amount of internal diversity. Moreover, they very often merge gradually with one another, so that any dividing line on a map has to be drawn more or less arbitrarily. Linguistic situations like that in Figure 3.1 are therefore never found in reality. Actual situations approach it in varying degrees, but never very closely.

Consider first the arbitrariness of any dividing line. In some cases, a reasonable dividing line can be drawn without much distortion of the facts. The border between Mexico and the United States, for instance, will serve fairly well as a line of demarcation between English and Spanish. But even here some important qualifications must be added. Many people living near the border on the American side speak Spanish better than English, and many speak only Spanish. Furthermore, many people on the

Mexican side know English. Between the area where English is spoken to the virtual exclusion of Spanish and the area where the opposite situation obtains, there is a sizable region where both are used, where English words creep into Spanish conversations, and so on. Even here, any sharp line of demarcation represents an oversimplification.

In other cases, the difficulties involved in drawing a dividing line are much greater. Among the Australian aborigines, for example, one finds distinct language areas arranged geographically like the links of a chain. The speech of any two adjacent language areas is quite similar, and if one were to start at one end of the chain and progress from one area to the next until reaching the other end, at no point would the linguistic transition from one area to the next be sharp enough to justify positing a boundary between two separate languages. It would never clearly be reasonable to say, "Aha! I've just left language X behind; now I'm in the territory where they speak language Y." Given a continuum of this kind, it hardly seems justified to speak of two separate languages. Yet if we were to compare directly the speech of the two areas at the ends of the chain, ignoring the intervening links, we would observe major differences and would no doubt conclude that two separate languages were involved. Situations like this are quite common. Often the speech of two adjacent areas is mutually intelligible while the speech found at the two ends of a continuum is not.

It is evident, then, that any lines like those in Figure 3.1 are bound to be artificial to some degree, since the geographical boundary between two languages is never sharp. The transition may be relatively abrupt, very gradual, or anywhere in between. This qualification does not mean that we cannot speak of separate languages, but it does mean that in so speaking we are abstracting to a greater or lesser degree from reality.

The other implication of Figure 3.1 is that there is linguistic uniformity within each subarea marked off by the boundary lines. Even in the United States, where there is comparatively little linguistic diversity, we find that this implication does not hold true, even if we leave aside such obvious exceptions as the people who speak more than one language and the areas (mainly in large cities) where Spanish, Chinese, Italian, or other foreign languages are spoken. The speech of Texas is not the same as the speech of New England; Midwesterners do not talk the same way as Southerners. We are all aware of these surface differences to a certain extent, even having some fun occasionally at the expense of other dialects.

The differences are of various sorts. Most familiar, perhaps, are the variations in pronunciation discerned between virtually any two speakers of the same language. Some people pronounce *roof* and *root* to rhyme with *goof* and *shoot*, while others pronounce them with the vowel sound of *put*. The word *greasy* is generally pronounced to rhyme with *fleecy* in the northern parts of the country; in the South, it rhymes with *easy*. In many parts of the East and South, *r* is not pronounced at the end of a word or before a consonant, while it is in the West and Midwest. In many dialects where it is not, for instance, *par* rhymes with *pa*, and *startle* with *throttle*. Examples of this sort could easily be multiplied. There are also many variations in vocabulary and syntax. In some parts of the country the term *hot cakes* is preferred for what are called *pancakes* or *griddle cakes* in other areas. Some people *stand in line* and others *stand on line* (while in England they *queue up*). In western Pennsylvania, people say **This blouse needs pressed**; in most dialects, one would say instead **This blouse needs to be pressed** or **This blouse needs pressing**.

These are only a few examples of the thousands of details on which Americans differ in their speech. In the strictest possible sense, then, it cannot be maintained that the area where American English is spoken is characterized by linguistic uniformity. And in many other parts of the world, areas we would be inclined to mark off on a map as areas in which a single language is spoken display even more internal linguistic diversity than our country does. Thus we must complicate our picture of language areas to accommodate the reality of linguistic variation.

dialects

One obvious way to make the picture more realistic is to subdivide a language area into dialect areas; within the geographical domain of American English, for instance, we might want to mark off a Southern dialect, a New England dialect, a Midwestern dialect, and others. This slightly more realistic picture, where dialect divisions within a language are indicated, is schematized in Figure 3.2. Language A is here divided into dialects A_1, A_2, and A_3, and languages B and C are similarly divided. Naturally, the lines indicating dialect boundaries deserve to be treated with as much caution as the lines indicating language boundaries. Seldom if ever can we point to a line on a map and say with accuracy that one dialect abruptly ends at that location and another begins.

The basis for distinguishing various dialects of a language is that the linguistic system used by speakers of one dialect differs in certain respects from that used by speakers of the others. To take a hypothetical example, dialect B_1 of Figure 3.2 might be considered a distinct variety of language B because of these differences and a number of comparable ones: (1) the

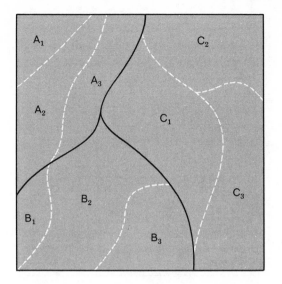

figure 3.2

speakers of B_1 use the sound [u] (as in **shoot**) in words that other speakers of B pronounce with [ʊ] (the vowel of **put**); (2) [i] is used in words where other dialects have [ɪ] (this is the difference between **beet** and **bit**); and (3) the word **tawpa** is used to designate a certain kind of bird, whereas speakers of B_2 and B_3 use the word **kenso**.

Matters are not really this simple, however. When one tries to draw dialect boundaries on the basis of points of difference in linguistic systems, one gets different results depending on which traits of the linguistic system are used as criteria in establishing the lines of demarcation. If we had looked, not at the particular examples above, but at other traits of pronunciation, vocabulary, and syntax on which speakers of B vary, B might have been partitioned in quite a different manner. Moreover, the alternative boundaries would be as valid as the first, both having been established on similar grounds.

Linguists use the term **isogloss** to refer to the geographical boundary of a linguistic trait. Even within a relatively homogeneous speech area, quite a large number of isoglosses can be traced. There is no necessary relation between any one isogloss and any other; they crisscross and diverge and often present a rather bewildering picture.

Figure 3.3 is a conceivable linguistic map on which three isoglosses are marked. The linguistic traits in question are lexical ones. Some speakers call a certain sparrow-like bird found in the region **finu**; others use the word **tawen** to designate this kind of bird. The isogloss running vertically

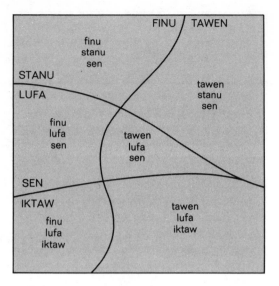

figure 3.3

demarcates roughly the subareas characterized by these alternate lexical items—speakers to the left of this line in general use *finu*, while those to the right use *tawen*. Similarly, the *stanu/lufa* and the *sen/iktaw* isoglosses indicate the extensions of the use of alternate lexical items.

The three isoglosses divide the region represented in Figure 3.3 into six subregions, each of which is distinct from the other five. In one subregion, speakers use *finu*, *stanu*, and *sen*; in another they use *tawen*, *stanu*, and *sen*. Where, then, is there a dialect boundary? There is really no satisfactory answer to this question. Dialect boundaries are established on the basis of different linguistic traits, but the three linguistic traits indicated in Figure 3.3 contradict one another as to where a dialect boundary lies. The dividing line will be drawn in one place if the criterion is the *finu/tawen* distinction, in another if it is the *stanu/lufa* alternation, and in still another if it is the *sen/iktaw* distinction. If we added more isoglosses to Figure 3.3, the situation would be worse yet.

One way out of the difficulty is to say that six dialect areas are represented in Figure 3.3, not two. In other words, we can define a dialect in such a way that two people speak different dialects if their linguistic systems differ with respect to at least one trait. Thus a person from the *finu/lufa/sen* area speaks a different dialect from the one spoken by a person from the *tawen/lufa/sen* area, since one person uses *finu* while the other uses *tawen*.

The problem with this definition is that no two persons have absolutely identical linguistic systems. Any given pair of speakers will differ with respect to some points of syntax, phonology, and vocabulary, whether or not they are normally conscious of these differences. It is probably true, for instance, that no two speakers of English know exactly the same set of words. One speaker will invariably happen to have learned some word that the other has not. Therefore, if we follow to its logical conclusion the proposition that a single trait is sufficient to establish a dialect boundary, we end up claiming that every speaker has his own dialect, one that no other speaker shares.

Thus we arrive at a definition of **dialect** that, while perfectly reasonable, is extremely narrow. It does not permit us to speak of the New England dialect of American English, for example, because no two New Englanders possess exactly the same linguistic system. But obviously it is often useful to be able to speak of dialects in the broader sense, in which the term is not restricted to the linguistic system of just one person. The term **idiolect** is therefore commonly used to designate the dialect of one person, and the term **dialect** is defined more loosely, so that it is proper to speak of a New England dialect. Some other rationale must then be found for carving up a language area into dialect areas.

We implicitly used such a rationale earlier in discussing Figure 3.2. We justified demarcating region B_1 as a separate dialect area of language B because the speakers in area B_1 shared, not one, but a large number of linguistic traits not characteristic of other dialects of language B. In other words, the line dividing B_1 and B_2 represents a whole bundle of isoglosses that roughly coincide. Along or near the line dividing B_1 and B_2 are the [u]/[ʊ] isogloss, the [i]/[ɪ] isogloss, the *tawpa/kenso* isogloss, and various other isoglosses as well. The speakers of B_1 retain many individual differences, but they cohere as a group at least in the sense that they have in common many linguistic traits that set them apart from other speakers of the same language.

Defining dialect boundaries in terms of bundles of isoglosses rather than single isoglosses leads, therefore, to fairly reasonable results. However, a dialect map like Figure 3.2 still represents a considerable abstraction from reality, just as Figure 3.1 does. It is a gross oversimplification to draw dialect boundaries that exhaustively partition a language area into non-overlapping subareas. Consider Figure 3.4, in which each of the numbered lines represents an isogloss. Isoglosses 7, 8, 9, 10, and 11 run together roughly as a bundle. We are thus justified to some extent in speaking of a major dialect boundary between the areas on either side of this bundle. At the same time, however, isoglosses 3, 4, 5, and 6 form a bundle that is equally suitable as the basis for establishing a basic dialect division. If we

figure 3.4

insist on dialect areas that do not overlap, we are faced with an arbitrary decision about which isogloss bundle or bundles to choose as the criteria. If all of them are defined as criteria simultaneously, they will intersect to yield very many small dialect areas. In any case, the picture is always quite complex, and the linguistic facts of a region usually do not lend themselves to a natural division of the region into dialect areas. Whatever choice we make will be somewhat arbitrary and will leave some facts out of consideration. There will always be stray isoglosses like 1 and 2 to complicate the situation. Dialects, then, are more a product of our conceptualization and desire for simplification than a natural linguistic phenomenon.

Linguistic diversity cannot be discussed fully in geographical terms; it has at least two other dimensions. One is the dimension of social groups and classes. Within a given geographical area, particularly an urban one, there are speech differences correlated with social structure. Denizens of high society and workers of the lower economic classes commonly differ quite noticeably in their speech. In university towns, the members of the academic community (most of whom come from other areas) can be quite distinct linguistically from the townspeople native to the region. People who work together or who have a common occupation or hobby often share many specialized vocabularly items not known by the community as a whole. Policemen, for example, have a professional jargon, as do football fans and members of the underworld.

The other dimension of linguistic diversity is to be found within individual speakers. Not only does a single speaker possess his own unique linguistic system; he has different **styles** of speech that he employs in different circumstances. The style he uses when being interviewed for a job differs considerably from the style he uses in conversation among close friends, for instance. We are attuned to differences in style, even if they seldom come to our conscious attention. Witness the mildly humorous effect of mixing styles: *It is incumbent upon me to humbly submit to your attention the request that you get the hell outta here*. Thus we encounter linguistic diversity even when we restrict ourselves to considering only one speaker and ignore the fact that a person's linguistic system undergoes at least minor changes throughout his lifetime.

We have stressed linguistic diversity to the point of calling into question the validity of the very notions of **language** and **dialect**. Strictly speaking, no two linguistic systems are identical, so that any description of a linguistic system has to be a description of the linguistic system of a single individual. And even here there are qualifications. We must not conclude from all this, however, that there is nothing uniting all the varieties of speech that we call English or Japanese. Linguistic diversity will naturally seem extremely important when we examine it alone, without attempting to ferret out features on which all or most of the idiolects of a language are in agreement. The more deeply we pry into the structure of a language, though, the less impressive idiolectal differences appear to be. Speakers of English have vastly more linguistic traits in common than traits in which they differ. The differences, moreover, tend to be of a rather peripheral nature. It is important to have some appreciation of the complexities of language use, but at the same time we must not concentrate on differences to the point where we are blind to similarities.

standardizing tendencies

Linguistic diversity exists because languages are learned and used and because language learning and use are creative processes involving an extremely complex system. When a child learns to talk, the linguistic system he masters is virtually identical with the one used around him. Inevitably, however, there will be some differences between the linguistic system the child assimilates and the ones his models use. In the first place, the child cannot observe the systems of his models directly; he can only observe their linguistic performance, and on the basis of this rather indirect evidence he must proceed (largely subconsciously) to formulate a linguistic system that reproduces their linguistic competence. Given the vast amount of detail that a language comprises, minor discrepancies will inevitably arise. Moreover, we have seen that no two people possess precisely the same linguistic system, and the child usually learns to talk from more than one person. On the points where his models diverge, he must make some decision as to which model to follow. The child's idiolect, therefore, will normally represent a mixture of the idiolects of the various people most influential in his learning to talk, not a carbon copy of any single idiolect.

Every act of speech is to some extent a creative one. A language is an instrument of communication, but a language itself does not communicate. To express an idea, a speaker must assess the situation and use the linguistic system at his command to encode the idea in a signal from which the hearer will be able to reconstruct at least approximately the idea that prompted the utterance. The communicative potential of the language must somehow be exploited in a manner appropriate to the context. In arriving at an utterance that will do what he wants it to do, the speaker has to make his language fit the situation, no matter how unusual; to construct a phrase or a sentence to express what no single word is available to express; and sometimes even to innovate, to alter the linguistic system to make it more nearly adequate to present needs. The seeds of linguistic diversity are thus to be found in the application of the abstract linguistic code to concrete situations for specific communicative purposes. If the word a speaker needs is not available, he may coin a suitable one; a listener watching someone scraping paint off a table will probably understand you if you say that the table is being *depainted*. People often resort to metaphorical expressions to get their ideas across, and some of these stick as part of the innovator's idiolect and may even spread to other speakers. Languages are full of expressions of metaphorical origin, such as *the heart of the matter, bridge the gap, let off steam,* and *stir up trouble.* Quirks of pronunciation are also sometimes adopted for their stylistic or expressive value.

The tendency of linguistic diversity to grow is checked by several forces, however. Since a language is used primarily for communication, a speaker is not free to innovate without limit; his linguistic system must remain similar enough to the systems of the people around him to enable them to understand him. Besides this essentially negative factor, a speaker is subjected to certain positive forces tending toward standardization.

Whatever the psychological motivations may be, people commonly model their speech after the speech of the people they communicate with. They may sometimes do so simply out of a desire for change. A more important motivation, no doubt, is the desire to fit in well with a social group, to be one of the gang linguistically as well as in other ways. This tendency toward linguistic uniformity within a group is probably for the most part unconscious, and it is certainly not without exceptions. One member of a group, for example, may try to enhance his group standing by deliberately adopting unorthodox modes of speech.

The prestige motive is perhaps the most potent of all. A person will imitate someone he admires and would like to resemble, in speech as in other ways. He is not likely to imitate someone who stands low in his estimation. The speech of prominent or admired people is often adopted as a standard or model, although there is no reason to think that any dialect of a language has intrinsic merit over the others. Sometimes the dialect of a certain region or social class takes on special prestige for the community or nation as a whole. Parisian French, for example, has more prestige throughout France than the other local dialects. To a somewhat lesser extent, British English enjoys special favor in the eyes of many Americans. Boston English is considered by many people to be more prestigious than Southern speech or Brooklynese.

When a dialect comes to be accorded special prestige by the community as a whole, it can serve as a standardizing influence. Parisian French is a good example. It was originally just a local dialect, like many other local dialects spoken in what is now France. They were all continuations of spoken Latin, and there is no reason to claim that any one was intrinsically more adequate, logical, or pleasing than any other. Paris, however, gradually became a social, economic, and political center of great importance. Moreover, the Parisian dialect was written and served as the medium for a flourishing literary tradition. Parisian French, in short, came to be held in high regard in France, but for purely external reasons; it is not inherently better than any other local *patois* and it has no claim to historical priority. For most Frenchmen, though, this dialect is *the* dialect, the one to be emulated. The other, equally legitimate dialects are looked down upon as provincial and inferior, or even as corrupt versions of the standard language (which they are not at all).

Whatever its precise causes may be, the high prestige of the Parisian dialect is a powerful factor in the linguistic attitudes and practices of French society. One is not likely to rise to national prominence in France without speaking the dialect of Paris, and an individual may even be hampered by a provincial accent, despite an otherwise perfect command of this dialect. A writer cannot hope for wide fame if he writes in one of the *patois*. Furthermore, Parisian French has been institutionalized as a standard language. It is the language authorized by the Académie Française, taught in schools, used on formal occasions, and (quite importantly in our age) projected throughout France by radio, television, and the press. Under the strong influence of the standard language, the local *patois* are gradually dying out; everyone is exposed to standard French, if only through the schools, and there are strong practical and social reasons for learning it. When so many factors combine to favor one particular dialect, its influence may be enough to override the tendency toward linguistic diversity and effect a trend toward linguistic uniformity, particularly in our age of mass communication, when spoken and written messages in the standard language reach millions of people.

A dialect that is accorded special prestige frequently comes to be regarded as more correct, more adequate, or purer than less prestigious dialects. It should be clear by now that these attitudes will not stand up to objective critical scrutiny. There is a sense in which it is proper to speak of correctness in language. A speaker often makes mistakes in speaking; if these really are mistakes (that is, distortions of his linguistic system as this system is reflected in performance), he will be able to recognize them as such if they are called to his attention and to correct them. But this is true of all dialects and constitutes no basis for setting one dialect apart from the others as being the most correct. Every dialect is adequate to its job; if it were not, its users would modify it until it were. The process of keeping a dialect in tune with communicative needs goes on continually, in fact. We adopt new words and phrases throughout our lives. Thus one dialect could hardly be more adequate than another. Nor is any dialect a corrupt form of another, purer dialect. Languages change; they do not degenerate (or we would have abandoned speech long ago in favor of grunts). Southern American English, for instance, is not a degenerate version of any other variety of American English, but is on a par with the others in all respects.

The idea that there are correct and incorrect varieties of a language is fostered to a considerable degree by pedagogical practice. American school children, for instance, are told not to say *ain't*, to avoid double negatives, to distinguish between **shall** and **will** in a rather complicated way, and so on. Until the general public can be educated to accept linguistic diversity, a person may well be handicapped socially and professionally by speech traits considered incorrect by people he has to deal with. Schools should help to foster the acceptance of linguistic diversity and avoid artificial corrections. A child who drills and drills to add to his linguistic system a **who/whom** distinction that was not there in the first place is likely, unless he is otherwise informed, to come to the erroneous conclusion that one version of a language is intrinsically more correct than any other, including his own.

It is doubtful that fine grammatical points of English like the distinctions between *shall* and *will*, *who* and *whom*, or *like* and *as* would have survived (to the slight extent that they have survived) if speakers had been left to their own devices. Despite grammatical instruction, many speakers of English are not at all sure when to use *who* and when to use *whom*. When attempting to speak "very properly," for example, a speaker may use *whom* where *who* is required, since *whom* sounds more formal and hence seems, fallaciously, more correct. This phenomenon of a speaker going astray by trying too hard to conform to the requirements of a dialect more prestigious than his own is called **hypercorrection** and is not at all unusual where linguistic norms are taken seriously.

To what extent linguistic practice can be legislated, by teachers or by governments, is an open question. The very fact that people still worry about *who* and *whom* and try to avoid split infinitives is evidence that such attempts are not wholly without success. On the other hand, the pronouncements of prescriptively oriented teachers and grammarians are quite without effect on the vast majority of spontaneous conversation; in general, people are content to communicate successfully, regardless of whether or not they do so "correctly." Nothing is really changed when a grammarian breaks down and allows *like* to be used to introduce an adverbial clause instead of insisting on *as*; most English speakers are way ahead of him, since they have been using it that way all their lives.

The matter is much more serious when language reform is adopted as governmental policy. The lack of a common linguistic medium can be a serious bar to national unity, or even to efficient administration. French, Italian, Swiss German, and Romansch coexist harmoniously as "official" languages in Switzerland, but there only four languages are involved. The bewildering array of languages in widespread use in India, by way of contrast, constitutes a serious obstacle to national progress. What can a government do in such a case? With a strong educational system that provides effective language instruction over a long period of time, there is at least hope that one or a small number of languages will become sufficiently well established on a large scale to be functional as genuine national languages. The prospect is at best doubtful, though, even if we disregard the understandable hostility of people who are disappointed that their language was not chosen for a national language. Formal instruction is seldom able to compete effectively with the constant influence of spontaneous language use. We have seen, however, that a tendency toward linguistic uniformity can arise naturally from the dynamics of social intercourse; one might hope to channel this tendency in some way. In any event, linguistic practice is much more likely to follow its own course than the dictates of those who would presume to direct it.

Although we draw isoglosses on a map and talk of languages and dialects shared by thousands or millions of people, the real story of trends toward linguistic diversity and uniformity is to be found at the level of individual speakers. The innovation of a linguistic trait presupposes a speaker who makes that innovation. If an innovation spreads, it does so because people with whom the innovator communicates, and subsequently people who communicate with them, adopt the new trait and incorporate it into their personal linguistic systems. If no one chooses to adopt it, the innovation will die out or be restricted to its originator. When an inno-vation catches on, its isogloss tends to spread out in a gradually widening circle from the innovator, who occupies the center of the circle. The pre-cise shape of the isogloss will depend on the form of the network of channels of communication linking the speakers involved, on the density of communication along the various channels, on the relative prestige of the speakers, and so forth.

This process occurs not just with new linguistic creations, but with all linguistic traits on which speakers vary. Where there is communication via language, there is a tendency for features of one idiolect to creep into the speech of people exposed to it. Isoglosses are therefore by no means static. Over a period of years, the position of an isogloss on a map can shift noticeably. As one might expect, isoglosses tend to spread outward from a high-prestige dialect, even forming concentric circles around the area where this dialect is spoken. If two or more prestige dialects are influential in a region, the isoglosses emanating from them will flow together and intersect, like ripples on a pond when a handful of pebbles are tossed into the water. Hence the proneness of dialect areas to inter-sect and overlap, as in Figure 3.4.

The diffusion of linguistic traits depends ultimately on communication and on the willingness of people to change their speech patterns after the example of others. Where little or no communication takes place, there can be little in the way of a trend toward linguistic uniformity. Geographi-cal obstacles, such as oceans or mountains, can therefore be quite effective in preserving dialect differences. Isoglosses cannot cross a mountain unless people or their messages do so with some regularity, and the same is true of political or social boundaries. Isoglosses will thus tend to pile up in bundles along gaps in the network of communication channels. This ten-dency will emerge as an important factor in our later discussion of lin-guistic relatedness.

writing

Most languages have existed as purely oral forms of communication. People had been talking successfully for thousands of years before writing was invented, and millions of people today get along fine with their language even though it has no written form. Written languages like English are the exception, not the rule.

Language is speech and the linguistic competence underlying speech. Writing is no more than a secondary, graphic representation of language, but one with certain advantages. A written message is relatively permanent, whereas speech is quite ephemeral. Once emitted, a speech signal is gone forever (although electronic recording techniques are changing that to a certain extent); a written message can be kept and consulted at any future time. Facts and ideas committed to writing can be preserved without being a burden on memory. Moreover, written messages can be read by any number of people at different times and places. It is much easier to distribute pieces of paper than to train messengers to memorize long messages and to travel about presenting them orally.

The debt of modern society to writing is enormous. Writing is not just a convenience; our highly integrated, technologically oriented civilization could hardly exist in anything like its present form without the ability to record and preserve linguistic messages. To realize this, it is perhaps sufficient to try to imagine the chaotic state of affairs that would result if all written representations of language were to disappear permanently. The mail system that ties society together would be nonexistent. There would be no newspapers or magazines to tell us of current events. The vast store of knowledge and culture that is preserved in writing would be wiped out. One could not go to a library to read and do research, but would have to resort to personal interviews. We could not organize our thoughts and render them coherent by committing them to writing; everything would have to be worked out in our heads. All written records would disappear. Bureaucratic machinery would come to a halt. One could not even post a FOR SALE sign. Electronic communication devices could take up some of the slack, but this is really beside the point. It is safe to say that the technology responsible for them could never have been developed if man had not first learned the art of writing, which made possible the accumulation of a large body of scientific and technical knowledge.

Granted the practical importance of writing, it does not follow that written messages deserve to be treated with more reverence than oral ones. Oral communication is even more important than writing, which is still only a secondary representation of language. Nevertheless, the written word is commonly regarded with great, perhaps excessive, respect. The written form of language even exerts some influence on its spoken form, notably in the phenomenon of **spelling pronunciation.** The word *often,* to take just one example, is pronounced by most people without a [t] sound, but because of the way it is spelled some people have introduced a [t] in their pronunciation of this word. Also noteworthy is the popular practice of forming a new word by pronouncing as a word the sequence of letters used to abbreviate a longer title. In this way the word **NATO** was obtained from the cumbersome *North Atlantic Treaty Organization.* **SEATO, UNESCO, BART, SALT**, and many more have been formed in similar fashion. An even more common variant of this practice is simply to pronounce the sequence of letters one at a time, as in *F.B.I., C.I.A., U.N., U.S.A., G.I., D.A.R., U.C.L.A.,* and countless others.

People sometimes regard the written word with special reverence, even going so far as to believe that something must be true if it occurs in print. Since most people do not write books or articles that get printed, there is perhaps a natural tendency to regard printed words with wonder or admiration and to forget that they carry no guarantee of truth or quality. False or stupid things can be printed as easily as anything else, and often are. A more common instance of our reverence for the written word is the concern, so prevalent in our society today, over correct spelling. There is really no compelling reason why a word has to have a unique spelling; we could get along perfectly well if everyone spelled words as he thought they should be spelled. That was the practice in earlier centuries, and it led to no particular difficulties. Why, then, do we spend so much time and effort trying (and in many cases failing) to learn to spell correctly? Why these endless pilgrimages to the dictionary?

Whatever the explanation, this attitude is no doubt connected with the more general idea, discussed earlier, that some versions of a language are more correct or proper than others. Correct spelling is regarded as an integral facet of the correct use of language, and the written dialect, as manifested in books, magazines, and newspapers, is the dialect to be emulated. This dialect is the one described in grammar books, and its words are neatly listed in compendious dictionaries complete with their pronunciations, spellings, definitions, syllabifications, and even etymologies. We consult dictionaries when in doubt as to how to use or spell a word, or where to hyphenate it at the end of a line. We stand corrected if the dictionary says that a word means something other than what we have always thought it meant or is pronounced in a way we would never have dreamed of pronouncing it. This attitude is not necessarily bad, but it is not the only possible one, nor even the most rational. When in conflict with a dictionary, we always have the alternative of claiming that the dictionary does not accurately reflect our dialect.

Writing can be an important factor in establishing or maintaining a dialect as a standard one. A written language has great prestige, as we have seen. When represented in writing, a language or dialect is better able to serve as a model, since it has greater permanence. People who compile dictionaries and grammar books prefer to work from written documents, and their descriptions are in practice interpreted as prescriptions to be observed in speaking and writing correctly.

A dialect thus established tends to take on an existence of its own, one maintained independently of developments in the spoken language. Languages, especially in their primary (spoken) form, are continually changing. Written languages are for the most part more conservative than their spoken progenitors, for a number of reasons. People usually write with more care and formality than they speak with, so that innovations are slower to appear in writing. The tradition of correctness in spelling keeps changes in pronunciation from being reflected in written messages. Because writing is relatively permanent, writings from the past (unlike past speech) continue to remind people of the way things used to be done and thus act as a restraining influence. People concerned with the correctness or purity of language will regard developments in the spoken language as evidence of linguistic corruption and resist their incorporation into writing.

As a result, the written language and its spoken counterparts sometimes drift quite far apart. It even happens that few if any people speak as their native dialect the spoken analog of the literary language; the literary language sustains itself solely through formal instruction in such cases. The spoken and the literary tongues are noticeably different in French; there is quite a jump from the standards of speech and writing taught in the schools and adopted for formal occasions to the informal conversational idiom. The formal Latin of Cicero differs considerably from the spoken Latin of the time, as reflected in the works of Plautus, who used the vernacular, and in casual scribblings that have been preserved. The spoken and literary languages may even diverge so far as to be mutually incomprehensible.

The isolation of liturgical languages from their spoken origins is a similar phenomenon. There is, of course, even greater resistance to change in a language used as the vehicle of religious doctrine and devotion than in a literary language. Moreover, the religious significance is sometimes sufficient to preserve a liturgical language long after its spoken counterpart has ceased to exist in other domains. Latin, as the language of Roman Catholicism, has been preserved in something like its classical form, though Latin as a spoken language has evolved into the modern Romance languages, which are quite different. Sanskrit is no longer spoken as a vernacular, but it remains as a language of religion and scholarship. Hebrew has been reestablished as a spoken language in Israel, but for many centuries it survived only as a liturgical language.

types of writing systems

The technique of writing grew out of the more general institution of pictorial art. The crucial difference between a pictorial representation of a situation and a written representation is that a pictorial representation is direct, whereas writing represents a situation through the mediation of language. We can describe a situation by drawing a picture or by talking about it, and writing combines aspects of each, being a graphic representation of a spoken message.

A picture may be worth a thousand words, but drawing pictures is not a very practical means of graphic communication. Besides being cumbersome, a pictorial system is inadequate to deal with many messages. For instance, how would you draw a picture to convey to someone the information represented in the sentence *Harvey's father-in-law's second wife will not be able to sympathize with the anti-war demonstrators until the views they sometimes advocate become more respectable in the eyes of those with firm commitments to morality and the future welfare of the nation?* Perhaps it could be done. It is much easier to write it, though, and the possibility of misinterpretation is much reduced when words are used instead of pictures.

The transition from direct representation to language-mediated representation came about when certain conventional pictures, or signs, were understood as designating words instead of things or ideas. Rather than drawing a picture of a man plowing a field, for instance, one would simply write in linear order the stylized signs normally used to designate a man, a plow, and a field. In this case it is not the event that is directly depicted; if it were, the man would be shown in the field with the plow. Instead, the three symbols are strung out in linear order corresponding to the words in the sentence describing the situation. The graphic signs now represent parts of the sentence, which in turn describes the event.

In all writing systems, symbols designate linguistic units rather than ideas or things. The distinct advantage of such an arrangement is that anything that can be said can be written (if the writing system is adequate). There are limitations, of course. Most writing systems lack any satisfactory way of indicating intonation, for instance. Gestures cannot be represented. On the whole, however, these minor deficiencies do not bother us.

Writing systems differ in two fundamental ways. First, they differ in their choice of symbols. The English, Greek, and Russian alphabets, for example, have quite different inventories of symbols, although there is some overlap among them. This difference is actually a superficial one, however; the three systems are of basically the same character, where one letter stands for one sound type. A more important difference in writing systems involves the kinds of units their symbols designate. On the basis of this distinction, three kinds of writing systems can be differentiated, although any one writing system will to some extent represent a mixture of two or more of these types.

Chinese orthography is the usual example of a **logographic**, or word-writing, system. Essentially, each symbol or character stands for a word; it has no phonetic value except by virtue of the fact that the word it stands for has a characteristic pronunciation. A word-writing system is advantageous in one way. Written Chinese can be understood over a wide area, even though the spoken dialects in this area are not all mutually intelligible, because differences in pronunciation are not reflected in the orthography, the symbols of which indicate words and not specific sounds. Although a given word may sound quite different in two dialects, the corresponding written character will be the same. But word-writing systems also have many disadvantages, mainly because so many symbols—literally thousands—are required. Learning to read and write involves much more time and effort than with other kinds of writing systems; for each word that is to be used and comprehended in writing, a separate symbol has to be memorized. One cannot figure out how to write a word, or what a character stands for, by means of any fixed relationship between symbols and sounds. The difficulties that the thousands of characters of a word-writing system present for purposes of printing are obvious.

Many writing systems are **syllabic**, or syllable-writing, systems: each symbol represents a single syllable or syllable type. If English were written syllabically, for instance, the word *macaroni* would be written with four symbols, one each for *ma, ca, ro,* and *ni.* Each symbol in a syllable-writing system has a particular phonetic value, and it is used in any word that contains the phonetic sequence it stands for. Thus it is possible to figure out how a word is pronounced from the way it is written, and vice versa. The signs of a syllabic system will be counted in the dozens, not in the thousands, which makes such a system much less cumbersome than a word-writing system. Japanese is a well-known example of a language written syllabically.

Most familiar to us are **alphabetic** writing systems. Basically, each symbol in an alphabetic system represents, not a whole syllable, but a single sound segment. The English word *cat*, for instance, contains three letters, one each for the sound segments [k], [æ], and [t]. Since the number of sound types that are systematically distinguished in a language is relatively small, the number of symbols required in an alphabetic writing system is also comparatively small; we get along with twenty-six letters for English.

The above characterizations of the three main types of writing systems are idealized and oversimplified in various ways. For example, some of the characters of Chinese resemble syllabic signs rather than word signs. Thus the same character is used for both 'wheat' and 'come,' since both are pronounced *lai*. Most Japanese writing is not purely syllabic but involves a mixture of syllabic signs and word signs (of Chinese origin). We even use word signs in English; $ is a word sign for the same word that can be written *dollars* using alphabetic symbols. Numerals, such as 3 and 7, are also word signs.

Furthermore, writing systems are seldom as rational as the descriptions might lead one to expect. English is often cited as a language whose orthography is plagued with irrationality and irregularity. One letter may stand for a sequence of sounds (x = [ks]), and a sequence of letters may stand for one sound (*th* for the initial sound in *thing* or *thin*). A single letter or sequence of letters can have many different phonetic values (*ough* is very different in *through, rough, cough, bought, hiccough, dough*, and *bough*). Conversely, the same sound sequence can be represented in many different ways (*cite, site, sight*). In no strict sense, then, does English orthography manifest a simple, regular pairing of one symbol with one sound type. On the other hand, it would be misleading to point out these irregularities of English orthography without at the same time mentioning the regularities; we can only speak of irregularity in the context of a coherent, basically regular system.

A great many letters used in English orthography have constant phonetic value. For example, the letters *m, f, v, z, b, d, r*, and *l* almost always stand respectively for the sounds [m f v z b d r l]; most of the exceptions are cases of a letter not being pronounced, like the first *m* in *mnemonic*. Observe that even the deviations from the one-sound/one-symbol pairing tend to fall into standard patterns. Consider *thing, philosophy*, and *shell*, for instance. The initial sound of each of these words is represented by two letters (*th* = [θ], *ph* = [f], and *sh* = [š]). But these three sounds are very similar (linguists call them **fricatives**—compare them with [a] or [t]), and at the same time their orthographic representations are similar, each consisting of two letters the second of which is *h*. The fact that *c* stands for [s] in *cite* but for [k] in *care* is not wholly idiosyncratic; the use of *c* is quite regular. Leaving aside the special sequence *ch*, we can observe the following: *c* always represents [s] before the letters *i*, *e*, and *y* (*medicine, city, cent, notice, cycle,* and *juicy*); elsewhere it represents [k] (*car, coil, cut, electric, act, success,* and *acrid*). As a subregularity, notice that the pronunciation of *c* is modified from [s] to [š] when *ci* or *ce* is immediately followed by a vowel, as in *facial, special, vicious,* and *ocean*; this does not happen, though, when the first vowel after *c* is accented (thus we have *sócial*, with [š], but *society, scíon,* and *scíence* with [s]). There are very few exceptions.

The orthographic representation of English vowels is also full of regularities, although it has often been criticized as irregular. Upon encountering the nonsense words *vack* and *vake*, for example, you will probably have no trouble deciding how to pronounce them. If English vowel orthography were not highly systematic, you would have no basis for this knowledge. But you do, since *-ack* and *-ake* are systematically used with constant phonetic values. Compare *vack* with *back, lack, rack, whack,* and *stack*; and *vake* with *wake, cake, lake, take, rake, stake,* and *flake*. It should also prove instructive to examine the pairs *rack/rake, man/mane, fat/fate, pal/pale, Sam/same, tap/tape,* and *mad/made*. On the whole, then, English spelling is quite reasonable and we have no real cause for complaint.

a brief history of writing

The art of writing first developed in the Middle East, sometime around 3000 B.C. The Sumerians were apparently the first to use a writing system, and the practice soon spread. It is quite possible that all writing systems stem ultimately from the Sumerian achievement, but we cannot conclude this with certainty.

The Egyptian writing system developed under Sumerian influence. It was a mixed system, part word-writing and part syllable-writing. Although the natural evolution seems to be from word-writing systems to syllable-writing systems, probably no system has ever been purely logographic. Right from the start, word signs come to be used as syllabic signs by means of the rebus principle. For example, suppose word signs were available for *ray* and *sing*, but not for *racing*. The natural thing to do when the word *racing* was needed in a written message would be to represent it by combining the signs for *ray* and *sing*. When this system is followed consistently, the signs involved lose their status as word signs and take on purely phonetic significance. In this way a basically syllabic system can develop from a basically logographic one.

Out of the Egyptian writing system grew various syllabic ones used by

West Semitic peoples from the second millennium B.C. Hebrew, Aramaic, and Phoenician, among other languages, were written with these syllabic systems. The writing practices of the Semites in turn spread to the Greeks, apparently through the Phoenicians. It is to the ancient Greeks that we owe the principle of alphabetic writing.

What the Greeks did was to systematize a device often used to render syllable-writing more precise. Syllabic signs were sometimes ambiguous; for instance, the same sign could designate *ta, ti, te,* and *to.* Vowel signs were therefore added to the ambiguous syllabic signs to avoid confusion. Thus, if the sign for *ta* could also be used for *ti, te,* and *to,* one would add to it a sign for *a* to indicate that *ta* was meant. In effect, then, *ta* was written *ta-a, ti* was written *ti-i,* and so on. When this device was used systematically, the original ambiguous syllabic signs came to be reinterpreted as signs for single consonants. The sign for *ta,* when accompanied consistently by the *a* sign, was interpreted as standing for the single segment *t.*

Alphabetic writing in various forms has spread throughout the world, although other kinds of writing systems are also in use. The Latin alphabet developed on the Greek model; modified in only minor ways through the centuries, it has been adopted throughout Western Europe and the New World. All other alphabetic writing systems can be traced back to the Greek invention in one way or another. Its success has been phenomenal.

Writing has become an indispensable component of modern society, and in all probability we will rely on it even more heavily in the future than we have in the past. As civilization becomes more complex and greater quantities of information have to be stored and transmitted, the written word will become even more indispensable than it already is. Language will continue to be a basically oral competence whose written representation is only secondary, but even now the development of languages is often influenced by their written representations. We must expect the connection between speech and writing to become even more intimate.

suggestions for study and discussion

1. Look for examples of hypercorrection and spelling pronunciation in contemporary English to add to those cited in the text.

2. Think about the varieties of English you use in different social situations. What lexical choices would you use in some situations but not in others? Are

there features of pronunciation that you try to avoid in certain social contexts? What points of grammar do you try to observe in formal situations more than in informal ones? Do you tend to use more complex sentences in more formal circumstances? To what degree are you aware of these stylistic differences in normal language use? How conscious are you of such differences in the speech of others?

3. Here is a map of a hypothetical region on which forty locations are identified by numbers. Suppose that data on linguistic variation has been collected from speakers representing each of these forty locations, and that the six speech traits listed below, on which the speakers vary, have been identified.

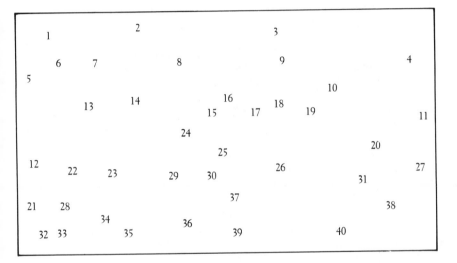

Trait A
   Subject pronouns may optionally be deleted at points 7, 8, 13–18, and 24.
   At all other locations, subject pronouns may not be deleted.

Trait B
   An object noun must obligatorily be marked with a special object suffix at points 3, 4, 10, 11, 20, 27, 30, 31, and 33–40.
   At all other locations, the object suffix is optional.

Trait C
   The most common word for 'sword' is [sez] at point 37.
   The usual word for 'sword' is [karf] at points 11, 20, and 26–40.
   At all other locations, [lalm] normally designates 'sword.'

Trait D
   The most common word for 'beaver' is [mim] at points 14–17.
   At all other locations, [fas] is the usual word for 'beaver.'

Trait E

A word-final [d] is changed to [t] at point 16.

At all other locations, word-final [d] is pronounced [d].

Trait F

[p] is pronounced [p] when it occurs between two vowels at points 5, 12, 21, 22, 28, 32, and 33.

[p] is pronounced [v] when it occurs between two vowels at points 31 and 35–40.

At all other locations, [p] is pronounced [b] when it occurs between two vowels.

Trace the isoglosses that mark the boundaries of each of these speech traits. Which points seem to be most influential as sources of linguistic innovations? Does the data provide sufficient justification for positing major dialect boundaries?

4. If you are a member of a linguistics class or some other group interested in language variation, you may wish to do some dialect research of your own. Find some words that differ in pronunciation among the members of the group. Are the differences systematic to any degree, in the sense that comparable differences are found in other vocabulary items? You may also want to look for cases where group members use different lexical items to express the same concept, or for instances of grammatical variation. Can the linguistic variation be correlated in any way with social or geographical factors? If the variation is geographical in character, plot the data for each trait on a map and trace the isoglosses. Do different isoglosses tend to coincide to the extent that it is reasonable to speak of dialects?

5. Hypothetical dialect maps have been used in this chapter for ease of presentation and discussion. For more extensive exemplification of dialect geography, with real language data, you may wish to consult a linguistic atlas, which is a collection of maps indicating the geographical distribution of speech traits. Here are some references: Hans Kurath, *Linguistic Atlas of New England* (Providence, R. I.: Brown University, 1939–43); Hans Kurath, *A Word Geography of the Eastern United States* (Ann Arbor: University of Michigan Press, 1949); Hans Kurath and Raven I. McDavid, Jr., *The Pronunciation of English in the Atlantic States* (Ann Arbor: University of Michigan Press, 1961); Jules Gilliéron and E. Edmont, *Atlas Linguistique de la France* (Paris, 1902–10); Marvin I. Herzog, *The Yiddish Language in Northern Poland: Its Geography and History*, Indiana University Research Center in Anthropology, Folklore, and Linguistics Publication 37, supplement to *International Journal of American Linguistics*, 31:2 (1965).

6. Discuss what would be involved in carrying out a major reform of English spelling. If you think such a reform would be feasible and desirable, formulate plans for its implementation. You might consider the following matters, among others: Would it be desirable for spelling to be a direct reflection of pronunciation? If spelling reflected pronunciation directly, would the spellings appro-

priate for different dialects be similar enough to one another to be recognizable? If not, should the pronunciation of one dialect be taken as the model? How is this dialect to be chosen? Does it matter that related words (like *photograph* [fówtəgræf] and *photography* [fətágrəfi]) would look rather different in a phonetically accurate writing system? If it does matter, how can the problem be avoided? Would a spelling reform meet with general acceptance? Should it be sudden or gradual? Could speakers cope with a period during which the new system and the old one coexisted? Would children really have an easier time learning to spell? Would children who learn only the new system be able to read material printed under the old system? If not, would they have to be familiarized with the old spelling system? Would the necessity for this familiarization offset the pedagogical advantages provided by the new system? Would it be economically feasible to reprint all or most existing works using the new spelling, and would it be culturally feasible not to do so? What would the effect of spelling reform be on the many people around the world who have learned to read English under the old system but who are not very familiar with the details of its pronunciation? All things considered, is it really worth the trouble?

7. Devise a syllabic writing system for English—that is, a writing system in which the basic symbols stand for syllables rather than single sounds. What are the advantages of a syllabic system for English, if any? What problems arise? What alternative means might be considered for representing consonant clusters?

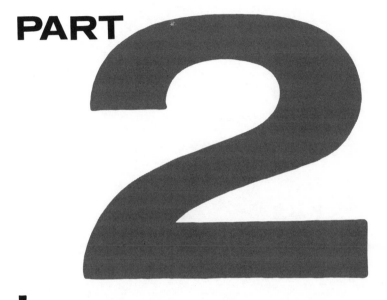

PART 2

language structure

CHAPTER

4

the organization of grammar

simple lexical items

the discreteness of linguistic units

We can conceive of a language as a code that specifies an infinite set of sentences, each of which pairs a meaning with a sound sequence. A sentence consists of a string of words. The meaning of a sentence depends on the meanings of the words it contains, just as the pronunciation of a sentence depends on the pronunciations of its words.

In characterizing a sentence in this way, we are making the assumption that linguistic units are basically discrete, that it is possible and correct to divide a sentence into word-like units, each of which is further divided into a linear string of individual sound segments. The discrete character of linguistic units may seem obvious, but the acoustic examination of a speech signal would not in itself lead one to this conclusion. In purely physical terms, there is for the most part no clear break between adjacent words in an utterance or between the sound segments of a single word;

73

indeed, these units often merge with one another and temporally overlap. Thus a speech signal is more nearly like a continuous stream than like a string of beads. It is true that we can pause between words in uttering a sentence, or even in the middle of a word, but for the most part we do not.

Yet we feel intuitively that a sentence can be broken up into words and that words can be broken up into individual sounds. Our writing system reflects such an assumption of discreteness, for in general we leave spaces between words and represent each sound of a word with a separate symbol. There can be no real doubt that linguistic units are in fact basically discrete, despite the testimony of the speech signal itself. A language, remember, is not sound waves in the air; a language is the competence, the set of principles mastered by a speaker in which resides his grasp of an infinite set of sentences. On the basis of this competence, a speaker somehow constructs sentences and pronounces them, thereby producing the physical speech signal. Thus there is no conflict in claiming that linguistic units are discrete although the speech signal is continuous. The claim of discreteness is made for the units of linguistic competence, for the psychological representation of linguistic structure that underlies verbal behavior. Let us now proceed to examine these units.

words and morphemes

Up to now we have been using the common term **word** to designate an intermediate unit of structure smaller than a whole sentence yet larger than a single sound segment. Words seem to have psychological validity; we might misspell *antipathy*, but we would probably not do so by leaving a space before *thy* to indicate a word boundary: *antipa thy*. Moreover, when we pause in uttering a sentence, there are some places where it is more natural to pause than others. The sentence *Frederick is very antipathetic toward communists* could be interrupted naturally after every orthographically marked word, but hardly after *Freder*.

In studying the structure of a language, however, we readily recognize the existence of units of grammatical structure smaller than words. The word *gardens*, for instance, divides naturally into the components *garden* and *s*. *Garden* can appear by itself as an individual word, as well as in the words *gardening*, *gardener*, and so on. The plural *s* of *gardens* also appears in *cars*, *furs*, *telephones*, *ideas*, and many other nouns. The *tele* of *telephones* shows up in *telegraph*, *television*, *teletype*, and *telescope*. The word *unfaithfulness* decomposes into *unfaithful* and *ness*. *Unfaithful* decomposes into *un* and *faithful*, which in turn consists of *faith* and *ful*.

Each of the four components—*un, faith, ful,* and *ness*—appears in other words or can stand alone as an independent word (as in *unprepared, faith, careful, stubbornness*).

Minimal units of grammatical structure, such as the four components of *unfaithfulness*, are called **morphemes**. *Telephones* thus has three morphemes, while *telephone* contains two and *phone* just one. A morpheme usually has a fairly clear and constant meaning in all its uses, although it is easy to find exceptions. *Un* has negative force in *unfaithful, unemployed, unenthusiastic, unremorseful, unable, unerring,* and many other words. *Er* has a constant meaning in *painter, teacher, fighter, beholder, writer, passer, protester,* and *speaker.* On the other hand, it would be hard to pin down any constant meaning for *spect* in *respect, inspect, circumspect,* and *spectacle,* or for *pro* in *protest, prospective, profess, protract, progress, process,* and *proceed.* *To* really has no meaning in sentences like *I want to go,* although it must be present for such sentences to be grammatical. *Do* in *What do armadillos eat?* and *it* and *that* in *I dislike it that your factory dumps thousands of gallons of sulfuric acid in the river every hour* are similarly without apparent meaning.

Morphemes sometimes vary in their phonetic manifestations. *Pro,* for instance, is pronounced differently in *profess* and the noun *progress.* The plural morpheme is pronounced [s] in words like *lamps, ropes, births, puffs, nuts, racks,* and *fights.* In words like *ideas, bras, cards, pencils, dams, cans, bibs,* and *pills,* however, it is pronounced [z], and it is pronounced a third way in *churches, judges, juices, roses, flashes,* and *rouges.* The plural morpheme has no phonetic form at all with some nouns; consider, for example, *I stole a lot of sheep* and *I caught four fish.* Then there are completely idiosyncratic forms such as *oxen, children,* and *brethren.* It is not always obvious whether or not a given sound sequence should be considered a morpheme. For instance, should *animal* be said to consist of two morphemes, *anim(a)* and *(a)l,* or just one? (Consider *animate, nature/natural.*) Is *woman* to be broken up into *wo* plus *man*? In any case, a sound sequence that is a morpheme in some words does not necessarily constitute a morpheme wherever it appears. *Un* is clearly a morpheme in *unremorseful* and *unfaithful,* but it is not a morpheme in *under* or *sun.*

types of morphemes

Linguists sometimes distinguish between **lexical** and **grammatical** morphemes, between **free** and **bound** morphemes, and between **roots** and affixes. Although these distinctions are rather superficial, they are worth discussing if only to illustrate the various ways in which morphemes differ from one another in their behavior.

Consider the string *Man chop wood axe*. This string is not a grammatical sentence of English, although it consists of English morphemes. On the other hand, it is fairly easy to grasp the general import of this ungrammatical string. With no difficulty we can picture to ourselves a man holding an axe and using it to chop some wood. This ungrammatical sentence is more or less meaningful—it is somewhat vague, but to a large extent we can reconstruct the conceptual situation the sentence portrays.

To make *Man chop wood axe* into a grammatical sentence, we could add the morphemes *the, **PAST*** (indicating the tense of the verb), *some, with,* and *a(n),* giving us *The man chopped some wood with an axe.* The sentence is now well formed and quite a bit more precise, but the added morphemes seem to introduce a lesser amount of semantic content. They bring the conceptual situation portrayed by the sentence into sharper focus, but the meaning they contribute somehow seems secondary. The essential components of meaning were provided by the morphemes *man, chop, wood,* and *axe.*

Lexical morphemes are forms like *man, chop, wood,* and *axe*; **grammatical** morphemes are forms like *the, some, with, a(n),* and the past-tense morpheme. Lexical morphemes are nouns, verbs, adjectives, and adverbs. They have more or less independent meaning, so that one or a series of lexical forms in isolation can be fairly meaningful. *Axe* suggests something quite definite to us, as does *Man chop wood axe. With, a(n)* or *The some with a(n)* by itself leaves us in the dark. Classes of lexical morphemes contain hundreds or thousands of members. There are thousands of nouns in English, for example, and it is very common for new ones to be added to the lexicon of a language. Grammatical morphemes are elements like prepositions, articles, conjunctions, forms indicating number, gender, or tense, and so on. Such classes contain relatively few members, and new members are added to a language rather infrequently.

The distinction between lexical and grammatical morphemes is handy and correct up to a point, but it should not be pushed too far. It is somewhat artificial, for there is really a continuum from morphemes with semantic content, like *wood,* to morphemes devoid of semantic content, such as *it* and *that* in *I dislike it that your factory dumps thousands of gallons of sulfuric acid in the river every hour.* Prepositions are classed as grammatical morphemes, yet they are not all empty of semantic content. The sentence *The coins are on the desk,* for instance, is changed significantly in meaning when *on* is replaced by *under, over, by, near, in, off, around,* or *for.* Grammatical morphemes such as the *ly* of *rapidly,* the *un* of *unable,* and the *er* of *gardener* have definite semantic content. The conjunctions *and, or,* and *but* are by no means synonymous. On the other hand, not all lexical morphemes have independent meaning. What is the meaning of *stand* in *understand,* for example, or of *with* in *withhold?* The numerical differences are not very clear-cut either. English prepositions are fairly numerous, at least when compared with the single-morpheme adverbs of place, such as *here* and *there,* or with the single-morpheme adverbs of time, such as *now, then,* and *soon.*

Free morphemes are those that can stand alone as independent words; all others are said to be **bound** morphemes. *Dog, sad, rapid, berry,* and *able* are thus examples of free morphemes, while the plural morpheme *s* of *dogs,* the *ness* of *sadness,* the *ly* of *rapidly,* and the *un* of *unable* exemplify bound morphemes. Most lexical morphemes are free (at least in English), and many grammatical morphemes are bound, as the above examples show. But the two distinctions do not coincide; there are exceptions in both directions. *And, or,* and *but* are grammatical morphemes, yet they constitute independent words. *Cran* and *boysen* would be considered lexical morphemes, but they are bound to *berry* and do not occur alone.

A great many words are constructed by the addition of one or a succession of grammatical morphemes to a lexical morpheme. We have seen that *ful* is added to *faith* to give *faithful,* which can subsequently be expanded to *unfaithful* and then to *unfaithfulness.* To the lexical morpheme *quick* we can add the grammatical morpheme *ly* to obtain the word *quickly.* S is added to *dog* to give *dogs.* The Aztec word *nitetlazotla* means 'I love' or 'I love someone.' *Tlazotla* is a lexical form, the verb 'love.' *Ni* and *te* are grammatical forms. *Ni* indicates that the subject of the verb is 'I.' *Te* indicates that the object of the verb is human but specified no further. The Aztec word *tlamatini* means 'wise man' or 'knower.' The verb *mati* means 'know.' The grammatical morphemes *tla* and *ni* are added to this to form *tlamatini. Tla* is similar to *te;* it indicates that the object of the verb *mati* is not specified but that it is nonhuman. *Ni* is added to the end of the verb form *tlamati* and contributes agentive meaning in the same way that the *er* of *gardener* does. Notice, incidentally, that the *ni* of *nitetlazotla* and the *ni* of *tlamatini* are not the same morpheme, despite the fact that they have the same phonological shape. Similarly, the *er* of *gardener* and the *er* of *stronger* are different morphemes; apart from pronunciation, the properties of these endings are quite different.

The lexical morpheme that constitutes the core of such words is called a **root,** while the grammatical morphemes that are added to a root to form larger units are called **affixes.** Thus, *faith* is the root to which are added the affixes *ful, un,* and *ness* to form *unfaithfulness.* In *quickly, quick* is a root and *ly* an affix. The affixes *tla* and *ni* flank the root *mati* in *tlamatini*. An affix that precedes the root, for example *tla*, is called a **prefix**; *ly*, which follows the root *quick*, is a **suffix**. In some languages, an affix can be inserted inside a root. For instance, the affix *ar* is placed inside a verb root in Sundanese, a language of Java, to indicate that the verb has a plural subject; the plural of *niis* 'to cool oneself' is thus *nariis*. Such affixes, called **infixes**, are much less common than prefixes and suffixes.

inflection and derivation

Affixes have varying effects when they are added to roots. When *s* is added to *dog* to form *dogs*, the effect is to further specify *dog* with respect to the number of animals being referred to. Both *dog* and *dogs* are nouns; adding the plural morpheme does not change the grammatical class (or, to use an older term, does not change the part of speech) of the word. Similarly, suffixing the past-tense morpheme to the verb *chop* gives us another verb, *chopped*. On the other hand, *quick* and *quickly* belong to different grammatical classes; *quick* is an adjective, but *quickly* is an adverb. The Aztec verb form *tlamati* means 'know something'; the addition of the suffix *ni* gives us *tlamatini* 'wise man, knower,' which is not a verb but a noun. By the addition of the proper affix, an adverb can be derived from an adjective, or a noun from a verb. Other affixes relate still other grammatical classes.

Accordingly, linguists often distinguish between **inflectional** and **derivational** affixes. *Boy* and *boys*, to speak in loose, rather intuitive terms, are alternate forms of the same entity, as are *chop* and *chopped*, or Latin *laudō* 'I praise,' *laudās* 'you praise,' *laudat* 'he praises,' *laudāmus* 'we praise,' *laudātis* 'you (plural) praise,' and *laudant* 'they praise.' The endings added to *boy, chop,* and *laud* in the above forms are inflectional affixes. English nouns like *boy* can be inflected for number. *Chopped* contains an inflectional ending to indicate past tense. Latin verbs are inflected to agree with the subject in person ('I' versus 'you' versus 'he') and in number (singular versus plural). The Spanish adjective *hermosas* 'beautiful' contains two inflectional suffixes. It agrees with the noun it modifies in number and gender; *a* indicates that the noun is feminine and *s* that it is plural.

Derivational affixes are rather different in character, though the distinction between derivational and inflectional affixes is not always clear-cut. The derivational affix *ly* serves to derive the adverb *quickly* from the adjective *quick*. The Aztec suffix *ni* is a derivational suffix that derives a noun from a verb, as in *tlamatini*. Affixes like these do not serve to mark agreement, as many inflectional affixes do. Nor do the various derived forms of a root lend themselves very well to a paradigmatic display having general validity for the language, such as the six present-tense forms of Latin *laud* cited above and in Chapter One. When both derivational and inflectional affixes accompany a root, there is a strong tendency for the derivational affixes to be closer to the root than the inflectional ones. In the word *darkens*, for example, the suffix closest to the root, *en*, derives the verb *darken* from the adjective *dark*; the inflectional suffix *s* is then attached to the derived verb. In the Aztec verb *quimictias* 'will kill him,' the derivational suffix *tia* 'cause, make' is attached to the root *mic* 'die' to form the verb stem *mictia* 'kill.' The inflectional affixes *qui* 'him' and *s* 'FUTURE' are then attached to the stem to form the full word *quimictias*.

The processes of word formation in English exploit derivational affixes quite heavily. Consider, for instance, some of the affixes that can be used to derive nouns from verbs. *Ing* is very productive, giving us *hunting, dating, dancing, singing*, and many others. *Ment* yields *argument, placement*, and *establishment* from the corresponding verbs. The agentive suffix *er* yields *gardener, singer, swimmer, robber*, and countless others. Verb/noun pairs that illustrate other affixes of this type include *refuse/refusal, illustrate/illustration, criticize/criticism*, and *impose/imposition*.

Derivational affixes do not always effect a change in grammatical class. The derivational prefix *de*, for example, relates *populate* and *depopulate*, yet both are verbs. Also compare *apply/reapply, imaginative/unimaginative*, and *possible/impossible*. Nor is a shift in grammatical class always signaled by an overt marker. *Star* and *face* are basically nouns, but they can also be used as verbs, with no affix: *The governor will star in a new movie; Some people can never face reality.* The adjectives *major* and *minor* function in academia as either nouns or verbs. Thus one can either *have a major* in linguistics or simply *major* in linguistics. Likewise, one can either *minor* in physics or *have a minor* in it.

complex lexical items

affixation

The **lexicon** of a language is its inventory of morphemes, together with information about how these morphemes can be combined to form more complex lexical items, such as words. In some cases, the combination of morphemes into complex lexical units is very regular. The past-tense morpheme, for instance, can be added to virtually any English verb. Thus we have *chop/chopped, slice/sliced, see/saw, buy/bought, can/could, am/was, bite/bit, raise/raised,* and so on. (One exception is *beware,* which can be used only in the present tense as an imperative.) The phonetic effect of putting a verb into the past tense varies from verb to verb; for some verbs, the addition of the past-tense morpheme has no phonetic effect at all—*cut,* for example (compare *I cut meat every day* and *I cut meat yesterday*). The point to note, however, is that there is almost always some way to do it. In general, the formation of words through the addition of inflectional morphemes is quite regular.

The combination of roots with derivational affixes tends to be less regular. One can *untie* a knot or *unhand* a maiden, but not *unclose* a door. A person can be *impish, boyish, foolish, childish,* or *waspish,* but not *geniusish, enemyish,* or *antish.* Something can be *reapplied, reassembled, reheated,* or *reapportioned,* but hardly *resaid, rereceived, reseen,* or *rebitten.* One who dances is a *dancer;* one who golfs is a *golfer;* but one who exists is not an *exister,* and one who operates on a patient is called a *surgeon* rather than an *operator.* Derivational processes, as opposed to inflectional ones, range from fairly regular to highly idiosyncratic and irregular.

The distinction between essentially regular linguistic phenomena and essentially irregular or idiosyncratic ones is quite significant, as we will see in our examination of syntactic and phonological systems. It bears directly on the question of the nature of language and language acquisition.

Suppose a friend of yours reports that he has discovered a special kind of native hut in the jungles of Brazil, and that he has decided to call it a *crut.* Now you know a new noun morpheme, *crut.* Without being told, you know that to speak of more than one *crut* the proper word is *cruts.* Plural formation in English is not an idiosyncratic property of individual nouns; it is governed by regular, general principles that you have mastered in becoming an English speaker. In learning English, you did not learn individually for thousands of nouns that *pencil* has a plural, that *apple* has a plural, that *box* has a plural, and so forth. You internalized the general structural principle that any common noun referring to a concrete, individual object has a plural. (*John, evaporation,* and *butter* are instances of nouns that normally do not have plurals. *John* is a proper noun or name, not a common noun; *evaporation* is not a concrete object; *butter* is not an individual object.) It is the possession of this general principle that tells you that *crut* has a plural. This principle projects to new cases, to new lexical items that you have never encountered before. What a speaker has to learn is simply the set of nouns of this type and the single principle that all such nouns can be combined with the plural morpheme.

On the other hand, the addition of the derivational affix *un*, meaning 'not,' to adjectives in English is not completely regular. Clearly, the same process of word formation is responsible for *untrue, unhappy, unintelligent,* and so on. The construction of these words is governed by a fairly general principle of English. Individual adjectives, however, behave idiosyncratically with respect to this process of word formation. There would seem to be no principle by which we say *untrue* but not *unfalse; unimportant* but not *unpressing* or *unurgent; unhappy* and *unjoyful* but not *unsad* or *unoverjoyed* and probably not *unecstatic; unintelligent* and sometimes *unsmart,* but not *unbright; unattractive* and *unpretty* but hardly *unugly* or *unbeautiful.* It is not enough, in learning English, just to learn the inventory of English adjectives and the principle of derivation whereby *un* can be attached to an adjective. It is also necessary to learn, along with each individual adjective, whether or not it can undergo this principle of derivation. What cannot be predicted by general linguistic principles must be learned separately for each lexical item.

compounds

The addition of affixes to lexical morphemes is one way of constructing complex lexical items from simple ones. There are various other ways of forming complex lexical units, and for the most part they are less regular than affixation.

Affixation, as we have seen, involves adding a grammatical morpheme to a lexical morpheme or to a larger unit containing a lexical morpheme. Some words, by way of contrast, are formed by combining two or more grammatical morphemes. By combining two prepositions, we obtain the English word *into* or *upon*. The French word *des*, if it is considered a separate word, represents the fusion of three grammatical morphemes. *Les* is *le* or *la* (the definite article 'the') plus the plural morpheme. *De* 'of' plus *les* is manifested as *des. Des* thus means 'of the (plural).'

More common, probably, are lexical units known as **compounds**. A compound is a lexical unit in which two or more lexical morphemes are juxtaposed. Although languages differ greatly in the number of compounds in the lexicon, English is very rich in them. To name just a few, we may cite *textbook, wasteland, grandstand, longbow, whitecap, slow-down, bedside, homing pigeon, blowtorch, sunburn, suction pump, gas mask, water tower, fingerprint,* and *dishwater*. Notice that in some cases a grammatical morpheme is attached to one of the lexical morphemes entering into the compound, for example in *homing pigeon* or *catcher's mitt*. In English, but not necessarily in other languages, compounds are characterized by a special stress pattern: the first lexical morpheme is pronounced with much greater emphasis than the second. Thus we distinguish by means of stress the adjective-noun sequence *red skin* 'skin that is red' and the compound *redskin*, where *red*, not *skin*, is pronounced with greater emphasis. Note also that the orthographic treatment of compounds is by no means consistent. Some are written as one word (with or without a hyphen), while others are written as two. This is perhaps to be expected, since compounds have something of an intermediate status. On the one hand they are single complex units, but at the same time they differ from other words, and resemble word sequences, in that they contain more than one lexical morpheme.

Compounding is extremely prevalent in Aztec. Let us take just two examples, *tizanamacac* and *apannemini*. *Tizanamacac* means 'chalk seller.' It consists of *tiza* 'chalk' plus *namacac* 'seller,' which is in turn derived from the verb *namaca* 'sell.' *Apannemini* is even more complex. The two lexical morphemes are *a* 'water' and *nemi* 'live.' *Pan* is a grammatical morpheme meaning 'on,' and *ni* is the agentive affix we have already encountered in *tlamatini* 'wise man, knower.' The entire compound thus means 'water-on-live-er,' or 'one who lives on (the) water.'

Although a number of regularities can be observed, compound formation tends to be idiosyncratic. Consider English compounds consisting of an adjective and a noun, for instance. The following seem quite regular: *longbow, madman, Frenchman, wildflower, dirty work, deaf mute,* and *white man*. They can all be paraphrased by an expression of the form **NOUN** *that is* **ADJECTIVE**. Thus a *longbow* is a *bow that is long*; a *madman* is a *man that is mad*; and so on. This is a recurrent pattern of compound formation in English; in other words, an adjective-noun compound can be formed given the existence of a corresponding expression of the form **NOUN** *that is* **ADJECTIVE**.

A person learning English must learn more than just this principle of compound formation, however. He must at the same time learn a wealth of unpredictable, arbitrary facts about compounds of this type. It is just an arbitrary fact that *dirty work* is an English compound, but not *clean work, dry work,* or *wet work*. Why do we have *madman* but not *sadman, saneman, shyman,* or *dumbman*? Further, many compounds that are superficially of this type do not mean what we would predict on the basis of the regular pattern. A *redskin* is not a skin that is red but an Indian.

A *bigwig* is not the same thing as a *big wig*. Other examples of this kind are **greenhorn, tenderfoot, dumbbell, redcoat, yellowjacket, sourpuss,** and *paleface.* Similar observations could be made for compounds other than those consisting of an adjective and a noun.

idioms

Another kind of complex lexical item is the **idiom**. An idiom is a phrase whose meaning cannot be predicted from the individual meanings of the morphemes it comprises. If you **beat a dead horse**, you do not necessarily strike a carcass. A person can *die with his boots on* with his boots off. A **red herring** is not necessarily a fish. Nor is a pail always involved when someone **kicks the bucket**. Languages are full of idioms. Some others from English are **hit the sack, bury the hatchet, come up smelling like a rose, stick to the straight and narrow, hit the nail right on the head,** and **sing a different tune.** Almost by definition, idioms are idiosyncratic rather than regular in their formation.

Because they are constructed from morphemes that are also used non-idiomatically, most idioms can also be interpreted literally. If someone **beats a dead horse**, for instance, he may in fact be engaged in striking the carcass of a certain kind of animal. **Beat a dead horse,** in other words, is ambiguous between this literal interpretation and the figurative interpretation of harping on an issue that has long since been decided. It is interesting to observe that idioms are not just semantically different from the corresponding string of morphemes taken in the literal sense; the semantic peculiarity of idioms is often accompanied by special syntactic properties. In the literal sense, to take an example, **Penelope kicked the bucket** has the passive variant **The bucket was kicked by Penelope.** When *kicked the bucket* means 'died,' it is incorrect to resort to this passive locution.

Most idioms are easily recognized as "frozen" or standardized metaphors. The metaphorical character of **beat a dead horse, let off steam, stir up trouble, keep one's eyes peeled, take the bull by the horns,** and so on is readily apparent. Once they are established in a language as fixed lexical units, frozen metaphors tend to lose their vividness, and speakers often lose sight of their metaphorical origin. Thus the nature of the metaphors underlying **off the cuff, cock and bull story,** and **kick the bucket** is not apparent to most speakers. Some idioms result not from metaphor but from ellipsis. The Spanish **No hay de qué,** literally 'There is not for what,' means 'You're welcome' or 'Don't mention it.' This expression is puzzling until one realizes that the full expression would translate literally as 'There is not anything for which to thank me' or something similar. The French *Il n'y a pas de quoi* is exactly parallel.

Idioms and standard metaphors (not to mention other complex lexical items) are clearly hammered out on the anvil of language use. Metaphorical expressions, if well suited to the occasion, are more colorful and effective than straightforward, prosaic statements. Successful metaphors are picked up and reapplied, so that they eventually become well established in the language. We use hundreds of them daily without even noticing them. The high redundancy of most common communication situations, coupled with the natural desire for brevity and the path of least resistance, renders very understandable indeed the tendency toward ellipsis that results in such expressions as *No hay de qué*. We can see perhaps the same tendency at work in the adoption of compounds; it is much simpler to say *suction pump* than *pump that works by suction*.

Words that are constantly associated in usage sometimes begin to cohere as lexical units. *Bread and butter* is such a common expression that it is somewhat odd to hear *butter and bread. Ham and eggs* is another example; *eggs and ham* just isn't the way to say it. Other examples are *bread and wine* and *bread and water. The stars and stripes* refers to more than just any aggregation of stars and stripes; *stripes and stars* does not have this special significance. The same can be said of *hammer and sickle.* The morphemes *in, so,* and *far* are used together so often that they have virtually fused into one word. We can write either *in so far as* or *insofar as. Nevertheless* has a similar origin. Those who know French will recognize *cependant* 'however' and *parce que* 'because' as fused forms of the same type.

phonological, semantic, and syntactic representations

When a person learns a morpheme, what he does, essentially, is tie together three kinds of information: phonological, semantic, and syntactic.

Suppose, for example, that he masters the English morpheme *cat*. In so doing, he must master a certain amount of phonological information, the information that the pronunciation of this morpheme is *cat* ([kæt]), and not *milk, liberty, dog, act, tack,* or anything else. More precisely, he has to learn that this morpheme consists phonologically of three sound segments (not two or four or seven); that these are [k], [æ], and [t] (not [s], [æ], and [t] or any other combination); and that these are ordered [k]–[æ]–[t] (not [æ]–[k]–[t], [t]–[æ]–[k], or any other way). We can say that, as part of the process of learning a morpheme, a person learns a **phonological representation** for that morpheme. The phonological representation of *cat* includes at least the information given above.

We have seen that some morphemes are semantically empty; *to,* for instance, has no obvious meaning in **I want to go.** Most morphemes do have meaning, however, and this meaning must be learned as part of the process of learning a morpheme. We do not at present know how to characterize the **semantic representation** of a morpheme, to say what kind of information must be associated with a morpheme for it to have a certain meaning as distinct from all other possible meanings. It is clear, however, that morphemes do have semantic representations of some kind and that the pairing of a semantic representation and a phonological representation in a morpheme is in most cases fully arbitrary or conventional. English would work just as well if the semantic representation of *cat* were associated with some other phonological entity.

A morpheme is not fully defined by its semantic and phonological properties alone. A morpheme also has syntactic properties, some **syntactic representation** that determines how it functions with respect to the grammatical processes of the language. *Cat,* for example, can function only as a noun, and never, say, as an adjective. Thus the sentence **That fat cat spat at flat black mats** is grammatical, but the sentence **It is very cat** is not. Consequently, morphemes can be viewed as bundles of semantic, phonological, and syntactic properties.

The picture is not really this simple, however. **Route,** for example, has two alternate pronunciations, sometimes even within the same idiolect; it can be pronounced to rhyme with either *shout* or *shoot. Economics* can start with the vowel of either *peck* or *peek,* and some people use the two variants interchangeably. **Light** can be the semantic opposite of either *dark* or *heavy,* not to mention *filling* (**Ice cream is light, but pie is very filling**). **Square** can function syntactically as a noun, verb, or adjective (**Mark an X in the proper square; It is useless to try to square the circle; The table is square**). It is the exception for a common lexical morpheme to have a single phonological representation, a single semantic representation, and a single syntactic representation, as a glance at any page in a dictionary will show. In describing the lexicon of a language, we must somehow make provision for these alternate possibilities.

The question naturally arises as to how these entities that seem to be variants of the same morpheme are related to one another. For cases like *route* and *economics*, there is not much to be said. For some speakers, each of these words has two alternate vowels in its phonological representation; the speaker has a choice whenever he goes about pronouncing these forms. Much more interesting are those cases where the same phonological representation is associated with different semantic or syntactic representations.

We can observe first that there are many forms with identical phonological shape that have little or nothing further in common. In these instances, we are justified in saying that the forms are different morphemes. The two *ni* morphemes of Aztec are a good example. One indicates that the subject is 'I,' the other is an agentive suffix, and they have nothing in common except pronunciation. The two *er* suffixes of English (in *stronger* and *dancer*) are another example. *Read* and *reed*, both pronounced [rid], clearly have no special affinity, and neither do *ant* and *aunt*, both pronounced [ænt] in some dialects. The existence of such phonologically identical sets of morphemes in a language can be considered purely coincidental.

In other cases, though, the similarities are such as to suggest, with varying degrees of force, some special relationship between identically pronounced forms. Consider, for example, the phrases *sharp razor, sharp mind, sharp focus*, and *sharp outfit*. In the strict sense, these four instances of *sharp* are semantically different; they might be paraphrased respectively as 'having an edge that cuts well,' 'quick, intelligent,' 'not blurry,' and 'stylish, smart.' But in a broader sense these four versions of *sharp* display a special semantic relationship that justifies treating them as variants of a single morpheme. On purely intuitive grounds, one could maintain that *sharp* in the sense of 'having an edge that cuts well' is somehow basic and that the other versions of *sharp* are secondary, being derived from it as essentially metaphorical creations. A mind is sharp in that it cuts with ease through difficult problems; a picture is in sharp focus when the lines are thin and well defined, like the blade of a keen knife; a sharp outfit is one that stands out in sharp focus against the background of mediocrity.

Examples of such metaphorical extensions are legion. Compare *clear water, clear issue, clear presentation*, and *clear weather*; or *I bumped my head, head of a pin*, and *head of a department*; or *The car struck a pole, Harvey struck his mother, The clock struck twelve, Strike that from the record, strike a match, strike out*, and *strike oil*. Even restricting ourselves to simple lexical units consisting of a single morpheme, we encounter the widely pervasive influence of metaphor. However, the relationship between two senses of the same morpheme is not always one of basic meaning and metaphorical extension. The *drive* of *drive a car* and the *drive* of *drive a golf ball* are to a certain extent similar in meaning (they both involve imparting motion to the thing driven), but neither seems to be a metaphorical extension of the other.

Most difficult and intriguing of all are those variants of what seems to be the same morpheme that differ semantically according to syntactic use. There is an evident relationship between the noun *circle* in **He drew a circle in the sand** and the verb *circle* in **The Indians circled the cabin**, or between the noun *fire* (**I will light a fire**) and the homonymous verb (**fire the pottery**). It would be tempting to suppose that the difference in meaning is attributable directly to the difference in syntactic use: to say, for instance, that the two versions of *circle* have the same semantic representation and that the difference between *circle* as a geometrical figure and as movement in a path resembling that geometrical figure resides solely in the difference between nouns and verbs. This may be part of the truth, but it cannot be the whole truth. It is sufficient to observe that no constant semantic effect is associated with the functioning of a morpheme as a noun, as a verb, or as any other part of speech. The semantic difference between *circle* as a noun and as a verb is one of movement. Whatever the precise difference between *fire* as a noun and as a verb may be, it is not one of lack of movement versus movement. The semantic distinction between the noun *skin* (**My skin is soft**) and the verb *skin* (**I skinned my knee**) is of another sort entirely. Squaring a circle and circling a circle are very different enterprises.

meaning and its manifestation

In coming to grips with linguistic structure, we have so far directed our efforts mainly at dissecting language to see what kinds of parts it has. We have seen that sentences are divisible into lexical items of various sorts, some of which can be further divided into smaller lexical units. We have seen that a linguistic system as a whole can, at least for convenience of discussion, be broken up into semantic, syntactic, and phonological subsystems. A lexical item can be analyzed for its semantic, syntactic, and phonological representations, each of which corresponds to one of these subsystems. It is time that we shifted the emphasis from dissection to anatomy and physiology in order to get some kind of overview of how the components of a language are organized in a coherent system and how they interact. Semantic considerations must play a prominent part in this discussion. In Chapters Five and Six we will examine in more detail the nature of syntactic and phonological systems.

Let us return to our original conception of a language as a device for

MEANING

↑
↓

PRONUNCIATION

figure 4.1

pairing meanings and sound sequences. It is the possession of such a device that enables a speaker to translate his thoughts into sequences of sounds for communication to others and to understand the sound signals emitted by other speakers, to reconstruct (at least approximately) the thoughts that prompted the emission of these signals. This device for linking meanings and sound sequences consists in a set of conventions and principles. By using these conventions and principles in some complex way that is not at all clearly understood, a person manages to create and understand utterances. Our immediate concern is not with how these conventions and principles are used in practice, but rather with their intrinsic character. In other words, our task is to understand linguistic competence as best we can; little is known about linguistic performance, and in any case it is beyond the scope of this book. The following paragraphs, then, will not outline step by step what a speaker does when he produces or perceives an utterance, but rather will sketch the organization of the system that underlies his performance, that enables him to function in the dual capacity of speaker and hearer.

Consider the sentence *The cat scratched the dog*. It has both a meaning and a pronunciation. The problem is to state how, by what organizational scheme, this meaning and this pronunciation (and all similar pairs) are connected. If we depict the situation as in Figure 4.1, the problem is that of characterizing the relationship symbolized by the arrow. The relationship is complex, even for the simplest of sentences, so we will examine it a little bit at a time.

the role of phonological rules

We will start from the phonological end. *The cat scratched the dog* consists of a string of morphemes. Letting **PAST** symbolize the past-tense morpheme, and putting a plus sign between successive morphemes of the string, this sentence can be represented as *the+cat+scratch+PAST +the+dog*. Each of these morphemes has some phonological representation, as we have seen. The morpheme *cat*, for instance, is defined in part

MEANING

the + cat + scratch + PAST + the + dog

Phonological Rules

PRONUNCIATION

figure 4.2

by the information that it consists of three sound segments, [k], [æ], and [t], arranged in that order.

The phonological representations of these individual morphemes do not themselves specify fully the pronunciation of the sentence in all its phonetic detail. A language, remember, is characterized by a phonological system, by general phonological principles that do not pertain to individual morphemes but hold across the board for all morphemes of the language. These principles combine and interact with the phonological representations of individual morphemes in determining the full, detailed pronunciation of a sentence. A sound segment has different pronunciations, for example, depending on what sound segments are adjacent to it in the string. English [n] is not phonetically the same in *tenth,* where it occurs before [θ], and in *ten,* where it does not. The English [k] is pronounced differently at the beginning of a word (where a slight puff of air is released as it is articulated) and after [s] (where the puff of air is much weaker or is missing altogether). General phonological principles such as these combine with the special phonological properties of individual morphemes in determining precisely how a sentence is pronounced.

Retaining *The cat scratched the dog* as our example, we can modify the above diagram to the one shown in Figure 4.2. The phonological system of the language is responsible for determining the full pronunciation of this sentence on the basis of the phonological representations of its individual morphemes. The principles of the phonological system do such things as specify that the (word-initial) [k] of *cat* is pronounced with a slight puff of air and that the [k] of *scratch* (which occurs after [s]) is not. These principles are called **phonological rules.** (**Rule** is simply a less cumbersome term than **principle**—it implies nothing more or less than the latter.) The nature of phonological rules and representations will be discussed more fully in Chapter Six.

conceptual and surface structures

Given the representation of a sentence as a string of morphemes, then, each with some phonological representation, the phonological rules of the language determine its detailed phonetic form, or pronunciation. The next point we must examine is the relationship between a thought that a speaker wants to express (or that a hearer reconstructs) and the string of morphemes that corresponds to it. How are meanings and strings of morphemes connected? This is, to say the least, a difficult question. In fact, it is the crucial question that linguists are faced with today in their investigation of linguistic organization. Answering it involves clarifying the relation between **syntax**—the principles or rules specifying the set of grammatical sentences of a language and their structures—and **semantics** —the study of meaning. The difficulty is rendered even more acute by the close connection between semantics and human psychology in general; to describe meaning, or even to say what sort of thing meaning is, we are forced to talk about the structure of thought and cognition. Very little of substance is known about the principles of psychological organization, however. It is fairly easy to observe the motions of our speech organs to see how sounds are produced, but it is not so easy to observe and characterize the operation of the mind. While we can with some assurance say quite a bit about the relation between meaning and strings of morphemes, there are many large and serious gaps in our knowledge.

What is the relation between the string *the+cat+scratch+PAST+the+ dog* and the meaning of this sentence? The first thing to notice is that both entities are highly structured. *The+cat+scratch+PAST+the+dog* is not just a jumble of morphemes randomly thrown together; it is a group of morphemes arranged in a very particular way. For one thing, these morphemes are arranged in a specific linear order, one after another. Changing this linear order gives either an ungrammatical string or another sentence. Moreover, certain adjacent morphemes of the string cohere in some sense to form distinct substrings. *The+cat* seems to be some sort of special group; this substring functions as a unit in a way in which *PAST+the*, for example, does not. Similarly, *scratch+PAST+the+dog* is some sort of unit (with subgroups *scratch+PAST* and *the+dog*), while *cat+scratch+PAST+the* is not. We are dealing, therefore, with a rather abstract structure, of which the linear sequence of morphemes is only one facet. This structure will be called the **surface structure** of the sentence.

It is equally clear that the meaning of the sentence *The cat scratched the dog* is structured, but it is not so easy to say just how. What does the meaning of a sentence look like, anyway? This is a fair question, but one to which we cannot at present give a very satisfying answer.

As organisms with complex central nervous systems, we possess vast stores of conceptual knowledge, knowledge that is highly organized and integrated. Thinking is the manipulation of concepts, the activation of subparts of our total conceptual apparatus. A sentence is meaningful, if at all, just because it relates to aspects of our psychological structure, because it is capable of evoking or being evoked by some conception of a situation.

We use sentences to talk about conceived situations, which arise in various ways. The situations we conceive of may be based squarely on immediate perceptions. If A is giving to B a play-by-play account of a fight between a cat and a dog, he may have occasion to use the sentence *The cat scratched the dog* by way of reporting on something he has seen happen only seconds before. In this case, A's conceptualization of this situation results directly from sensory experience. He is thinking of a cat and dog because he is watching an event in which they are participating, and he thinks of them as having engaged in the act of scratching because he has just watched such an action unfold. B thinks of an act of scratching because A says to him *The cat scratched the dog*. On the basis of the sentence he perceives, he constructs some conceptual picture of the happening. If the act of communication is successful, B's conceptual picture will have much in common with the one that prompted A to make the report; they will differ in fine detail, no doubt, but not in fundamentals.

The conceptualization of a situation may arise without being evoked by immediate perceptions at all, linguistic or nonlinguistic. A person may conceive of a situation from memory and proceed to report on the remembered state of affairs. Or he may manipulate his store of concepts so as to conceive of something he has never witnessed at all; our mental processes have a considerable degree of freedom from sensory control. If you know what cats and dogs are, and what it is for something to scratch something, you are capable of conceiving of a cat scratching a dog, even if no such event has ever occurred in your experience or been reported to you via language. By rearranging and restructuring familiar conceptual entities, we can make up new ones that have hitherto never occupied our consciousness. Such is the origin of unicorns (with or without flowers growing from their nostrils) and of all products of human creativity.

The meaning of a sentence is thus a conceptual situation, and it is structured. The meaning of *The cat scratched the dog* is not the precise mental picture that A had last Tuesday when he uttered the sentence for

B, nor is it the precise mental picture that B constructed when he heard it. Maybe A was thinking of a Siamese cat and a collie when he produced the sentence, and he was interested in the fact that the Siamese used its left front paw to do the scratching, but these details are clearly not part of the meaning of the sentence itself; if B had no information other than the sentence to go on, he could not deduce these details from it. To the extent that *The cat scratched the dog* has a definite meaning at all, it has one because the particular conceptual situations that it evokes or that evoke it have certain fundamental properties in common. If we could extract all the irrelevant frills and complications involved in any actual conceptualization underlying a sentence, the conceptual picture that would be left could reasonably be called the meaning of that sentence.

Conceptual pictures are highly structured. The conceptual situation represented by *The cat scratched the dog* is far from being just a random arrangement of ideas. It consists of parts arranged in a very specific way. One component of this complex thought is the conception of a cat; another is the conception of a dog. These components are combined as participants in the envisaged act of scratching. The activity is conceived of as being located in time prior to the present. If these components were combined differently, a different thought would result. For example, the same components structured in another manner would constitute the conceptual situation represented by *The dog scratched the cat* or by *In the presence of the dog, the cat scratched itself*. Similarly, our conception of a bicycle does not consist simply in the association of the concepts wheel, pedal, handlebar, frame, seat, and so on, but rather in the arrangement of these in a coherent, familiar structure. Without the configuration, we have nothing but a pile of junk.

Both the string of morphemes constituting a sentence and the conceptual situation underlying it are structured entities, therefore. We have called the former the surface structure of the sentence. Let us adopt the term **conceptual structure** to designate the latter. The semantic and syntactic systems of a language comprise the principles that relate conceptual structures and surface structures. For every sentence of a language, these principles specify the relationship between its form as a string of morphemes and its conceptual import. We can now revise our diagram (Figure 4.2) of the way in which the components of a language interact to pair meanings and pronunciations in the form of sentences. The result is Figure 4.3, in which the terms **meaning** and **pronunciation** have been replaced by slightly more descriptive ones; we can say that a sentence represents a **conceptual structure** and has a **phonetic manifestation**.

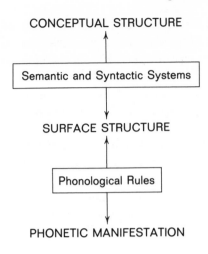

figure 4.3

lexical choices and syntactic rules

In Chapter Two, we took a brief look at semantic and syntactic systems. We saw that lexical items have meaning, or conceptual import, and that the meaning of a sentence depends ultimately on the meanings of its lexical items. This aspect of a language was said to be its semantic system. The syntactic system of a language was characterized simply as the set of principles or rules specifying which strings of lexical items, out of all possibles ones, are grammatical sentences. The syntax of a language can be viewed, in other words, as a system of rules for constructing the infinite set of strings that are grammatical in the language. We can now describe more precisely how these systems function to link conceptual structures with surface structures.

A sentence can be used to talk about some conception of a situation because the morphemes that make it up have individual conceptual import, or semantic representations. Morphemes can thus be used to designate components of a complex thought or aspects of its configuration.

Suppose, once again, that A is reporting to B on a battle between a cat and a dog. A sees the cat scratch the dog, and a moment later he goes about reporting this to B. As the result of recent sensory experience, A has conceived of a rather complex situation. He has conceived of an event involving two participants with certain characteristics. In order to translate this complex notion into linguistic form, he chooses morphemes to desig-nate subparts of it. The conceptual import of the morpheme *cat* matches one component of the conceptual situation; that of **dog** another; and that of *scratch* a third. Furthermore, A conceives of the event as having taken place prior to the present moment. He can therefore choose the morpheme **PAST** to indicate the temporal location of the event. Estimating that B's attention has already been focused on a particular dog and a particular cat, he chooses the definite article **the** to precede **dog** and **cat** (as opposed to *some, a,* or some specification as to which dog and cat are involved).

The assignment of lexical items to represent parts of a conceptual structure is of course only one facet of the relationship between the conceptual structure of a sentence and its surface structure, which phonological rules connect with a phonetic manifestation. Conceptual and surface structures are by no means identical, and consequently there must be some set of principles that relate them. These principles are the syntactic rules of the language, its syntactic system.

A few examples will demonstrate that the conceptual and surface structures of sentences are not identical. In some cases, components that are present in a conceptual structure are simply not present in the corresponding surface structure. English imperative sentences are a good example. **Come here!** does not display overtly any noun designating the person or thing that is to come. Yet the conceptual import of this sentence most certainly includes some entity that is being ordered to change location with respect to the speaker. Conversely, there are sentences that contain in their surface structure elements that have no place in the conceptual structure. The **to** in **I want to go** is an example; it is quite devoid of meaning. **Harvey broke the window** and **The window was broken by Harvey** have different surface structures, but they have basically the same meaning, the same conceptual structure. **Biting dogs can be bothersome** can result from either of two radically different conceptual structures (do the dogs bite or get bitten?), but the surface structure is the same or very similar under either interpretation. The surface and conceptual structures of sentences therefore cannot be identical.

We have now arrived at the scheme of linguistic organization depicted in Figure 4.4. In learning a language, a person must learn a set of lexical items, a set of syntactic rules, and a set of phonological rules. Each lexical item involves a semantic representation, a phonological representation, and a syntactic representation. A conceptual structure is connected with a surface structure by the choice of lexical items, whose semantic representations make them suitable to designate parts of the conceptual structure, and by syntactic rules. Phonological rules connect the surface structure of a sentence with its phonetic manifestation on the basis of the phonological representations of its lexical items.

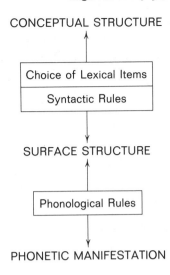

CONCEPTUAL STRUCTURE

Choice of Lexical Items

Syntactic Rules

SURFACE STRUCTURE

Phonological Rules

PHONETIC MANIFESTATION

figure 4.4

linguistic and psychological constraints

To complete this outline of the organization of linguistic systems, let us return to the notion that the syntax of a language consists of rules specifying an infinite set of grammatical sentences, differentiating those strings of morphemes that are well-formed sentences from those that are not.

The sentences of a language form an infinite set because there is, in principle, no limit to their length; just as there is no highest number, there is no longest sentence. As languages are organized, then, sentences of any desired degree of complexity can be constructed. The source of this property of human language is twofold. First, the human mind is in principle capable of conceiving thoughts of any desired degree of complexity. Second, the syntactic rules of a language are capable of connecting conceptual structures, regardless of their complexity, with surface structures. This feature of syntactic rules will be examined in some detail in the next chapter. The first point should be clarified before we go any further.

Our psychological mechanisms are such that conceptual situations of unlimited complexity can, in principle, arise. A person can conceive of a cat having scratched a dog. He can also conceive of someone believing that some state of affairs obtains. These two conceptions can in turn serve as components of a more complex thought, the thought of person A believing that the cat scratched the dog. This thought in turn can be a subpart of a still more complex conceptualization, in which person B hopes that A believes that the cat scratched the dog. And so on. It is easy to see that these conceptual situations are structured, that the component ideas are not just randomly piled together. For B to hope that A believes that the cat scratched the dog is not at all the same as for A to hope that B believes that the cat scratched the dog or for the cat to believe that A hopes that the dog scratched B. It should also be apparent that there is no *intrinsic* limit to the possible complexity of such conceptual situations.

To say that there is no intrinsic limit is not to say that human conceptual powers have no bounds. Obviously, they are highly constrained in many ways, although no one knows precisely what these constraints are. Try to visualize something that is round and square simultaneously, for instance. It cannot be done. It is possible to visualize something that is simultaneously round and red, say, but not round and square. It is only possible to visualize a round figure, or a square one, or to switch rapidly back and forth between a round and a square figure, or to visualize a square figure superimposed on a round one. There must be many similar constraints. Moreover, there are bounds on cognitive performance, just as there are bounds on linguistic performance. In trying to conceive of a very complicated situation, we are likely to get confused, to put the components together in the wrong way, and so forth. We can handle ideas of only so much complexity before we start to make mistakes. There are definite limits on the amount of information we can hold in mind and operate with at one time.

Consequently, some thoughts are just too complicated to handle all at once. In playing chess, for example, it is easy to think of the next move, and it is not too hard to think two moves ahead. When we try to conceptualize all the possibilities and their consequences for three, four, or five moves in advance, however, we quickly lose track and have to start over again, taking it one step at a time. Some thoughts, therefore, are just too complex for us to entertain, even though they are possible thoughts, just as some grammatical sentences are too complex for us to produce. This constraint is radically different in kind from the one that precludes our visualizing square circles. The possibility of visualizing square circles is flatly ruled out by the principles of human psychological organization. It has nothing to do with complexity or memory limitations. But none of the components of the complex conceptualization involved in planning eleven moves ahead in chess is ruled out by psychological constraints, and neither is their arrangement; there are simply too many for us to remember simultaneously.

With this distinction in mind, let us return to the notion of grammaticalness. Some sentences are likely never to occur simply because of performance limitations of the kind just discussed. No sentence three billion words long has any real chance of ever being uttered, although such a sentence could, in principle, be constructed; we simply could not handle a sentence that long. Even sentences of reasonable length can be so involved that we cannot easily operate with them. *The car that the woman bought stalled* is a relatively simple sentence that should bother no one. *The car that the woman that the dentist flattered bought stalled* is much less likely to be understood on the first try. *The car that the woman that the dentist that my mother recommended flattered bought stalled* is too involved for most people to grasp immediately, although they can figure it out if it is written down and they have enough time. All three sentences are equally grammatical and meaningful. It is important not to confuse ungrammaticalness with the excessive complexity that makes a sentence difficult or impossible to use. By virtue of speaking a language, we have a grasp of infinitely many well-formed sentences that are too complicated for us to handle with ease, just as we are capable of multiplying any two numbers even though there are many multiplications that are too difficult for us to carry out in our heads. This is one of the reasons for distinguishing between competence and performance.

Deviant or ungrammatical sentences are those which violate some constraint; whether or not they are too complex to be used readily is irrelevant in this regard. We may distinguish between ungrammaticalness in a narrow and in a broad sense.

In the narrow sense, a sentence is ungrammatical if it violates some syntactic rule of the language. For example, *The boys am stupid* is ungrammatical in this narrow sense. It is a syntactic principle of English that the verb of a sentence agrees with the subject in number and person. The subject of *The boys am stupid* is third person plural, but the verb form *am* is a form taken only by a first person singular subject (*I*). Another syntactic principle of English is that a simple adjective, such as *stupid*, must precede the noun it modifies, not follow it. *The stupid boys* is thus a well-formed expression, but *the boys stupid* is ungrammatical.

Other sentences are deviant in some sense, but not because they violate any syntactic rule. In this broader sense, sentences like the following are ungrammatical: *That circle is square; Harvey rode the fragrance around the room; I heard a purple symphony*. These sentences violate psychological constraints of some kind, not syntactic ones. That is, the conceptual structures that would have to underlie these sentences are simply not possible thoughts. We cannot conceptualize something that is both round and square at the same time (although there are various ways to cheat and make it seem that we can, say by switching back and forth rapidly between the conception of a circle and that of a square). The only way we can conceive of a person riding on a fragrance is by mentally turning a fragrance into something concrete, like a ribbon of smoke, and to imagine this as having enough body to support a rider as it floats around the room serving as a magic carpet. A symphony can be purple only if one performs a similar mental transformation. When we turn a fragrance or a symphony into something concrete, we are, of course, no longer conceiving of a fragrance or a symphony; we have used our conceptual powers to dream up some new kind of physical object. *The brick elapsed* is deviant in the same way. No possible conceptual situation qualifies as the conceptual structure underlying this sentence, and in this case it is even difficult to dream up a metaphorical kind of brick that would be the sort of thing that could elapse. We can interpret these sentences if we try hard enough, but only in a secondary or metaphorical sense. It is necessary to modify the conceptual import of one of the lexical items just for the sake of making the conceptual structure a psychologically possible one.

A sentence will be said to be **ungrammatical** only when it is syntactically deviant, that is, when it violates some syntactic rule. Sentences like *I heard a purple symphony* are more naturally said to be semantically deviant or to violate psychological constraints. It may not always be clear whether a sentence is syntactically or semantically deviant, if only because there is much concerning syntactic rules and psychological processes that is still unknown. The distinction seems to be a reasonable one, however. Some sentences, of course, are syntactically and semantically deviant simultaneously, for example *I are listening to a purple symphony*. Others deviate so far from the syntactic patterns of a language, or from possible manifestations of conceptual structures, that one would hesitate even to call them sentences. *And but though chocolate or thrice willow noose abstract square square asunder Harvey* is an English sentence only in the sense that it is a string of English words. It would be completely arbitrary to single out any particular syntactic or psychological constraints as those violated by this string.

suggestions for study and discussion

1. Idioms tend to be more or less fixed in form; consequently, they usually do not permit all of the syntactic options allowed by the corresponding non-

idiomatic expressions. For example, the idiom *let off steam* is parallel in structure to the nonidiomatic sequence *let off passengers*. But while *let passengers off* is a grammatical variant of the latter, *let steam off* is less acceptable in the idiomatic sense. *Off* can be expanded to *on and off* with *passengers*, but not with *steam* (*The driver let passengers on and off*, but not *The boys let steam on and off*). *Passengers* can be put in "focus" position, as in *It's passengers that the driver let off*, but *It's steam that the boys let off* does not seem fully grammatical. *Passengers*, but not *steam*, may be replaced by a pronoun (*The driver let them off*, but not *The boys let it off* in the sense of *let off steam*).

List a number of common English idioms. Is their origin transparently metaphorical, or did they possibly originate in some other way? What are some syntactic options that are not permitted by the idioms but are permitted with the corresponding nonidiomatic sequences?

2. In the text, a distinction is made between sentences that are ungrammatical by virtue of violating some syntactic rule and sentences that are grammatical but too complex for speakers to create or comprehend spontaneously. Do you think this distinction is valid? Can you find cases where it is difficult or impossible to distinguish between ungrammaticalness and excessive complexity?

3. The text distinguishes between ungrammatical sentences that violate syntactic rules and sentences that are grammatically well formed but deviant because they violate semantic or psychological constraints. Is this a valid distinction? Can you find instances where it is not apparent whether the deviance of a sentence is syntactic or semantic in character? Construct several expressions (like *purple symphony*) that represent "impossible thoughts." How do such expressions relate to the notion "metaphor"?

4. Carefully examine a poem or some other literary work whose impact is heavily dependent on the nonnormal use of language. Determine what kinds of linguistic or psychological constraints have been violated to achieve the literary effect of the work. Are any of the violations systematic in character? Determine what kinds of constraints (such as rhyme or meter) the writer has observed in addition to those that characterize normal language use.

5. The words listed below are from Luiseño, a Uto-Aztecan language spoken in southern California. Each word consists of two morphemes. Identify the morphemes exemplified in the data and state their meanings. The symbol [ʔ] stands for a glottal stop (see Chapter Six).

nokaamay	'my son'	pokaamay	'his son'
ʔoki	'your house'	poki	'his house'
potaana	'his blanket'	notaana	'my blanket'
ʔohuukapi	'your pipe'	pohuukapi	'his pipe'
ʔotaana	'your blanket'	nohuukapi	'my pipe'
noki	'my house'	ʔokaamay	'your son'

6. Identify the additional morphemes exemplified in the Luiseño words listed below and state their meanings. One morpheme has two slightly different phonetic forms; what determines which form is used in a given word?

ʔomkim	'your (plural) houses'	pompeewum	'their wives'
nokaamayum	'my sons'	pomki	'their house'
popeew	'his wife'	čampeewum	'our wives'
ʔopeew	'your wife'	čamhuukapim	'our pipes'
ʔomtaana	'your (plural) blanket'	ʔomtaanam	'your (plural) blankets'
čamhuukapi	'our pipe'	pomkaamay	'their son'

7. The words listed below are from Warao, a language of Venezuela (data from Henry A. Osborn, Jr., 'Warao III: Verbs and Suffixes,' *International Journal of American Linguistics* 33:1 [1967], pp. 46–64). Identify the morphemes in the data and state their meanings. Do not assume a morpheme-by-morpheme correlation between the Warao forms and the English glosses.

nahoropuhu	'can eat'
mipumeherepute	'they will want them to see'
kapatameheremoana	'has not yet wanted (him) to cut'
narumeherete	'will want (him) to go'
mitu	'one who sees'
narukuna	'would go'
noruhupute	'they will sit down individually'
narupumoana	'they have not yet gone'
narumehere	'want (him) to go'
ruhupuhu	'can sit down'

8. Most morphemes consist of a linear sequence of sound segments, but not all do. Some morphemes have no segmental shape of their own and are manifested instead by the modification of other lexical items. For example, the plural morpheme of English is sometimes manifested phonologically by the modification of the noun root rather than by the addition of a suffix. Thus *mice* is the plural of *mouse,* *men* the plural of *man,* and so on. Morphemes manifested through the modification of other lexical items are known as "process morphemes."

The words listed below are from Clallam, a Salish language spoken in northern Washington (data from Laurence C. Thompson and M. Terry Thompson, 'Metathesis as a Grammatical Device,' *International Journal of American Linguistics* 35:3 [1969], pp. 213–19). The forms in column II are derived from those in column I by the addition of a process morpheme that translates roughly into English as 'be . . . ing.' Describe this process morpheme. The superscript [ʷ] indicates that the preceding sound is labialized, and [ʔ] that it is glottalized; [q] is like [k] except that it is articulated farther back in the mouth, and [x] is like [k] except that it is a fricative rather than a stop; [c] stands for a voiceless alveolar affricate; and [ə] symbolizes a mid central vowel (see Chapter 6 for explanations).

	I			II	
čkʷut		'shoot'	čukʷt		'be shooting'
qʔxʷit		'tie up'	qʔixʷt		'be tying up'
tʔcət		'shatter'	tʔəct		'be shattering'
mtəqʷt		'put in water'	mətqʷt		'be putting in water'

9. The lexical items of a language can be divided into classes on the basis of their differing grammatical and phonological properties, and an enumeration of the class memberships of lexical items is a necessary aspect of any full linguistic description. A class is defined by any structural property that characterizes some lexical items but not all, and a given lexical item belongs simultaneously to numerous intersecting classes as determined by its various properties.

The past-tense form of most English verbs is derived by the suffixation of [d]; this suffix is rendered phonetically as [d], [t], or [əd], depending on the nature of the final consonant of the root (see Chapter Six). For example, **rub**, **kick**, and **boot** have the following past-tense forms: **rubbed** [rʌbd], **kicked** [kɪkt], **booted** [butəd]. However, some verbs form the past tense in other ways, hence English verbs can be divided into a number of classes on the basis of past-tense formation. Find as many of these classes as you can, and list representative members of each.

10. The interaction of lexical items with the syntactic and phonological rules of a language is especially important for determining lexical classification. Consider, for example, the syntactic rule called Dative Movement in English. Each of the following sentences has two objects, a direct object and then a "dative" or indirect object marked by **to** or **for**:

   I gave a book to Helen.
   I sent a card to Helen.
   I bought a present for Helen.
   I communicated my ideas to Helen.
   I created difficulties for Helen.

Dative Movement optionally permutes the direct and indirect objects, deleting the preposition that accompanies the latter. When this rule applies, optional variants of sentences like those above are the result:

   I gave Helen a book.
   I sent Helen a card.
   I bought Helen a present.

However, not all verbs taking direct and indirect objects permit Dative Movement to apply. **Give, send,** and **buy** permit it, but not **communicate** or **create**; the following are ungrammatical for most speakers:

   I communicated Helen my ideas.
   I created Helen difficulties.

Divide verbs taking direct and indirect objects into classes on the basis of their behavior with respect to Dative Movement. Is there any way to predict, in most cases at least, which class a given verb will belong to? Judgments about the grammaticalness of sentences derived by Dative Movement vary somewhat from speaker to speaker; explore this dialectal variation.

11. Additional problems in lexical, syntactic, phonological, and historical linguistic analysis can be found in Langacker, *Fundamentals of Linguistic Analysis.*

CHAPTER 5 syntactic systems

surface structures

The function of syntactic rules is to link conceptual structures with surface structures. We know very little about conceptual structures, since we know so little about human cognition in general. In comparison, the nature of surface structures is relatively easy to ascertain, and our examination of syntactic systems will consequently start with them. Although we will concentrate on English, much of the following discussion will prove valid for all languages.

A sentence, as we have seen, can be segmented into a series of morphemes. *The cat scratched the dog* can be represented as *the+cat+scratch +PAST+the+dog. An old man gave the airplane to Helen* consists of the morpheme sequence *an+old+man+give+PAST+the+air+plane+to +Helen.* The morphemes of a sentence are not randomly arranged but are combined in a very specific way to form a surface structure. We can note three aspects of the configuration of surface structures: their linear arrangement, their hierarchical arrangement, and the types of units they contain.

linear and hierarchical arrangement

The linear ordering of the morphemes of a sentence is self-evident. In the first string above, *the* precedes *cat* precedes *scratch* precedes *PAST*, and so on. Changing the order of the morphemes in a sentence results either in an ungrammatical string or in another sentence. *Cat the dog the scratched*, for instance, is an ungrammatical string. *The dog scratched the cat* is grammatical, but it is simply not the same sentence as *The cat scratched the dog*.

The morphemes of a sentence are also arranged hierarchically. We observed earlier that the morphemes of *The cat scratched the dog* cohere to form larger units. *The* and *cat* function as a group in some sense, whereas *PAST* and *the* in no way stand apart from the rest of the string as a unit. A string of morphemes that constitutes such a unit is called a **constituent**. *The+cat* is thus a constituent of *The cat scratched the dog*, but *PAST+the* is not.

The entire string *the+cat+scratch+PAST+the+dog* can be considered a constituent, since it constitutes a special kind of unit, a sentence. This string can be broken down into two smaller constituents, *the+cat* and *scratch+PAST+the+dog*, and the latter has the subconstituents *scratch+ PAST* and *the+dog*. Finally, each individual morpheme is a constituent. The hierarchical grouping of the morphemes of a sentence can be illustrated in a diagram such as Figure 5.1. In this **tree structure**, *the+cat*, *scratch+PAST*, and *the+dog* are shown to be units, since the members of each pair are attached to intersecting **branches**. By the same token, *scratch+PAST+the+dog* is shown to be a unit, and the entire sentence is a higher-level unit composed of the subparts *the+cat* and *scratch+PAST +the+dog*. *PAST+the*, on the other hand, does not form a unit; the branch leading from *PAST* and the one leading from *the* do not intersect. Similarly, *the+cat+scratch* is shown not to be a constituent, since the branch leading from *the+cat* fails to intersect with the branch leading from *scratch*.

The ambiguity of certain sentences can be explained with reference to their tree structure. Consider, for example, the sentence *Steve or Sam and Bob will come*. This sentence can be interpreted in either of two ways. It can mean that Bob will come and that either Steve or Sam will come too; or it can mean that either Steve will come or Sam and Bob will. This difference in interpretation corresponds directly to a difference in tree structure. The first interpretation corresponds to the first structure of Figure 5.2, while the second interpretation corresponds to the second

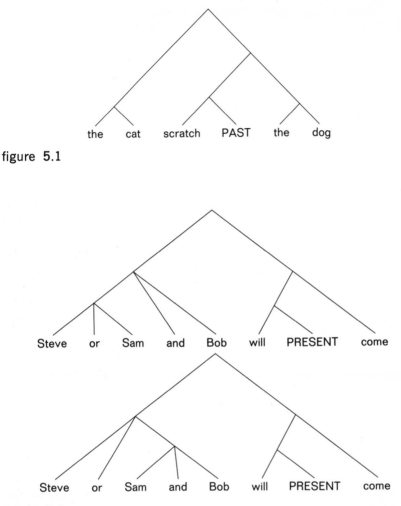

figure 5.1

figure 5.2

structure. (In both structures, **PRESENT** stands for the present-tense morpheme, which determines that the modal verb is manifested as *will*, instead of as the past-tense form *would*.)

The morpheme sequence *Steve+or+Sam+and+Bob+will+PRE-SENT+come* thus represents either of two surface structures. These surface structures differ not in the identity or order of morphemes, but rather in tree structure. In the first structure of Figure 5.2, **Steve or Sam** is a sub-constituent of **Steve or Sam and Bob**. In the second structure, it is **Sam and Bob** that is a subconstituent. Using parentheses to enclose the elements of a constituent, we can represent the contrasting structures as

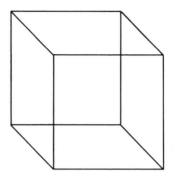

figure 5.3

(Steve or Sam) and Bob and *Steve or (Sam and Bob)*. These contrasting surface structures manifest different conceptual structures.

Another example of this type of structural ambiguity is *little girl's bike*. As *(little girl's) bike*, it is the bike of a little girl. As *little (girl's bike)*, it is a girl's bike that is little. Or consider *The policeman killed the woman with a gun*, which is also structurally ambiguous. *The policeman killed (the woman with a gun)* means that the woman was armed, while *The policeman killed (the woman) (with a gun)* has another interpretation. This structural ambiguity is exactly parallel to that of certain geometrical figures. Figure 5.3, for instance, can be viewed in either of two ways, just as *little girl's bike* can.

constituent types

We have not said everything there is to say about a surface structure when we have described the linear ordering of its morphemes and their hierarchical arrangement. Consider Figures 5.1 and 5.2 once more. The tree diagrams indicate that certain morpheme sequences belong together as constituents and that others do not, but they do not show what type of constituent a given sequence is. For instance, they do not indicate that *the cat* and *the dog* are constituents of the same kind, as opposed to, say, *scratched* or *will come*. Nothing shows that *Steve or Sam and Bob*, *an old man*, and *the dog* are similar, that *will come, gave the airplane to Helen*, and *scratched the dog* are similar, but that *an old man* and *scratched the dog* are constituents of different types.

To supply this information, we can simply label the constituents, giving constituents of the same type the same label. In Figure 5.4, the labels identify the constituents of *The cat scratched the dog*. Some of the labels

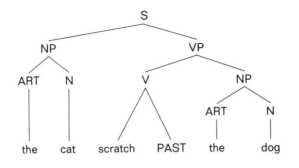

figure 5.4

are obvious. S stands for sentence, N for noun, V for verb, and ART for article. NP stands for noun phrase, a constituent whose main member is a noun. By the same token, VP labels a verb phrase, a constituent built around a verb. *The cat* and *the dog* are shown to be constituents of the same type, since both are labeled as noun phrases. *The cat* and *scratched*, on the other hand, are shown to be different types of constituents.

Figure 5.5 represents the surface structure of *An old man gave the airplane to Helen*. ADJ stands for adjective, and P for preposition. We will use the term prepositional phrase (PP) to designate a constituent consisting of a preposition plus a noun phrase. *Helen* of course is a noun, as the label N indicates, but notice that it is also labeled as a noun phrase. Since *Helen* is a constituent whose main member is a noun, it meets the definition of a noun phrase given above.

We see, then, that a single-word noun like *Helen* can function as a noun phrase as well as more complex structures such as *an old man* or *Steve or Sam and Bob*. Similarly, a verb phrase may consist of just a verb, like *exists*, or it may be more complex, like *gave the airplane to Helen*. The reason why such diverse structures as *Helen, an old man*, and *Steve or Sam and Bob* are labeled as the same type of constituent is that they behave alike with respect to syntactic rules. To take just one example, consider the rule for forming questions in English. In a question, the first verb word precedes the noun-phrase subject; this contrasts with the usual word order, in which the verb follows the subject. The question form of *Helen will come*, therefore, is *Will Helen come?*, the order of *Helen* and *will* being the opposite of their noninterrogative order. In the same way, the question form of *An old man will come* is *Will an old man come?*, and that of *Steve or Sam and Bob will come* is *Will Steve or Sam and Bob come?* In each case, the question differs from the noninterrogative sentence only in the relative order of *will* and the string of morphemes said to be a noun phrase. Since *Helen, an old man*, and *Steve or Sam and*

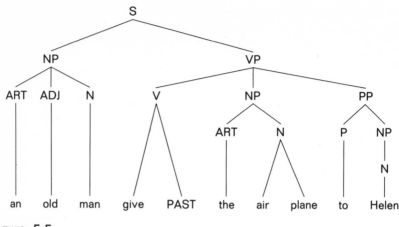

figure 5.5

Bob function alike with respect to the rule of question formation, and with respect to many other syntactic rules of English besides, we are justified in treating them as constituents of the same type.

One should not conclude that surface structures are fully understood or that it is always an easy matter to ascertain the precise tree structure to be associated with a given string of morphemes. Even at this relatively overt level of syntax, much remains to be worked out, and various details are bones of contention. Nevertheless, some things are fairly clear: the morphemes of a sentence are arranged in a hierarchical structure of some kind, the major outlines of which can be sketched with reasonable assurance, and we must identify types of constituents by labeling or by some comparable device.

complex sentences

The powers of human conceptualization enable us (in principle at least) to form thoughts of any desired degree of complexity. Regardless of how complex a conceptual structure may be, the syntactic rules and lexical choices of a language allow us to construct a grammatical sentence to represent it. The grammatical sentences of a language thus form an infinite set, since there is no intrinsic limit to the length or complexity of the meaningful sentences that the grammar of a language specifies to be well formed. In this section, we will examine more closely those aspects of syntactic systems which project our linguistic competence to an infinite set of sentences.

complex conceptual structures

Sentences, like the thoughts they represent, vary greatly in complexity. *Pete fainted* is a simpler sentence than *Alice broke the fancy chamber pot which had been given to her by her great-aunt,* in terms of both conceptual and surface structure. The latter sentence is in turn less complex than *Linguists are no different from any other people who spend more than nineteen hours a day pondering the complexities of grammar and its relationship to practically everything else in order to prove that language is so inordinately complicated that it is impossible in principle for people to talk.*

We are concerned here with a special kind of complexity. Specifically, many sentences are complex in the sense that they are constructed out of simpler ones. For example, *I believe Shirley hopes the rattlesnake bit me* can be decomposed into the simpler sentences *I believe, Shirley hopes,* and *The rattlesnake bit me.* By combining with *but* the simple sentences *Eggplant turns me on* and *Rhubarb nauseates me,* we obtain the more complex sentence *Eggplant turns me on, but rhubarb nauseates me.* Traditionally, the simple sentence-like components that go into the construction of complex sentences are known as **clauses**; a clause, roughly defined, is a constituent that contains a verbal element of some kind and could (perhaps with slight modification) stand alone as an independent sentence. We can therefore define a **complex sentence** as one that consists of more than one clause.

By and large, the clauses of a complex sentence correspond to components of the underlying conceptual structure. Thus the conceptual structure of *Eggplant turns me on, but rhubarb nauseates me* involves two main propositions, one pertaining to the speaker's reaction to eggplant, and the other his reaction to rhubarb. These propositions correspond directly to the two surface clauses *eggplant turns me on* and *rhubarb nauseates me.* Similarly, the semantic structure of *I believe Shirley hopes the rattlesnake bit me* contains three main components that correspond directly to surface clauses. One component pertains to a belief on the speaker's part, the second to a hope on Shirley's part, and the third to the biting of the speaker by the rattlesnake.

The correlation between surface clauses and components of meaning is at best imperfect, however. While the surface clauses of a complex sentence almost invariably correspond to semantic propositions, not every semantic proposition is realized as a separate clause in surface structure. For example, consider the sentence *Pete fainted after the nurse took his temperature.* The conceptual structure of this sentence involves at least three separate propositions: that Pete fainted, that the nurse took his temperature, and that the first of these events followed the second. But the sentence contains only two surface clauses: **Pete fainted** and **after the nurse took his temperature**. The single word **after** conveys the meaning of one proposition; this word is part of a clause, but it is not a clause in its own right. The same is true of the adjective **black** in the sentence **A black dog bit him**. This sentence has only one clause in surface structure, but semantically it is complex, since it involves two propositions: that a dog bit him, and that the dog was black.

Some components in the conceptual structures of sentences have no direct surface realization at all. This is true, for instance, in the imperative sentence **Open the crypt at once!** It is part of the meaning of this sentence that the speaker is giving a command to the hearer, but the sentence has no surface clause, such as **I order you**, that expresses this meaning directly. Nor is there any lexical item present with that meaning. The sense of **I order you** must be deduced by the hearer on the basis of the form of the sentence (it lacks an overt subject), its intonation, and the context. Interrogative sentences provide another example. In a question such as **Does she really have fleas?** there is no surface clause that directly expresses the sense of **I ask you**, yet it is intuitively clear that this sense is part of the conceptual structure of the sentence. Once again, the interrogative force of the sentence must be deduced from its form (the subject follows the auxiliary verb **does**), its intonation, and the context.

We see, then, that the conceptual structures of sentences are often more complex than their surface structures would indicate. Semantic components that could be expressed as separate clauses sometimes surface instead as smaller units, or have no direct surface realization at all. In fact, it is not unreasonable to speculate that every sentence has a complex conceptual structure with more than one component proposition, even though many sentences are noncomplex on the surface. It has been suggested, for instance, that the conceptual structure of every sentence involves a specification (such as **I order you, I ask you**, or **I say to you**) of the type of **speech act** it represents, even though this specification often fails to surface as a separate clause. It has also been suggested that specifications of tense (that is, the location of an event in time relative to the time of utterance) constitute separate propositions at the level of semantic structure. If these suggestions are correct, even the simplest sentence can be analyzed as consisting semantically of several propositions. And a simple, everyday sentence like **Three small wombats sneezed**, with only one surface clause, has at least five propositions in its conceptual structure: that the speaker is making a statement (as opposed to asking a question or giving a command), that sneezing is being predicated of wombats, that the event of sneezing is located in the past, that the wombats were small, and that there were three of them.

Let us now return to the observation that some sentences are complex in the sense that they are constructed out of simpler ones. Taken informally, this statement is correct and expresses a fundamental insight about the nature of sentence structure. When we say that the sentence *I believe Shirley hopes the rattlesnake bit me* is constructed out of the simpler sentences *I believe, Shirley hopes*, and *The rattlesnake bit me*, we are correctly characterizing certain aspects of its syntactic structure. For this reason, in fact, linguists commonly use the same symbol, S, to designate sentences and clauses; clauses are conceived of as simple sentences used in the construction of more complex ones.

Strictly speaking, however, this conception is misleading in certain respects. For one thing, it pertains mainly to surface structure. In terms of surface form, *I believe Shirley hopes the rattlesnake bit me* does consist of the simpler structures *I believe, Shirley hopes*, and *The rattlesnake bit me*, but we have seen that surface form is only one aspect of the structure of a sentence. In terms of conceptual structure, the relation is not so simple; by merely combining the conceptual structures of the simple sentences *I believe, Shirley hopes*, and *The rattlesnake bit me*, we do not obtain that of the complex sentence. Notice, for example, that it is part of the meaning of *The rattlesnake bit me* that the speaker is asserting the truth of this state of affairs—the speaker would be insincere if he uttered the sentence while believing that he had not in fact been bitten by the rattlesnake. But this is not part of the meaning of *I believe Shirley hopes the rattlesnake bit me*. A speaker could utter the latter sentence with perfect sincerity even if he knew for a fact that the rattlesnake had not bitten him.

The notion that complex sentences are constructed out of simpler ones is somewhat misleading even in terms of surface structure, for the following reason. When a clause functions as part of a complex sentence, it is often modified by special syntactic rules and thereby assumes a form that it could not have were it to occur alone as a complete and independent sentence. For example, the clause *trolls hate water* may stand alone as an independent sentence, or it may function as part of a more complex sentence, perhaps as the subject of *is obvious*. If *trolls hate water* is used as the subject of *is obvious* in a complex sentence, a syntactic rule of English requires that it be preceded by the subordinator *that: That trolls hate water is obvious*. The clause must occur with *that* when used in the complex sentence, and it may not occur with *that* when used in isolation as an independent sentence (*Trolls hate water is obvious* and *That trolls hate water* are both ungrammatical sentences). Because of the syntactic principles of English, therefore, this clause differs in surface form depending on whether it stands alone or is incorporated in a more elaborate structure.

Relative clauses provide another example. (A relative clause is one that modifies a noun phrase.) Consider the sentence *Joan distracted the man to whom Marge was speaking*. This sentence consists of two clauses which, were they to occur alone as independent sentences, would have the form *Marge was speaking to a man* and *Joan distracted the man*. The first of these is used as a relative clause modifying *the man* in the second, and because it functions as a relative clause, its form is modified by various syntactic rules of English. Specifically, the prepositional phrase *to a man* occurs at the beginning of the clause instead of after the verb, and the relative pronoun *whom* replaces the noun phrase *a man* as the object of the preposition *to*. *To whom Marge was speaking* is not grammatical as an independent sentence, nor does *Marge was speaking to a man* constitute a well-formed relative clause.

In summary, all sentences are probably complex at the level of conceptual structure, being decomposable into component propositions. Individual propositions of a conceptual structure have varying surface manifestations as determined by syntactic rules and lexical choices; a proposition may surface as a clause, it may be manifested as some smaller unit, or it may have no direct surface realization at all. Because of these syntactic and lexical modifications, the surface structure of a sentence tends to be simpler than its conceptual structure and to conceal the true complexity of the latter. Some semantically complex sentences thus consist of only one surface clause. Others are complex in surface structure as well, consisting of multiple surface clauses that reflect components of the underlying semantic structure. When a clause is used in the construction of a complex sentence, it is often modified by syntactic rules that would not apply were it to stand alone as a simple sentence. For this reason, the clauses of a complex sentence are not always identical to the simple sentences from which (informally speaking) the complex sentence is constructed.

conjoining

In traditional grammar, a distinction is made between **coordination** and **subordination**. The clauses of a complex sentence are said to be in a relation of coordination when they have "equal rank," as in *The sparrow is flighty, and the lion is a beast*. Otherwise they are said to be in a relation of subordination. In the sentence *It is obvious that trolls hate* the sparrow be PRESENT flighty and the lion be PRESENT a beast

figure 5.6

water, for example, *it is obvious* functions as the **main** clause, while *that trolls hate water* constitutes a **subordinate** clause.

Figure 5.6 sketches the surface structure of ***The sparrow is flighty, and the lion is a beast.*** This complex sentence is constructed by combining with *and* the clauses *the sparrow is flighty* and *the lion is a beast.* Since this is a coordinate structure, the two component clauses are arranged "in parallel"—neither contains the other as a constituent. The two clauses are said to be **conjoined**, and each clause is a **conjunct** of the conjoined structure. Elements like *and,* which connect the conjuncts of a conjoined structure, are called **conjunctions**. Notice that there are three occurrences of the symbol S in Figure 5.6. Each of the two conjoined clauses is labeled S, since a clause is a sentence-like unit, and the topmost S identifies the entire structure as a (complex) sentence.

There is no intrinsic limit on the number of conjuncts a coordinate structure can have. By adding a third clause to the example, we obtain the longer sentence ***The sparrow is flighty, and the lion is a beast, and the doe is a dear;*** by adding a fourth conjunct, we obtain the still longer sentence ***The sparrow is flighty, and the lion is a beast, and the doe is a dear, and the caterpillar is a creep;*** and so on. It should be evident that we could continue the process indefinitely, for length alone never renders such a sentence ungrammatical. For this reason the process of conjoining is itself sufficient to extend our linguistic competence to an infinite set of sentences.

Schematically, then, we can represent the structure of a conjoined sentence as in Figure 5.7. A triangle is used to abbreviate the internal structure of each clause, since the important concern here is not the in-

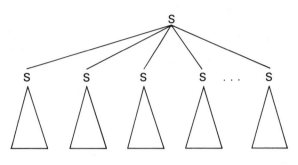

figure 5.7

ternal structure of the conjuncts, but rather their arrangement relative to one another. The three dots indicate that the sentence could be extended indefinitely by the addition of further clauses. Sentences like the ones discussed above, with two, three, and four conjuncts, are special cases of the sentence type depicted in Figure 5.7.

And is of course only one of the conjunctions of English. The other two major conjunctions are *but* and *or*, illustrated in the following sentences: *All men are equal, but some are more equal than others; Get your hair cut at once, or at least buy a hair-net! And, or,* and *but* also combine with other words to form more complex conjunctions, such as *either ... or, both ... and, but then, or else,* and so on. The simple conjunctions can occur before every conjunct in a conjoined structure, as the earlier examples showed, with the exception that they may not occur before the first conjunct. A sentence like *And she is beautiful, and she is charming* is therefore ungrammatical (except in special contexts where it continues a previous enumeration), since *and* incorrectly appears before the first conjunct, *she is beautiful.* Notice that the English conjunctions are more closely bound to the following conjunct than to the preceding one, as shown by the greater naturalness of pausing before a conjunction than after it: compared to *Penelope is very shy—and Abernathy is too*, with the pause before *and*, the sentence *Penelope is very shy and—Abernathy is too* sounds very awkward and unnatural. (For this reason it might be more accurate to represent conjunctions as constituents of the following conjunct, rather than as independent elements between the conjuncts as in Figure 5.6.) In many languages, however, a conjunction is bound more closely to the preceding conjunct than to the following one.

Various syntactic principles affect the surface manifestation of coordinate structures. For example, one syntactic rule of English allows the omission of all but the last occurrence of *and* or *or* in a series of conjuncts. This principle allows *The sparrow is flighty, the lion is a beast, the doe is a dear, and the caterpillar is a creep* as a variant of the fuller sentence *The sparrow is flighty, and the lion is a beast, and the doe is a dear, and the caterpillar is a creep*. (This rule can never affect sentences conjoined with *but*, since *but* is restricted to cases where there are only two conjuncts.)

More drastic in their effect are various rules that simplify conjuncts by deleting repeated elements. For instance, the verbs of all conjuncts except the first may be deleted if the verbs of all the conjuncts are identical (and if certain other conditions are met). From the structure *Jane munched on snails, Joyce munched on roasted grasshoppers, and Julie munched on chocolate-covered caterpillars,* this rule produces the optional variant *Jane munched on snails, Joyce on roasted grasshoppers, and Julie on chocolate-covered caterpillars*. Another rule permits the deletion of everything but the subject and auxiliary verb in the second conjunct when the remainder is identical to the corresponding elements in the first conjunct. This rule determines the surface form of sentences like these: *Wilt can break a railroad tie with his bare hands, and Nate can also; Penelope is very shy, and Abernathy is too; Uranium will not dissolve in Coca-Cola, but teeth will; The linebacker should make the tackle, or else the safety should. Break a railroad tie with his bare hands, very shy, dissolve in Coca-Cola,* and *make the tackle* have been deleted from the second conjuncts of these respective sentences.

Thus far we have concerned ourselves only with conjoined clauses, but smaller constituents can also be conjoined. For example, *the cruiser and the old battleship* is a conjoined noun phrase formed by combining the simpler noun phrases *the cruiser* and *the old battleship*. The structure of the complex noun phrase is shown in Figure 5.8. The coordination of other types of constituents (verbs, adjectives, verb phrases, and prepositions) is illustrated in the following sentences: *She bit and scratched the mugger; I want to marry a man who is tall, dark, handsome, and rich; Alexander believes that all non-patriots should leave the country and thinks that anyone who casts aspersion on the flag should be shot immediately; She slid up and down the bannister*.

There is reason to believe that many instances of conjoined constituents other than clauses are best regarded as reduced versions of conjoined clauses. Consider, for example, the sentence *The cruiser and the old battleship need painting*. In surface structure, this sentence consists of only one clause and has a conjoined noun phrase subject. In terms of meaning, however, it is equivalent to the complex sentence *The cruiser needs painting, and the old battleship needs painting,* which consists of two conjoined clauses. Thus it is not unreasonable to claim that the two

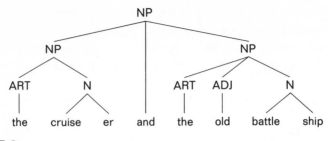

figure 5.8

sentences derive from the same complex conceptual structure. The second sentence reflects this conceptual structure fairly directly, but the first is modified by syntactic rules that delete the identical elements (**needs painting**) from one of the conjuncts and combine the two subjects, **the cruiser** and **the old battleship**, to form a conjoined subject. A similar analysis might be proposed for other sentences. Thus **She bit and scratched the mugger** can be regarded as a variant of **She bit the mugger and she scratched the mugger**; **I want to marry a man who is tall, dark, handsome, and rich** may be derived from the same conceptual structure as **I want to marry a man who is tall, who is dark, who is handsome, and who is rich**; and so on.

There are, however, sentences for which such an analysis appears to be inappropriate. For example, **John and Marsha met in New York** is certainly not equivalent to **John met in New York, and Marsha met in New York**; the latter, in fact, is semantically anomalous. By the same token, **We painted the football red, white, and blue all over** does not derive from the same conceptual structure as **We painted the football red all over, we painted the football white all over, and we painted the football blue all over**. Therefore, even if one accepts the hypothesis that conjoined clauses may be reduced by syntactic rules to single clauses containing smaller conjoined constituents, it is still dubious that all instances of conjoined constituents other than clauses arise in this way.

embedding

In a coordinate structure (like Figure 5.6 or 5.7), none of the conjoined clauses is contained in any other; by definition, the component clauses are all on a par. When one clause does function as a constituent of another, we speak instead of a relation of subordination. The subordinate clause is said to be **embedded** in the main clause.

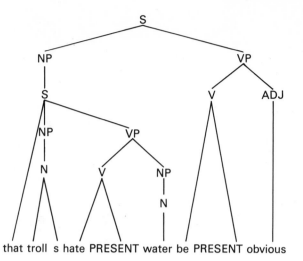

that troll s hate PRESENT water be PRESENT obvious

figure 5.9

The subordinate status of a clause is quite apparent when it functions as the subject or object of another clause. Such a clause is referred to as a **complement** clause. For example, *that trolls hate water* functions as the subject of *is obvious* in the sentence *That trolls hate water is obvious.* The surface structure of this sentence is shown in Figure 5.9. The structure of this sentence is quite analogous to that of *The answer is obvious*, except that the subject happens to be a clause rather than a simple article-noun combination. Evidence for analyzing this subject clause as a noun phrase is provided by the fact that it shares many (though not all) syntactic properties with clearly nominal constituents such as *the answer*. Notice, for instance, that both *the answer* and *that trolls hate water* can respond to the question word *what: What is obvious? The answer is obvious; What is obvious? That trolls hate water is obvious.* Moreover, the pronoun *it* can refer back to either one: *The answer is obvious, isn't it? Yes, it is obvious; That trolls hate water is obvious, isn't it? Yes, it is obvious.*

The subordinate status of relative clauses is also quite apparent. The surface structure of *Irving ruined the company which he inherited* is shown in Figure 5.10. (PRON stands for PRONOUN.) In this sentence, the relative clause *which he inherited* is embedded in the main clause *Irving ruined the company* and modifies its direct-object noun phrase, *the company*. As shown in Figure 5.10, the relative clause and the nominal it modifies combine to form a more complex noun-phrase object, *the company which he inherited.* Figure 5.10 claims that *the company which he inherited* bears the same relation to *ruined* that *my watch* does in the

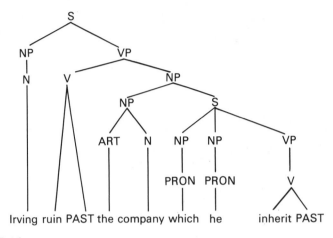

figure 5.10

simple sentence *Irving ruined my watch*—namely, both expressions are objects. It is not difficult to find evidence that supports this claim. For instance, the active sentence *Irving ruined my watch* has the passive variant *My watch was ruined by Irving;* the direct-object noun phrase *my watch* in the active sentence occurs as the surface subject in the passive variant. *The company which he inherited* functions just like *my watch* with respect to passivization: *The company which he inherited was ruined by Irving.* The constituent structure sketched in Figure 5.10 can be strongly justified on the basis of this and much other evidence.

There are many kinds of subordinate clauses in addition to relative and complement clauses, though it is not possible to deal with them systematically here. They include: adverbial clauses of time or location, typically marked by subordinators such as *when, while,* and *where (When we got there, the door was ajar; While doing push-ups, Felicita makes strange, grunting noises; Where I work, it is hard to find a parking space);* clauses specifying reason or intent, headed by subordinators such as *because, since,* and *in order to (Because she had a headache, I took my date home early; Since we were trailing by 37 runs in the eighth inning, I let my sister play; In order to appear calm for the interview, he guzzled down three quarts of Scotch);* and many others (for example: *Although she was rich, she was very happy indeed; Tom can mix martinis faster than Jerry can drink margaritas; Mars exploded, which led certain astronomers to the conclusion that it must have been inhabited by human-like creatures; They chose George to be the new sex symbol).*

The various devices for embedding one clause in another are like conjunction in that they extend our linguistic competence to an infinite set

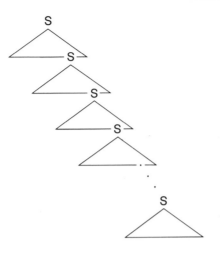

figure 5.11

of sentences. A subordinate clause embedded in a main clause to form a complex sentence may itself be complex, consisting of a main and subordinate clause; this new subordinate clause may in turn contain another one, which in turn contains another; and so on. Figure 5.11 shows the structure of such a sentence schematically; the three dots indicate that the embedding process could be extended indefinitely.

Let us use complementation for a concrete example. Figure 5.12 outlines the syntactic organization of the sentence *I think Joe hopes Harvey believes Marge feels Shirley knows the truth.* In this sentence, the complex structure *Joe hopes Harvey believes Marge feels Shirley knows the truth* functions as the direct object of the main clause verb *think.* Within this embedded structure, *Harvey believes Marge feels Shirley knows the truth* is the object of the verb *hopes. Believes,* in turn, has *Marge feels Shirley knows the truth* as its direct object, and *Shirley knows the truth* is the object of *feels.* Clearly, this sentence could be extended indefinitely (by adding a relative clause to modify *the truth,* by replacing *the truth* with yet another complement clause, or in any number of other ways).

Syntactic rules affect embedded clauses in various ways. In the case of complement clauses, one of their effects is to insert markings to indicate their subordinate status. One of these subordinators is *that,* illustrated previously in the sentence *That trolls hate water is obvious.* The insertion of *that* is obligatory when the complement clause is sentence-initial, but it may optionally be omitted in most other positions. Thus *I believe that Janice is pregnant,* in which the complement clause is noninitial, has the optional variant *I believe Janice is pregnant.* Other subordinators in-

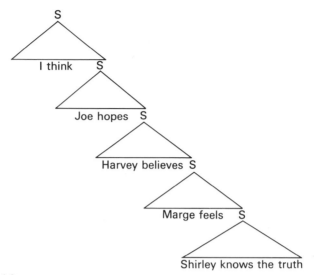

figure 5.12

serted by syntactic rules to mark complement clauses include *for . . . to* and
POSSESSIVE . . . ing, as in the following examples: *For us to get a
divorce would be tragic; I prefer for you to stay here; The President's
being so dense is astonishing; I dislike Joan's being so stubborn.* In the
combination *for . . . to, for* precedes the subject of the complement clause,
and *to* precedes the verb (and replaces its usual marking for tense).
Similarly, the subject of a complement clause is marked as a possessive
when *ing* is suffixed to the following verbal element (in place of the tense
marking). Notice that the choice among *that, for . . . to,* and *POSSES-
SIVE . . . ing* is determined in large measure by the predicate of the main
clause; a main-clause predicate may tolerate certain subordinators but not
others. The object of *advocate*, for instance, may be marked with *that* or
*POSSESSIVE . . . ing (I advocated that she leave; I advocated her leav-
ing)*, but not with *for . . . to (I advocated for her to leave* is ungrammatical). *Want*, on the other hand, tolerates *for . . . to (I want very much
for her to leave)*, but not *that* or *POSSESSIVE . . . ing* (note the ungrammaticalness of *I want that she leave* and *I want her leaving*).

Complement clauses are subject to other kinds of syntactic rules as
well. One such rule deletes the subject noun phrase of a complement
clause when it happens to be identical to some noun phrase in the main
clause (provided that the complement clause is marked by *for . . . to* or
POSSESSIVE . . . ing). Consider, for example, the sentence *I prefer for
you to stay here.* The subject of the main clause (*I*) and the subject of

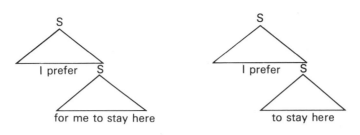

figure 5.13

the subordinate clause (*you*) happen to be different in this sentence, so no deletion is possible. Suppose, however, that the complement clause subject were also *I* (or its object form, *me*): *I prefer for me to stay here.* This sentence may be marginally acceptable, but normally the subordinate subject *me* would be deleted by virtue of its identity to the main clause subject, resulting in the sentence *I prefer to stay here.* (When the subject is deleted, *for* or the possessive marking is also deleted.) In other words, this deletion rule applies to the first structure in Figure 5.13 and yields the second structure as its "output." This way of viewing the surface structure *I prefer to stay here* reflects the fact that *I* is understood semantically to be the subject of both *prefer* and *stay*; it also has the advantage of showing that *I prefer to stay here* is basically analogous in structure to *I prefer for you to stay here.* In similar fashion, *I anticipated leaving* derives from the structure *I anticipated my leaving* through deletion of the complement-clause subject (compare *I anticipated her leaving*).

Two major syntactic rules affect the surface form of relative clauses. Both rules affect the noun phrase within the relative clause that is identical to the noun phrase the clause modifies. Let us return to the example *Irving ruined the company which he inherited.* If the relative clause were to occur alone as an independent sentence, it would have the form *He inherited the company* (or possibly *He inherited a company*). Since *the company* is the noun phrase in the relative clause that is identical to the noun phrase the clause modifies, it is subject to the two syntactic rules in question. The first of these advances the shared noun phrase to the beginning of the relative clause, and the second replaces it with the appropriate relative pronoun (*who, whom, which, whose,* or *that*). Because of these two rules, the surface structure of this sentence is the one shown in Figure 5.10, rather than Figure 5.14, which would result if the two rules did not apply. In most cases, an accompanying preposition may be moved to the beginning of the clause with the shared noun phrase, as in *Joan*

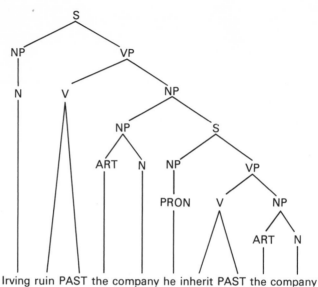

Irving ruin PAST the company he inherit PAST the company

figure 5.14

distracted the man to whom Marge was speaking. When the shared noun phrase is part of a larger nominal, the entire larger nominal may sometimes be transported; *I despised the man whose boots I was polishing* is an example.

the relationship between conceptual and surface structures

derivations

Up to this point, we have concentrated on surface structures, but the surface structure of a sentence represents only one facet of its syntactic organization. As we noted in Chapter Four, every surface structure manifests an underlying conceptual structure from which it is derived by syntactic rules and the choice of lexical items. To give a full account of how a sentence is put together, one must describe not only its surface structure but also its conceptual structure and the step-by-step **derivation** of the former from the latter. We do not yet know enough about human cognition to be able to describe conceptual structures in great detail, but it is clear that the relationship between conceptual and surface structures is often distant and indirect. The translation of a conceptual structure into

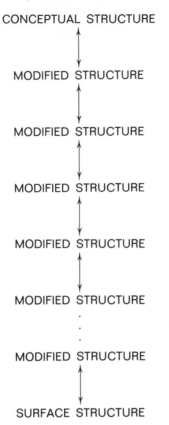

CONCEPTUAL STRUCTURE

MODIFIED STRUCTURE

MODIFIED STRUCTURE

MODIFIED STRUCTURE

MODIFIED STRUCTURE

MODIFIED STRUCTURE

MODIFIED STRUCTURE

SURFACE STRUCTURE

figure 5.15

its surface manifestation involves both the substitution of lexical items for conceptual components and the application of a long series of syntactic rules. The derivation of a sentence is schematized in Figure 5.15.

Each lexical selection and rule application modifies the abstract underlying structure in some way, making it less abstract and more like its ultimate surface form. The difference between the conceptual and surface structure of a sentence is thus the cumulative result of a great many small modifications effected by syntactic rules and lexical choices. Each of these modifications connects an underlying structure with one that is slightly less abstract.

ambiguous sentences

Because the relationship between conceptual and surface structures is very distant, the differences between two or more conceptual

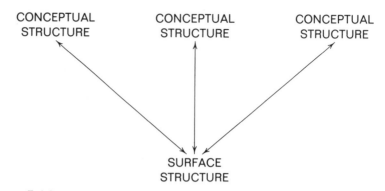

figure 5.16

structures will not always be evident on the surface. The application of syntactic rules and the choice of lexical items may obliterate the underlying differences so that a number of distinct conceptual structures have the same surface manifestation, as schematized in Figure 5.16. When a sentence can represent two or more different conceptual structures, we recognize it as being ambiguous, as having alternate semantic interpretations.

The quarrelsome Goths want another war is an interesting example. This sentence is ambiguous, but under either interpretation it consists of the same string of morphemes and has the same surface tree structure. *The quarrelsome Goths want another war* may mean that all Goths are quarrelsome and want another war; under this interpretation, it is related to *The Goths want another war and they are quarrelsome* and to *The Goths, who are quarrelsome, want another war*, which come from the same underlying structure. On the other hand, *The quarrelsome Goths want another war* may imply only that those Goths who happen to be quarrelsome wish to fight again. Under this second interpretation, it manifests the same conceptual structure as *The Goths who are quarrelsome want another war*.

Not every ambiguous sentence is like *The quarrelsome Goths want another war* in having precisely the same surface structure under its alternate interpretations. Consider *I'm standing near the bank*, for instance. This sentence is ambiguous because *bank* can represent either of two noun morphemes; one *bank* designates the land along a river, and the other designates a financial institution or the building housing it. Phonologically, the sentence is the same under either interpretation, since the two nouns *bank* are pronounced alike. The two surface structures of *I'm standing near the bank* are slightly different, however, since a surface structure is a structured string of morphemes and the two nouns *bank* are different morphemes. Similar examples of lexical ambiguity are legion.

Ambiguous sentences may also differ in surface tree structure under their alternate interpretations, as some previous examples show. For instance, the sentence *Steve or Sam and Bob will come* consists of the same string of morphemes under either of its interpretations, but the syntactic rules responsible for merging the two distinct underlying structures into the same morpheme string do not obliterate entirely the corresponding differences in tree structure. The two surface tree structures of *Steve or Sam and Bob will come* were illustrated in Figure 5.2.

Here are some other examples of ambiguity that may prove amusing or instructive: *The man decided on the train; I had a car stolen; Biting dogs can be bothersome; They are flying planes; I dislike fat men and women; It's too hot to eat; I demanded what he had stolen; The chauffeur will dust or wash and polish the car; The missionaries are ready to serve; Rodney broke the barn windows with his little sister; They fed her dog biscuits; I gave John what I wanted; It's the man that stole the candy; Sydney may leave; Tom thinks he is smarter than he is; Joan said she wanted to marry a Fascist; Everybody can't win in Las Vegas.*

synonymous sentences

Syntactic rules and lexical choices do not always have the effect of neutralizing underlying differences to produce relative surface uniformity. The opposite happens as well, so that a single conceptual structure often has divergent surface manifestations, as schematized in Figure 5.17. In such cases, the surface diversity that is introduced by syntactic rules and lexical choices conceals underlying uniformity.

The surface difference between *He fell into the sea* and *He fell into the ocean* is introduced by the choice of different lexical items, *sea* and *ocean*, to represent the same conceptual component. The two can be used interchangeably, since they have the same syntactic function and the same conceptual import. The two sentences thus manifest the same conceptual structure, although they consist of different strings of morphemes.

The surface differences that result from alternate lexical choices are sometimes more extensive. Consider, for instance, the idea of dividing something into two parts. The word *bisect* has this conceptual import, but so does the phrase *divide into two parts*. Consequently, the same conceptual structure that underlies *The East Germans bisected Berlin with a wall* has an alternate manifestation as *The East Germans divided Berlin into two parts with a wall*. No single lexical item in the second sentence has the same conceptual import as *bisect*. Instead, a number of lexical items are combined syntactically to achieve the same semantic effect. The sentences *Harvey is a bachelor* and *Harvey is a man who has*

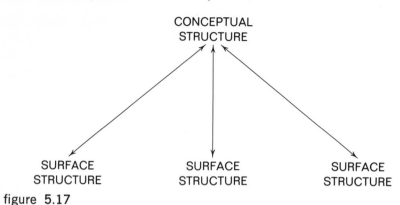

figure 5.17

never married constitute a more extreme example. The conceptual import of *man who has never married,* which consists of the noun *man* and a relative clause embedded after it, is represented in the first sentence by the single lexical item *bachelor.* The effect of alternate lexical choices in determining the surface manifestation of a conceptual structure can, therefore, be quite extensive.

The surface differences introduced by syntactic rules can also be quite extensive, as we will see later in some detail. For the moment, we will content ourselves with a single example. Consider the sentences *A detective hunted down the killer, The policeman looked over the situation,* and *The robber tied up the manager of the bank.* Each of these sentences contains a two-part verb constituent that consists of a verb and a preposition-like **particle.** *Hunted down, looked over,* and *tied up* are the verb constituents, and *down, over,* and *up* are their particles.

Each of these three sentences can be matched with another that manifests the same conceptual structure and contains the same lexical items. The matching sentences are, respectively, **A *detective hunted the killer down, The policeman looked the situation over,*** and **The *robber tied the manager of the bank up.*** A syntactic rule that we will call the Particle Shift rule accounts for the differences between these sentence pairs. This rule separates a verb and a particle by placing the particle after the following direct object noun phrase. Applied to the structure underlying *A detective hunted down the killer,* the Particle Shift rule produces the structure underlying **A *detective hunted the killer down*** by permuting the particle *down* with the noun phrase *the killer.* Similarly, this rule changes *(looked over) (the situation)* to *(looked) (the situation) (over)* and *(tied up) (the manager of the bank)* to *(tied) (the manager of the bank) (up).*

The derivation of the first pair of sentences is schematized in Figure 5.18, in which we can see that **A *detective hunted down the killer*** and **A *detective hunted the killer down*** result from the same conceptual

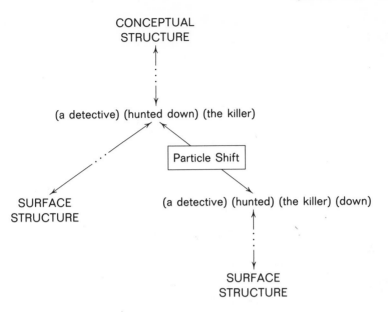

CONCEPTUAL
STRUCTURE

(a detective) (hunted down) (the killer)

Particle Shift

SURFACE
STRUCTURE

(a detective) (hunted) (the killer) (down)

SURFACE
STRUCTURE

figure 5.18

structure and involve the same lexical choices. By and large, the same syntactic rules apply in the derivation of these two sentences. The sole difference between them is that the Particle Shift rule applies in the derivation of one but not the other. Like many syntactic rules, this one is optional—it may apply but does not have to. When it does, the sentence A *detective hunted the killer down* results. When it does not, *hunted* and *down* remain adjacent in the string, yielding A *detective hunted down the killer*.

Notice that neither sentence is derived from the other. Rather, both are manifestations of the same underlying structure, represented in Figure 5.18 as *(a detective) (hunted down) (the killer)*. This underlying structure is not the shared conceptual structure itself, but an intermediate structure derived from it by previous lexical choices and rule applications. The same will be true of all our examples of syntactic rules. Surface structures are the product of syntactic rules; these rules do not *apply* to surface structures, but rather *derive* them from abstract underlying structures. At present, however, we can only speculate about the details of the more abstract representations of sentences, including the conceptual structures themselves.

syntactic rules

A number of syntactic rules were informally discussed in the preceding sections. We will now look at syntactic rules in a somewhat more systematic fashion. The rules we will be concerned with all have the effect of modifying a tree structure in some way, deriving from it a structure that is less abstract, as shown in Figure 5.15; such rules are called **transformations**. Three basic types of transformations can be distinguished: reduction rules, insertion rules, and rearrangement rules.

reduction rules

All languages have devices for avoiding the repetition of identical elements in sentences. For example, consider the sentence *My uncle has been dieting, and my aunt has been dieting, too*. This sentence is complex, manifesting a conceptual structure with two components. One component underlies *My uncle has been dieting*, while the other underlies *My aunt has been dieting*, which is conjoined with the first by *and . . . too*. There are many other ways in which this complex conceptual structure could be manifested, some of them involving radically different lexical choices and syntactic rules (for example, *Both my aunt and my uncle have been eating less than usual in order to lose weight*). However, we will be concerned only with three alternative sentences that result from the same basic lexical and syntactic options.

The similarity of the following four sentences is readily apparent:

My uncle has been dieting, and my aunt has been dieting, too.
My uncle has been dieting, and my aunt has been, too.
My uncle has been dieting, and my aunt has, too.
My uncle has been dieting, and my aunt, too.

Not only do they come from the same conceptual structure, but they are also very similar lexically and syntactically. Each sentence differs from the one that follows it only in that it contains one more verb word in the second conjunct. Thus, *My uncle has been dieting, and my aunt has been dieting, too* differs from *My uncle has been dieting, and my aunt has been, too* by the second occurrence of *dieting*. The second instance of *been* in the second sentence distinguishes it from *My uncle has been dieting, and my aunt has, too*. This differs from *My uncle has been dieting, and my aunt, too* by the second occurrence of *has*.

These four sentences come from a common underlying structure, in which the full verb sequence *has been dieting* is represented in the second conjunct. *My uncle has been dieting, and my aunt has been dieting, too* thus reflects this common underlying structure most directly, although the

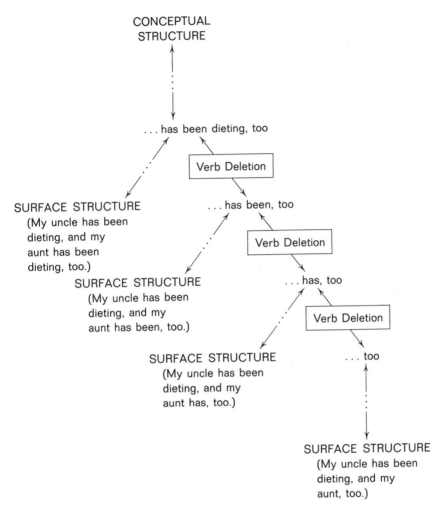

figure 5.19

relationship may be quite distant. A syntactic rule of English that we will call Verb Deletion applies to the common underlying structure and provides for its alternate manifestations, as shown in Figure 5.19.

The Verb Deletion rule applies optionally to the second conjunct of a complex sentence structure that involves conjoining with *too*. What this rule does (in somewhat simplified terms) is to delete the last in a sequence of verb words, provided that the same sequence of verb words also occurs in the first conjunct. The verb sequence ***has been dieting*** occurs in both conjuncts of the structure underlying ***My uncle has been dieting, and my aunt has been dieting, too***, so Verb Deletion can apply. If this rule applies just once, *has been dieting* is reduced to *has been* in the second conjunct. If it applies a second time, *has been* is reduced to *has,* since *been* is now the last verb word in the sequence. A third application of Verb Deletion reduces *has* to zero. All four sentences therefore derive from the same underlying structure, the choice depending solely on how many times Verb Deletion applies.

Reduction rules such as Verb Deletion are very common. Every language has syntactic rules which, under certain conditions, allow constituents to be deleted from a sentence structure when identical constituents occur elsewhere within the same sentence. When *has been dieting* is deleted to produce *My uncle has been dieting, and my aunt, too,* there is no doubt about what is predicated of the aunt. A speaker of English immediately interprets this sentence to mean that the aunt has been dieting, despite the fact that no verb phrase occurs overtly with *my aunt.* Because a duplicate of the deleted sequence occurs in the first conjunct, the full significance of the surface string *and my aunt, too* can be ascertained by examining the rest of the sentence. The reduction of duplicated elements thus eliminates a great deal of potential repetition without a loss of semantic content.

Verb Deletion is similar to two rules previously discussed (in fact, the three may be different manifestations of the same basic rule). One is the rule that derives *Jane munched on snails, Joyce on roasted grasshoppers, and Julie on chocolate-covered caterpillars* by deleting *munched* from the second two conjuncts. The other rule erases *dissolve in Coca-Cola* from one conjunct to derive *Uranium will not dissolve in Coca-Cola, but teeth will.* In all three instances, the identical elements are deleted without a trace. Sometimes, however, a remnant is left behind when one of two identical elements is reduced; such a remnant is called a **pro form**, since it stands for another, fuller expression. *One,* for instance, is a pro form that can stand in for a noun and certain of its modifiers. *This pretty black widow spider looks healthier than that pretty black widow spider* can thus be reduced to *This pretty black widow spider looks healthier than that one*; a reduction transformation replaces *pretty black widow spider* with the pro form *one.*

The reduction rules discussed so far are applicable when two constituents have the same meaning. Other reductions depend on **coreference** rather than identity of sense; that is, they are applicable only if the two elements in question are taken as referring to the same objects or individuals. For example, *himself* is a pro form that is coreferential to the noun phrase *a gray-haired man who looked like a lawyer* in the sentence

A gray-haired man who looked like a lawyer was admiring himself in the mirror. It is easy to see that the replacement of this complex nominal by the reflexive pronoun *himself* depends on coreference rather than identity of meaning. This sentence can only be interpreted to mean that just one man is involved (as both the subject and object of *was admiring*); if two different gray-haired men looking like lawyers were involved, the notion would have to be expressed differently. The reflexive pronouns (*myself, himself*, and so on) and the third-person personal pronouns (such as *he, she, them*, and *it*), whose occurrence depends on coreference, differ in this respect from the indefinite pronoun *one*, which requires only identity of meaning. In *This pretty black widow spider looks healthier than that one*, two different spiders are involved.

Two other reduction rules discussed earlier require coreference: the rule that deletes the subject of a complement clause and the rule that reduces a noun phrase to a relative pronoun. The derivation of *Joe prefers to be rich* from *Joe prefers for Joe to be rich* illustrates complement-subject deletion. This derivation is permissible only when the two occurrences of *Joe* are coreferential. *Joe prefers to be rich* cannot have the interpretation that one person named *Joe* prefers for some other person named *Joe* to be rich, only that he himself be rich. Similarly, *the man* and *who* must be coreferential in the sentence *Irma politely thanked the man who had rescued her from a horrible death*. The sentence cannot mean that one man rescued her and that she thanked another man—*the man* and *who* must designate the same individual.

In conclusion, it should be noted that some deletion rules do not depend on identity at all, but only on grammatical factors. For instance, the subject *you* may be deleted in an imperative sentence even if the sentence contains no other occurrence of *you*. Thus *Leave my wife alone!* is an optional variant of *You leave my wife alone!* Another example is the deletion of a preposition when it occurs directly before the subordinator *that*. Observe the following sentences: *I am sure of it; I am sure of this; I am sure of winning the election; I am sure of his honesty; I am sure that Winfred is still alive*. After the adjective *sure*, the preposition *of* occurs with many kinds of noun phrases (including *it, this, winning the election*, and *his honesty*). However, *of* is not permitted when the following nominal happens to be a clause headed by *that: I am sure of that Winfred is still alive* is ungrammatical. Instead we find *I am sure that Winfred is still alive*, derived by the obligatory deletion of the preposition before *that*. Finally, let us mention the deletion of a relative pronoun plus a form of the verb *be* when followed by an adjective or a prepositional phrase. By virtue of this rule (or rules), *a speech full of clichés* and *the spittoon near the door* may be derived from the fuller structures *a speech that was full of clichés* and *the spittoon that is near the door*.

insertion rules

Through the reduction of repeated constituents, large portions of an underlying tree structure may fail to be manifested overtly in surface structure (although their conceptual import can be reconstructed on the basis of the rest of the sentence). On the other hand, some syntactic rules have the effect of introducing into surface structure elements that are semantically empty or that duplicate information represented elsewhere in the sentence. Such elements may be regarded as **trappings** on sentences, as syntactically introduced embellishments with no independent semantic content.

The rules introducing *that, for...to,* and *POSSESSIVE...ing* as subordinators in complement clauses are examples of transformations that insert sentence trappings. In some of their uses, *there* and *it* are meaningless trappings added to sentences by insertion rules. When *be* has an indefinite subject, this subject may be replaced by *there* in surface structure; the original subject then occurs following *be* instead. Because of the *there*-insertion rule, we find sentences like *There is a hippopotamus in that cornfield* and *There are many people out of work* as optional variants of *A hippopotamus is in that cornfield* and *Many people are out of work*. *It* is regularly inserted in English in nonimperative sentences that would otherwise lack a surface subject. For instance, *is snowing* has no semantic subject in *It is snowing*; the *it* is inserted to give it a subject in surface structure. By the same token, *it* is a sentence trapping in *It's Penelope that shot my goat*.

Agreement rules insert markings that duplicate information represented elsewhere in the sentence. The markings they introduce therefore have no intrinsic meaning of their own and can be regarded as sentence trappings. The most common types of agreement rules are no doubt those that mark a verb to agree with its subject or object and those that induce agreement between a noun and its modifiers. Verbs agree with their subjects in English, though the overt indications of this process are very restricted; for most verbs, the only overtly marked distinction is between third-person singular subjects and all others (*eats* versus *eat*), and the distinction is made only in the present tense. Noun–modifier agreement in English is restricted to number agreement on demonstratives (*this truck* and *that cathedral* versus *these trucks* and *those cathedrals*). In other languages, however, subject–verb and noun–modifier agreement is much more elaborate, and various other kinds of agreement are possible as well.

rearrangement rules

Rearrangement rules modify tree structures by changing the linear order of elements or their arrangement into constituents. One of the simplest rearrangement rules, Particle Shift, was illustrated in Figure 5.18. The Particle Shift transformation optionally permutes a particle and a noun-phrase object to produce pairs of sentences like **A** *detective hunted down the killer* and **A** *detective hunted the killer down* as variant manifestations of the same underlying structure.

The effects of rearrangement rules are often more extensive. For instance, recall the rule that moves the shared noun phrase in a relative clause to clause-initial position, as in the derivation of **Irving** *ruined the company which he inherited* (compare Figures 5.14 and 5.10). In this particular example, the nominal that ultimately surfaces as *which* moves from object position to pre-subject position, but it remains within the same simple clause. Suppose, however, that the relative clause happens to be complex, as in Figure 5.20. This figure represents the structure we obtain by embedding the sentence shown in Figure 5.12—*I think Joe hopes Harvey believes Marge feels Shirley knows the truth*—as a relative clause modifying **the truth** in the simple sentence **The truth is a disturbing one.** The shared noun phrase in the relative clause, **the truth**, is in the most deeply embedded clause in Figure 5.20, yet it can still undergo the rule that transports the shared nominal to initial position in the relative, where it becomes a relative pronoun. In surface structure, *which* is found in the topmost clause of the relative, with **I** *think*: **The truth which I think Joe hopes Harvey believes Marge feels Shirley knows is a disturbing one.** It had to traverse several intervening clauses to reach this surface position, and it should be apparent that there is no intrinsic limit on how far a relative pronoun can move in this manner, depending on the complexity of the relative. Observe that the same rule (or a very similar one) also applies in the derivation of questions. In **What** *do you think Joe hopes Harvey believes Marge feels Shirley knows?*, the question word *what* functions semantically as the object of *knows*. (The sentence in Figure 5.12, in which **the truth** responds to *what*, is a perfectly good answer to this question.) Question words are transported to the beginning of the interrogative clause, regardless of how complex it may be.

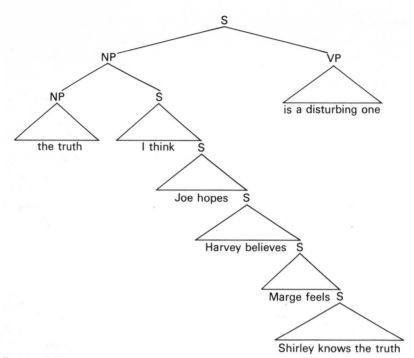

figure 5.20

Complement clauses are subject to two important rearrangement rules, commonly called Extraposition and Subject Raising. Extraposition simply moves a complement clause marked with *that* or *for...to* to the end of the main clause. Applied to the structure shown in Figure 5.9, for example, Extraposition derives the one in Figure 5.21; the former surfaces as *That trolls hate water is obvious,* and the latter as *It is obvious that trolls hate water.* The appearance of *it* in the second sentence is not due to the Extraposition rule itself, but rather to an insertion rule discussed earlier, which inserts *it* in sentences that would otherwise lack a surface subject (compare *It is snowing*). Here are further examples of pairs of sentences related by Extraposition: *For Mickey to want to join the Air Force would be shocking* and *It would be shocking for Mickey to want to join the Air Force; I advocate that you leave at once very strongly* and *I advocate very strongly that you leave at once; That for Mike to quit now would be terrible is obvious* and *It is obvious that it would be terrible for Mike to quit now* (in this last pair, Extraposition is applied twice).

Subject Raising affects the subject of complement clauses marked by *for...to* or *POSSESSIVE...ing.* It replaces the complement clause with its subject, moving the rest of the complement clause to the end of the

figure 5.21

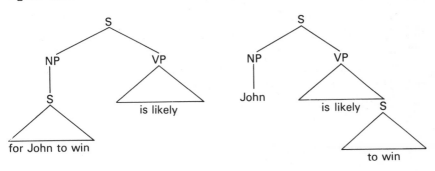

figure 5.22

verb-phrase constituent in the main clause. For example, Subject Raising derives the second structure in Figure 5.22 from the first, yielding *John is likely to win* as an optional variant of *For John to win is likely*. Similarly, Subject Raising derives *John stopped hallucinating* as a surface variant of *John's hallucinating stopped*. Notice that *for* and **POSSESSIVE** are erased when the complement clause subject is raised (just as they are when it is deleted). Notice also that Subject Raising can apply only with certain main-clause predicates, not just any predicate. *Possible* exemplifies a predicate that does not tolerate Subject Raising; *John is possible to win* is not a grammatical variant of *For John to win is possible*.

The above examples show Subject Raising with respect to subject clauses. The subject of an object clause can also be raised, replacing the clause in which it originates as the main-clause object. For instance, Subject Raising derives the second structure in Figure 5.23 from the first. Conceptually, **Bill** is not the object of **believes** in the sentence *Joan believes Bill to be rich*, but rather the subject of **be rich**. That is, what Joan

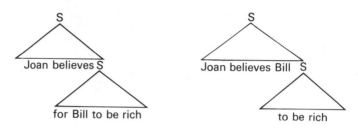

figure 5.23

believes is not Bill, but rather the proposition that Bill is rich. The structure on the left in Figure 5.23 thus reflects the meaning of this sentence more directly than does its surface structure, shown on the right. (The *for ... to* subordinator can occur with the complement of *believe* only when Subject Raising applies; if it did not apply, the sentence *Joan believes that Bill is rich* would result.) It is easy to show that **Bill** is the direct object of **believes** in surface structure. Notice, for example, that it can become the subject of **believes** in the passive: **Bill is believed by Joan to be rich**. This would not be possible unless **Bill** were part of the main clause.

derivations

The derivation of a surface structure from its underlying conceptual structure typically involves many different lexical choices and syntactic rule applications (see Figure 5.15). To conclude our brief discussion of syntax, we will do well to examine certain aspects of sentence derivation in more detail. We will take the insertion of lexical items for granted and concentrate on syntactic rules.

sequential rule application

Syntactic rules are posited to account for the discrepancies between conceptual structures and surface structures. It would be logically possible for all the differences between a given conceptual structure and its surface manifestation to be introduced by a single rule, but in fact this appears never to be the case. Instead, we invariably find that the derivation of a surface structure is the cumulative product of the application of many distinct syntactic rules. Each of these rules figures in the derivation of many other sentences as well, and for the most part the rules involved are

UNDERLYING STRUCTURE

the woman (the woman is nervous)

Relativization: the woman (who is nervous)

Relative Reduction: the woman (nervous)

Adjective Preposing: the nervous woman

SURFACE STRUCTURE

figure 5.24

independent, in the sense that one can apply regardless of whether or not any other does.

We can view these rules as applying sequentially (rather than simultaneously)—the "output" of one rule constitutes the "input" to the next. (Rule applications are sequential in an abstract, logical sense, much as the steps in a mathematical proof follow one another in a certain sequence; they are not sequential in any temporal sense, as no claims are being made here about linguistic performance.) Let us take for illustration the derivation of the nominal *the nervous woman*. This derivation is sketched in Figure 5.24, in which parentheses are used to mark an embedded clause.

Nervous is claimed to derive from an underlying modifying clause (a sentence like *I see the nervous woman* involves at least two propositions: that I see the woman, and that she is nervous); were this clause to stand alone as an independent sentence, it might appear as *The woman is nervous*. The first rules to affect this underlying structure are those that derive any relative clause; namely, the rules that transport the shared noun phrase to the beginning of the relative and reduce it to a relative pronoun. It happens that the shared noun phrase, *the woman*, is already in clause-initial position, so the transportation has no visible effect, but its reduction to a relative pronoun yields the modified structure *the woman who is nervous*. No other rules need apply, since this itself is a grammatical expression. However, the rule that deletes a relative pronoun plus the verb *be* (we will call it Relative Reduction) is eligible to apply, and if it does, the result is *the woman nervous*, in which the modifying adjective follows the noun. *The woman nervous* happens not to be grammatical, because simple adjectives are obligatorily moved in front of the noun they modify by a rule that we will call Adjective Preposing, which derives the surface structure *the nervous woman*. If the modifier were complex, on the other hand, it would remain after the noun, since Adjective Preposing affects only simple adjectives. For instance, *the woman nervous about having children* is derived by relativization and Relative Reduction, but Adjective Preposing cannot apply (*the nervous about having children woman* is ungrammatical, as is *the nervous woman about having children*).

Notice two things about this derivation. First, relativization, Relative

Reduction, and Adjective Preposing are basically independent processes, not just facets of a single rule; relativization can apply without the other two (yielding *the woman who is nervous*), and Relative Reduction sometimes applies without Adjective Preposing (as in the derivation of *the woman nervous about having children* or *the spittoon near the door*). Second, the application of the various rules must be regarded as sequential rather than simultaneous. Only after relativization has taken place are the conditions for Relative Reduction met, namely, the presence of a relative pronoun plus *be*. And only after Relative Reduction has applied does a simple adjective directly follow the noun it modifies, making possible the application of Adjective Preposing. Therefore we are dealing with separate grammatical processes, which nevertheless interact in a very specific way in the derivation of sentences.

rule ordering

The notion of rule ordering is implicit in the preceding discussion. In many instances, the rules which derive a surface structure must apply in a particular order, either because one rule creates the structures on which the next rule operates, or because the opposite order of application would yield incorrect results. (Once again, the ordering is an abstract, logical one, like the ordered steps in a mathematical proof, not a temporal one.)

Consider once more the derivation in Figure 5.24. The two rules of relativization must precede Relative Reduction in order of application, for they create the structure (relative pronoun plus *be*) on which the latter operates. Similarly, Relative Reduction must precede Adjective Preposing, since the sequence required by the latter (noun plus simple adjective) arises only through application of the former. The derivation of *It is obvious that trolls hate water* provides another example. Two rules, Extraposition and *It* Insertion, derive this sentence (Figure 5.21) from the structure that would otherwise surface as *That trolls hate water is obvious* (Figure 5.9). Extraposition applies first and moves the subject clause to the end of the sentence. Only then can *It* Insertion apply, since this rule inserts *it* as subject only in clauses in which the subject position is vacant.

In these examples, one rule creates the structures on which the next operates, so their application is necessarily ordered. Let us now look at an instance where two rules must be ordered in a particular way because the opposite ordering would yield incorrect results. Figure 5.25 sketches the derivation of *They are likely to lose. THEY* and *BE*, in capital letters,

	UNDERLYING STRUCTURE
	(THEY lose) BE likely
For...To Insertion:	(for THEY to lose) BE likely
Subject Raising:	THEY BE likely (to lose)
Subject-Verb Agreement:	THEY are likely (to lose)
Subject Case Marking:	they are likely (to lose)
	SURFACE STRUCTURE

figure 5.25

are used to designate the pronoun and verb before they are inflected by the rules under consideration.

For ... To Insertion is not our concern here, but rather the ordering between Subject Raising on the one hand and the two inflectional rules on the other hand. If Subject Raising applies first, as in Figure 5.25, no problems arise. *BE* agrees with the new subject, *THEY*, and is correctly marked as the plural form *are* (rather than the singular *is*). Moreover, *THEY* is inflected as *they* (rather than *them*), since it is not preceded by *for* when it is marked for case. However, the result would in both instances be incorrect if the two inflectional rules were to apply prior to Subject Raising. In the pre–Subject Raising structure *for THEY to lose BE likely*, the clause *for THEY to lose* is the subject of *BE*, and *THEY* follows *for*, so we would expect *BE* to be marked singular and *THEY* to be inflected as *them* (compare *For them to lose is likely*). Were Subject Raising to follow the inflectional rules, therefore, the result would be the ungrammatical sentence *Them is likely to lose*.

abstract structures

Perhaps the most fundamental point in our discussion of syntax has been the contention that surface structures must be viewed in relation to more abstract, underlying structures which they reflect only indirectly, through the mediation of various rules. Since surface structures and semantic structures clearly cannot be equated, it is hardly controversial that underlying conceptual structures of some kind must be posited. However, the justification for positing modified structures intermediate between conceptual and surface structures, as in Figure 5.15, may not be quite so obvious.

Two kinds of evidence can be offered to support these hypothesized intermediate structures, one of which has already been discussed. We have

UNDERLYING STRUCTURE

you imagine (you be rich)

For...To Insertion: you imagine (for you to be rich)

Subject Raising: you imagine you (to be rich)

Reflexivization: you imagine yourself (to be rich)

You Deletion: imagine yourself (to be rich)

SURFACE STRUCTURE

figure 5.26

seen that numerous distinct rules enter into the derivation of a given sentence. Moreover, some of these rules must apply before others can. These facts clearly imply the existence of structures that are the output of one rule and the input to another; in other words, they imply the existence of intermediate structures.

The second kind of evidence for intermediate structures is that they make it possible to eliminate apparent irregularities in favor of general rules. Let us consider just one example, the occurrence of the reflexive pronoun *yourself* in the imperative sentence **Imagine yourself to be rich**.

The normal rule for the occurrence of reflexives (in their nonemphatic use at least) is as follows: if two coreferential noun phrases occur in the same clause, the second one is marked as a reflexive pronoun. Thus **Joan admires Joan** reduces to **Joan admires herself** if the two instances of **Joan** are taken as designating the same person. However, **Joan imagined that someone bit Joan** cannot be manifested as **Joan imagined that someone bit herself**, since the two occurrences of **Joan** are in separate clauses. (Instead, simple pronominalization would derive **Joan imagined that someone bit her**.)

Given these observations, the appearance of *yourself* in **Imagine yourself to be rich** is surprising. There is only one noun phrase (*yourself*) in the surface structure of this sentence, and since Reflexivization requires two coreferential noun phrases, the occurrence of the reflexive cannot be explained in terms of surface structure alone. Nor can it be explained in terms of conceptual structure; conceptually, *you* is the subject of *imagine*, but the object of *imagine* is not *you*—rather it is the proposition *you be rich* (compare **Imagine that you are rich**). Therefore neither the surface nor the conceptual structure of **Imagine yourself to be rich** contains two coreferential noun phrases in the same clause, and the occurrence of the reflexive pronoun would appear to be irregular.

The difficulty vanishes when we consider the step-by-step derivation of this sentence through the appropriate intermediate stages. This derivation is given in Figure 5.26. All of the rules involved have been justified on the basis of other kinds of sentences. The important rule here is Subject Raising, which substitutes *you* for the complement clause as the object of *imagine*. The output of Subject Raising is the intermediate structure *you imagine you to be rich*, with both occurrences of *you* in the main clause. In this intermediate structure, and in it alone, the conditions for Reflexivization are met, so the new object of *imagine* is reflexivized to *yourself*. The subject *you* is later deleted, as it generally is in imperative sentences. The occurrence of *yourself* in this sentence is therefore not an irregularity at all. It follows from the general rule of Reflexivization— granted the existence of intermediate structures in a derivation.

suggestions for study and discussion

1. Divide the following complex sentences into their (surface) clauses:

> *Harvey says that his mother dislikes women who do not despise the title "Ms."*
> *Boys who believe that aggressiveness is good and that sentiment is bad are good, but girls who believe that kindness is bad and that toughness is good are bad.*
> *It is evident that for women who have children to succeed in business when no day-care centers are available is difficult.*
> *I didn't anticipate Martha's asking for a divorce or John's having a nervous breakdown, but I fully expected Pat to hope to try to start to attempt to save their marriage.*
> *That for the woman who the man that the girl who Peter slapped slandered likes to try to become liberated is improbable is true.*

Identify each clause as a conjunct, a main clause, a complement clause, a relative clause, or an embedded clause of some other type. What are some of the rules discussed in this chapter that apply in the derivation of these sentences?

2. Find as many alternate interpretations as possible for the ambiguous sentences listed on page 125. Think of other examples to illustrate each type of ambiguity they represent. Can you find sentences that display still other kinds of ambiguity? How are these ambiguities resolved in context? You might have a contest to see who can construct a sentence with the most interpretations (it would be advisable to set an upper limit on the length of the sentences permitted).

3. Three sentences are listed below. After each sentence, a sketch is given of its underlying structure and the rules discussed in this chapter that serve to derive its surface structure. Show the step-by-step derivation of each of these sentences by means of a diagram analogous to Figures 5.24, 5.25, and 5.26.

Sam thinks that my mother believes Harvey to be a crook.
Underlying structure: Sam think (my mother believe (Harvey be a crook))
Rules: For ... To Insertion, Subject Raising, *That* Insertion, Subject–
Verb Agreement

Men who are liked by women are admired by boys.
Underlying structure: Boys admire men (women like men)
Rules: Passivization, Relativization, Subject–Verb Agreement

*Men who change their names are believed by George to be thought by
Martha to be anxious to hold people up.*
*Underlying structure: George believe (Martha think (men (men change
their names) be anxious for (men (men change their names) hold up
people)))*
Rules: Particle Shift, Relativization, *For ... To* Insertion, Complement
Subject Deletion, Preposition Deletion, Subject Raising, Passivization, Sub-
ject–Verb Agreement

4. In the text, a rule of Preposition Deletion was described that deletes a
preposition when it directly precedes the subordinator *that.* Because of this
rule, we find surface structures such as *I am sure that Winfred is still alive,*
which derives from the underlying structure *I am sure of that Winfred is still
alive* (compare *I am sure of it*). Can you find other examples of Preposition
Deletion, involving different prepositions or different types of sentences?

The Preposition Deletion rule is actually more general, as shown by the
last sentence in question 3 above. Restate the rule so that it will handle data
such as the following: *I am anxious to attend the party; He's not sure whether
to bow or not; We weren't informed why that decision was made; I'm not
sure who delivered the package; Joe was disappointed at Joan's turning out
to be so ugly.* Can you find cases where the rule does not apply, though one
would expect it to on the basis of the other data considered? Can you find
cases where it applies only optionally?

Give arguments to justify positing underlying structures such as *I am
sure of that Winfred is still alive,* with a preposition that is eventually deleted.
In addition to the sentences already examined, you might consider data such
as this: *What I am sure of is that Winfred is still alive; Are you sure that
Winfred is still alive? Yes, I'm sure of it; What are you sure of? I'm sure
that Winfred is still alive.*

5. On the basis of the analyses presented in this chapter, posit underlying
structures for the sentences below and show their step-by-step derivation by
means of the appropriate rules, as you did in question 3 above.

*Tell me the name of the soldier who tried to kill himself with this rusty
bayonet.*
*Mary is thought by Joan to be believed by everyone to be said by the man
in the next room to want to make a fool of herself.*
*It is obvious that it is impossible for Pete to be sure that he loves Helen,
for her not to want to marry him, and for their parents to believe them
to be mature.*

6. Listed below are seven sentences of Samoan (given in the standard Samoan orthography). Find the semantic value of each lexical item. State the principles that determine word order for these sentences.

E sogi e le tama le ufi i le to'i.	'The boy cuts the yam with the axe.'
Sa sogi e le teine le ufi.	'The girl cut the yam.'
Sa fa'apa'ū e Ioane le to'i.	'John dropped the axe.'
E fa'apa'ū e le teine le peni.	'The girl drops the pen.'
Sa pa'ū le ufi.	'The yam fell.'
E pa'ū le to'i.	'The axe falls.'
Sa sogi e Ioane le ufi i le peni.	'John cut the yam with the pen.'

7. The phrases below are from Luiseño. Each word consists of two morphemes; isolate the morphemes and state the meaning of each. These examples illustrate agreement between a noun and an adjective that modifies it; describe this agreement. ([ŋ] stands for a velar nasal—see Chapter 6.)

kiik xwaayanik	'to (the) white house'
tooŋay yawaywiŋay	from (the) pretty rock'
tootal xwaayantal	'with (the) white rock'
kiŋa yawaywiŋa	'in (the) pretty house'
kiŋay yawaywiŋay	'from (the) pretty house'
tooik xwaayanik	'to (the) white rock'
tooŋa xwaayanŋa	'in (the) white rock'

8. In traditional grammar, an important distinction was made between "restrictive" and "nonrestrictive" relative clauses, and modern linguistic analysis has affirmed the correctness of this distinction. Restrictive clauses are normally represented orthographically with no special punctuation, but nonrestrictive clauses are set off by commas:

The girl who sold me the flower was pretty.
The girl, who sold me the flower, was pretty.

Who sold me the flower is restrictive in the first sentence, but nonrestrictive in the second.
        Find as many differences as you can—syntactic, semantic, and phonological—between these two types of relative clauses.

9. In the last section of this chapter, an argument involving Reflexivization was given to justify positing the existence of intermediate structures in a derivation. Similar arguments can be given to justify certain proposed underlying structures and syntactic rules.
        Felix wants to leave derives, it has been claimed, from an underlying structure in which *Felix* is the subject of both the main and the subordinate clause: *Felix wants (Felix leave)*. The subordinate-clause subject is said to be deleted by the rule of Complement-Subject Deletion when it is coreferential to the main-clause subject. Give an argument involving Reflexivization to sup-

port this analysis. (Hint: Notice the grammaticalness of *Felix wants to wash himself* and the ungrammaticalness of *Felix wants (for) Joan to wash himself.*)

Reflexivization can also be used to support the rule of Subject Raising. *Max believes Jacob to be a poor scholar* derives from an underlying structure in which *Jacob* functions as the subordinate-clause subject: *Max believes (Jacob be a poor scholar)*. However, it is claimed that *Jacob* functions in surface structure as the object of *believes* in the main clause, where it is moved by Subject Raising. Formulate an argument involving Reflexivization to back up this claim. (No hint this time.)

10. Determine whether the rules responsible for deriving the sentences discussed in question 9 must apply in any particular order.

11. Unfortunately, there is at present no introductory book dealing with modern syntax that can be recommended without reservation for beginning students. The following may prove most helpful: Palmer, *Grammar*; Langendoen, *The Study of Syntax*; Bach, *An Introduction to Transformational Grammars*; Jacobs and Rosenbaum, *English Transformational Grammar*; Chomsky, *Syntactic Structures*; Grinder and Elgin, *Guide to Transformational Grammar*.

CHAPTER phonological systems

articulatory phonetics

The sounds of speech can be studied from various points of view. One can investigate the physical properties of speech sounds as they are transmitted through the air, measuring the amount of energy present in the acoustic signal, its distribution over the frequency spectrum, how these measurements change in the course of an utterance, and so on. Another approach is to study sounds with respect to how we perceive them, asking questions like these: How much of a physical difference must there be between two sounds before a person can tell them apart? Which acoustic cues does the hearer rely on most heavily in speech perception? Which physical properties of sounds does he ignore altogether? A third way to study speech sounds is to examine the way they are produced, or **articulated**, by the speech organs. This approach is the oldest of all, going back at least to ancient India, and is also the most common. It is the one we will follow here.

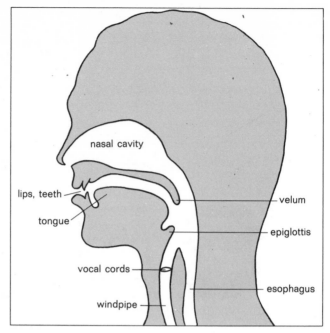

figure 6.1

the speech tract

The vocal organs of human beings all have more basic functions (such as eating and sucking), on which their articulatory functions are superimposed. Our vocal organs are thus not radically different from those of other primates. The fact that we vocalize in a highly systematic and coordinated manner, while they do not, must therefore be attributed to neurological factors rather than to gross anatomical differences. This is not to say that the other primates would sound just like us if they were comparably endowed neurologically; differences in the configuration and relative dimensions of the elements of the speech tract would make primate speech quite distinct phonetically from human speech.

When air is forced out of the lungs, it passes through the windpipe and exits through the mouth, the nose, or both. The outflow of air can be harnessed and channeled in various ways to form speech sounds. The path through which the air flows is sketched in Figure 6.1. This path resembles an obstacle course in which the obstacles can be inserted and removed. When we exhale normally, the air is allowed to exit freely. Speech sounds are produced when various obstacles are moved into position.

The first potential obstacle that the outflowing air encounters is the **vocal cords**, two elastic membranes situated near the top of the windpipe in the **larynx**, the little box that is popularly called the Adam's apple. These membranes can assume various positions. When relaxed, they are separated and allow air to pass through unobstructed. When taut, they come together to close off the windpipe and prevent air from flowing through. In still a third position, they are drawn together, but not so tightly as to prevent air from being forced out through them, setting them in rapid vibration. This vibration of the vocal cords, called **voicing**, is the source of vowel sounds, which are produced when no other obstructions significantly impede the outflow of air through the mouth. We will first examine the articulation of vowels and then consider the consonants.

vowel articulation

The sound produced by the vibration of the vocal cords is unavoidably modified by the configuration of the remainder of the vocal tract. For one thing, the tissues of the vocal tract absorb some of the original sound. More important, changes in the shape of the vocal tract affect its resonance properties. If the lips and tongue are in one position, the cavity through which the vibrating air passes will emphasize, or render more prominent, the sound components at certain frequencies. If the lips and tongue are in some other position, energy will be concentrated at other frequencies. (In similar fashion, an organ pipe emphasizes a tone at a frequency determined by its length and other characteristics.) The resulting differences in the distribution of energy over the frequency spectrum are what we perceive as differences in vowel quality. The vowels [i] and [a], for example, sound different because they are pronounced with the tongue in different positions, causing energy to be concentrated at different frequencies.

After the vocal cords, the most important organs in the articulation of vowel sounds are the tongue, the lips, and the **velum** (the fleshy rear part of the roof of the mouth). The tongue can assume many different postures and is of central importance in determining vowel quality. The lips can be rounded and protruded in various degrees or unrounded. The velum can be closed, as shown in Figure 6.2, blocking the opening to the nasal cavity so that air can pass out only through the mouth; or it can be lowered as in Figure 6.1, allowing air into the upper chamber. For the moment, let us ignore the action of the lips and the velum, taking the

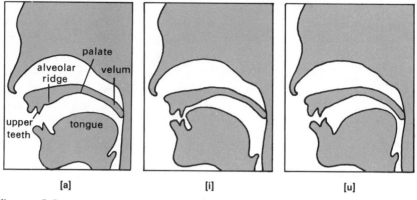

figure 6.2

latter to be closed. This will permit us to concentrate on the effect of modifying the position of the tongue.

It is customary to talk about the position of the tongue in terms of two dimensions, high-low and front-back. The tongue may be held low in the mouth, or it may be extended upward at some point toward the roof of the mouth, or **palate**. Accordingly, a vowel sound is said to be **low** or **high**. The sound [a], as in *father*, is a low vowel. [i] and [u], as in *feet* and *boot*, are high vowels. The position of the tongue during the articulation of these three vowels is very roughly indicated in Figure 6.2. Unlike [a], the sounds [i] and [u] are articulated with the tongue raised to constrict the vocal tract slightly at some point, though the constriction is not enough to cause any noticeable turbulence in the air passing through. [i] and [u] thus have a trait in common that distinguishes them from [a].

[i] and [u] are of course not the same. They differ with regard to the point of constriction. For [i], the constriction is formed by advancing the front of the tongue toward the **alveolar ridge**, the ridge just behind the upper teeth. For [u], however, the back of the tongue is raised and approaches the rear of the palate. [i] is said to be a **front** vowel, because the constriction is toward the front of the mouth, and [u] is a **back** vowel. Notice that [a] is like [u] with respect to the front-back dimension. It is at the rear of the mouth that the tongue is closest to the surface above it, although at no point are the two very near. [u] and [a] are both back vowels, therefore, and share a trait on which they differ from [i].

[a], [i], and [u] represent the extremes of vowel articulation. No vowel sound is pronounced with the tongue farther toward the front than it is for [i]; farther back than for [u] and [a]; higher than for [i] and [u]; or lower than for [a]. Between these extremes, of course, there are many possibilities. A vowel can be intermediate in height between high vowels like

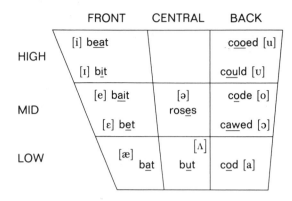

figure 6.3

[u] and low vowels like [a]. Or a vowel can be intermediate in the front-back dimension, coming between front vowels like [i] and back vowels like [u]. The position of the tongue during the articulation of various vowel sounds is represented in Figure 6.3. The location of a vowel with regard to the front-back and high-low dimensions is indicated by the phonetic symbol for that vowel. An English word containing each vowel sound is provided to illustrate the values of the phonetic symbols that are employed. Both dimensions have been divided into three regions, front–central–back and high–mid–low. These divisions are often made, but the scales are really continuous, so the zones are mainly for ease of reference.

The interpretation of Figure 6.3 should be fairly obvious. Starting from the vowel [i], one can produce in series the vowels [ɪ], [e], [ɛ], and [æ] by gradually lowering the tongue (and also the jaw). In the same way, [u] can be successively modified to [ʊ], [o], [ɔ], and [a]. Moreover, the height of the tongue is roughly comparable for [i] and [u], as well as for the pairs [ɪ ʊ], [e o], [ɛ ɔ], and [æ a]. To identify a vowel, we give its location along the two dimensions. [e], for instance, is a mid front vowel, [a] is a low back vowel, and [ə] is a mid central vowel. If greater precision is needed, we can divide the dimensions into smaller bands, making the grid finer.

The position of the tongue establishes the basic quality of a vowel. The precise phonetic character of a vowel, however, also depends on the lips and velum. These add two more dimensions to any fully adequate chart on which vowels are plotted.

Pronounce [i] and then [u]. Notice how radically different they are with respect to the shape of the lips. For [i], the corners of the mouth are drawn back as in a smile. For [u], on the other hand, the lips are rounded and protruded. [u], therefore, is said to be a **rounded** vowel, and [i] is **unrounded**. Of the vowels in Figure 6.3, [u ʊ o ɔ] are rounded, while all the others are unrounded. More often than not, a vowel is rounded if it is a nonlow back vowel and unrounded otherwise, but this is not always true.

The dimension of rounding is independent from the horizontal and vertical dimensions; no matter what the position of the tongue, a vowel can be either rounded or unrounded. For example, it is easy to make a vowel like [i] except that it is rounded, or a vowel like [u] except that it is not. These sounds are not used in English, but they are in many languages.

Any of the sounds so far discussed can be modified by lowering the velum so that air is allowed to pass through the nasal cavity. Vowels articulated in this way are called **nasal** vowels; those articulated with the velum closed are said to be **oral** vowels. Nasal vowels are very common, although they do not happen to be used in English. They are in French, to take one well-known example. Low vowels are more frequently nasal than high vowels, but again this is only a tendency. The nasal-oral dimension is independent from the other three.

A speech sound can therefore be viewed as a bundle of articulatory properties. [i], for instance, can be described as a high front unrounded oral vowel. Five terms are included in its description. The term **vowel** establishes that the articulation of the sound involves the vibration of the vocal cords and that there are no other major obstructions in the oral tract. The other four terms situate this sound in the classification of vowels just outlined; each term locates the sound along one dimension. To take another example, the French word *un* 'one' is manifested phonetically as a mid front rounded nasal vowel. Phonetic symbols, like [i], can be regarded as convenient notations for bundles of articulatory properties.

consonant articulation

There are many ways to make consonant sounds, and the mechanisms involved are sometimes quite intricate. Since this book is not a treatise on phonetics, we will have to be rather selective.

Perhaps the most fundamental of the consonants are the **stops**. These are sounds produced by closing off completely the flow of air, letting pressure build up behind the closure, and then releasing it suddenly in a burst. [p], for example, is articulated by closing the lips, thereby effecting a stoppage in the flow of air, and then opening the lips to let the trapped air escape. This sound occurs before the vowel [a] in the word *pa*.

The stoppage of air may be made with the lips, the vocal cords, or the tongue. A stop articulated with the two lips is called **bilabial**. One made by the vocal cords is a **glottal** stop. With the tongue, of course, there are many points in the mouth where the closure can be effected. For the most part, the point at which the closure is made determines what part of the tongue is used; the tip of the tongue, for instance, can easily make a stoppage against the upper teeth, but hardly against the velum. Stops articulated with the tongue are said to be **dental, alveolar, palatal,** or **velar** if the stoppage is made, respectively, against the upper teeth, the alveolar ridge, the palate, or the velum (see Figure 6.2). The English [p], then, is a bilabial stop. [t], the first sound of *to*, is an alveolar stop. *Key* begins with the velar stop [k].

A stop produced by means of a closure at a particular point can assume many different specific phonetic forms. Just as with the vowels, there are a number of secondary dimensions along which a stop consonant may vary. We will consider only some, and these fairly briefly. These modifications are most relevant for stops, but they pertain to other kinds of sounds as well.

The vocal cords may cease to vibrate during the articulation of a consonant. If they do, the consonant is said to be **voiceless.** If they continue to vibrate, it is said to be **voiced.** English [p t k], for instance, are voiceless stops. All three have voiced counterparts: [b], as in *bib*, is a voiced bilabial stop; [d], as in *dud*, is a voiced alveolar stop; [g], as in *gag*, is a voiced velar stop.

English voiceless stops are normally produced with the emission of a puff of air as the closure is released. Pronounce *pa*, holding your fingers directly in front of your mouth as you do so; it should be easy to feel the air emitted as [p] is articulated. Stops can be produced without the accompanying puff of air, and in fact, such sounds are very common. The stops of French and Spanish, for example, usually lack it. Stops accompanied by this puff of air are called **aspirated** stops; those that lack it are **unaspirated.** The [p] of English *pa* can now be described more precisely as a voiceless aspirated bilabial stop. The French [d] sound, as in *dans* 'in,' is a voiced unaspirated dental stop.

We should mention a few other modulations of stop articulations that, while relatively infrequent in the familiar European languages, are used in many languages of the world. A stop pronounced with an accompanying rounding of the lips is said to be **labialized.** (This is the same trait that characterizes rounded vowels.) Labialized alveolar and velar stops occur in English, but only in a few special environments. [t d k g] are labialized, for instance, when they precede the sound [w] (the initial sound of *wig*), in anticipation of the position of the lips required by the pronunciation of [w]. Examples are *twig, Edward, liquid,* and *iguana.* Sounds can also be modified by changing the size of the upper throat, or **pharynx.** By moving the root of the tongue back, the pharyngeal cavity can be greatly constricted. Sounds that are accompanied by this constriction are said to be **pharyngealized.** Arabic is one language that has pharyngealized consonants. **Glottalized** consonants are produced by the simultaneous action of the larynx (the box containing the vocal cords) and some other articulator. The larynx is raised with the vocal cords closed, causing an increase in air pressure along the upper vocal tract. The trapped air then rushes out when the consonant articulation is released. Many American Indian languages have glottalized consonants.

In the production of stops, the lips, tongue, or vocal cords effect a stoppage in the flow of air along the vocal tract, and this stoppage is subsequently released. Another mode of consonant articulation is to obstruct, but not block entirely, the flow of air. This is done by moving an articulator very close to the position it assumes in making a closure but leaving a small opening through which the outflowing air can pass. The constriction of the vocal tract induces turbulence in the flow of air through the narrowed passage, a turbulence that we perceive as a kind of hissing. Sounds produced in this way are called **fricatives**.

Like stops, fricatives can be characterized by the point at which the narrowest constriction is made. A fricative produced with both lips would be a bilabial fricative, a sound that is not used in English. The English sound [f] is a **labiodental** fricative, since its articulation has the upper teeth placed on the lower lip. [θ], the initial sound of *thing*, is a dental fricative; the tongue makes contact with the upper teeth, but, as is the case with [f], the flow of air is not completely blocked. [s], illustrated twice in *sis*, is alveolar. Articulated farther back on the tongue, and slightly behind the alveolar ridge, is the palatal fricative [š], the last sound of *fish*. English does not have a velar fricative; German and Russian do. [h], the first sound of *hand*, is a glottal fricative, although not much friction is produced as the air passes through the vocal cords. All of the above fricatives are voiceless. English also has a series of voiced fricatives, each of which matches a voiceless fricative in point of articulation. The voiced fricatives [v ð z ž] are the first consonants of *vile*, *this*, *zero*, and *azure* respectively.

A third mode of consonant articulation combines the features of stops and fricatives. A stoppage is made and then released, as for stops, but the release is made with the turbulence that is characteristic of fricatives. English has two of these sounds, called **affricates**. [č], the first and last sound of *church*, is voiceless. Its voiced counterpart, which occurs twice in *judge*, is symbolized [ǰ]. One is a voiceless palatal affricate, and the other is a voiced palatal affricate. The affricates used in English are, of course, only a small sample of those to be found in human languages.

Some consonants are articulated by making a closure in the mouth while lowering the velum to allow air to pass through the nasal cavity. These are called **nasal** consonants. Nasal consonants are distinguished from one another by the point where the oral closure is made. For English [m], as in *me*, the two lips are brought together, and [m] is thus a bilabial nasal. [n], as in *no*, is an alveolar nasal. The word *sing*, despite the orthography, ends phonetically in a single consonant, a velar nasal; this is symbolized as [ŋ]. Nasal consonants are usually voiced, but they do not have to be.

This brings us to the **liquids**, the *r*- and *l*-like sounds. We can only touch on the variety of liquids to be found in the languages of the world.

The various *l*-like sounds are called **laterals**. Pronounce an [l], as in *lip*. Notice that your tongue makes an alveolar closure in the center of your mouth. At the same time, however, air is permitted to escape on the sides, so that it is never completely blocked; hence the term lateral. The English lateral is voiced. Since no turbulence is caused by the closure in the center, and since the flow of air is continuous, it resembles vowels in acoustic quality. The same is true of voiced nasals and especially of the English [r] sound.

The English [r], as in *row*, involves no oral closure at all. It is therefore very much like a vowel. The articulatory trait that gives it its special character is the shape of the tongue. Either the front or the rear of the tongue is raised slightly toward the roof of the mouth in such a way that the upper surface of the tongue is shaped something like a cup. More commonly, *r*-like sounds are produced by flapping the front part of the tongue against the alveolar ridge, as in a very rapid pronunciation of [d]. One of the Spanish *r* sounds is produced in this manner. A common variant of this is the trilled *r*. A **trill** is a rapid series of flaps induced by the air stream as it is forced out. The Spanish word *pero* 'but' contains a flap *r*, while *perro* 'dog' has a trilled *r* in the same position. Trills are sometimes not produced with the tongue, but with the **uvula**, that slender finger of tissue that hangs down from the velum in the back of the mouth. This kind of *r* is used in many dialects of German and French.

We have now characterized all of the basic sounds of English except [w] and [y]. These are called **glides** or, because they are closely related to vowels, **semivowels**. The exclamation *wow* begins and ends with [w], and *yoyo* contains two occurrences of [y]. A glide is a rapid movement of the articulatory organs to or from the position they assume for the articulation of a certain vowel. The glide [w] is related to the vowel [u] in this way, and the glide [y] to [i]. The pronunciation of *wow*, for instance, starts from the articulatory position used to pronounce [u], with the lips rounded and the tongue high and back. Instead of actually articulating [u], however, the vocal organs glide rapidly into position for [a]. As [a] is being pronounced, the lips and tongue glide back where they came from, so that the word ends as they are approaching the [u] position. The articulation of [y] is parallel.

Usually, though not always, glides are related to high vowels, with [w]

	BILABIAL	LABIODENTAL	DENTAL	ALVEOLAR	PALATAL	VELAR	GLOTTAL
VOICELESS STOP	p			t		k	
VOICED STOP	b			d		g	
VOICELESS FRICATIVE		f	θ	s	š		h
VOICED FRICATIVE		v	ɣ	z	ž		
VOICELESS AFFRICATE					č		
VOICED AFFRICATE					ǰ		
NASAL	m			n		ŋ	
LIQUID				l	r		
GLIDE	w				y		

figure 6.4

and [y] being the most common. To take one other example, French has in addition to these a glide from the high front rounded position, as in *lui* 'him.' In English, the vowels [e] and [o] are normally pronounced with an accompanying glide. [e] is regularly followed by [y], and [o] by [w]. **Bait** and **boat**, for instance, are [beyt] and [bowt] phonetically. Other vowel-plus-glide combinations to be found in English are [ay] (*eye*), [ɔy] (*boy*), and [aw] (*cow*, though in many dialects the combination is [æw] instead).

Figure 6.4 summarizes the basic consonant sounds of English.

suprasegmental features

Thus far we have examined only sound segments. In closing, we should say a word about **length, stress,** and **tone,** phonological entities that can hardly be considered segments. They are commonly called **suprasegmental** phenomena in accordance with the practice of writing them phonetically by means of marks made above the symbols indicating segments.

Length is commonly regarded as a suprasegmental feature. Two sounds, particularly in the case of vowels, may be the same in every respect except duration. The vowel of English **bed**, for example, is slightly longer than the vowel of **bet**. In general, English vowels are longer before voiced consonants than before voiceless ones. In many languages, the length of vowels or consonants plays a more important role, serving to distinguish morphemes.

Vowels can also differ in relative prominence, as we have already observed with respect to English compounds. In the compound **redskin, red** is articulated with greater emphasis, but the opposite is true in the phrase **red skin**. The usual term for this prominence is **stress**. Thus **red** is said to be stressed in **redskin**, but **skin** is stressed in **red skin**. Stressed vowels typically differ from unstressed ones in that they are of greater length, higher pitch, and greater articulatory force.

We can raise or lower the pitch of our voices simply by increasing or decreasing the tension of the vocal cords. In many languages, differences of pitch are systematically used to distinguish morphemes. Chinese is the best-known example of such languages, which are called **tone** languages. A difference in tone may be a difference in pitch alone. For instance, the identification of a morpheme may depend on whether the vowel has high or low pitch. If a language has a number of tones, and not just two or three, the pitch **contour** becomes relevant. Speakers may distinguish, for example, among a high tone, a low tone, a falling tone, a rising tone, and a tone that falls and then rises. The maximum number of tones systematically used in any one language to distinguish morphemes is not definitely known, but it is on the order of eight to twelve.

distinctive differences

Human beings can make an infinite number of speech sounds. This is true simply because some articulatory dimensions are continuous rather than discrete. Between the positions for [u] and [a], for instance, there are an infinite number of possible tongue heights, and hence an infinite number of corresponding vowel sounds. The point of closure for stop consonants, to take another example, can come at any place along the oral tract. Most of these minuscule phonetic differences, naturally, are below the threshold of perception. Moreover, many grosser, clearly perceptible differences are not exploited systematically by the speakers of a language for purposes of communication.

We have come to a crucial notion: the systematic exploitation of certain phonological differences by the speakers of a language for purposes of communication. A language can serve as an instrument of communication because it establishes pairings between meanings and pronunciations. The building blocks of these pairings are the individual morphemes, which (in addition to syntactic properties) have conceptual import and phonological representations. The phonological representation of a morpheme determines its pronunciation.

For this communication scheme to function effectively, it must by and large be true that different morphemes have different pronunciations. It must be possible, on the basis of its phonological shape, to identify a morpheme and recover its meaning; otherwise the hearer would have no way of knowing what a sentence said and the speaker would have no reason to produce it. To take an extreme case, we could hardly communicate with one another if all the morphemes of our language were pronounced identically. A few identically pronounced morphemes present no real difficulties (for example, *fire* 'flame' and *fire* 'dismiss'). Massive identities of phonological shape, on the other hand, could seriously disrupt communication.

Therefore it must be possible to tell morphemes apart on the basis of their pronunciations. In what ways, then, do the morphemes of a language differ from one another phonologically? One way is in the number of sound segments they contain. **Red** and **ready**, for instance, differ in that the former has three segments and the latter has four. Obviously, though, the identity of the segments is of vastly greater importance. **Tan** can be recognized, distinguished from other morphemes, when the first segment is identified as [t], the second as [æ], and the third as [n]. This information separates **tan** from, say, **can**, which has a different initial segment, as well as from other morphemes that resemble **tan** even less.

But in what sense is it meaningful to talk about identifying a sound segment? In purely objective terms, no two uttered sounds are ever exactly alike in all their phonetic detail. Whenever a sound is pronounced, that exact sound is pronounced for the first (and last) time. The differences between two uttered sounds may be minute, almost immeasurable, but they are always there. In what sense, then, do we identify sounds, since every one is unique?

The answer is that, as speakers of a particular language, we systematically ignore certain differences between sounds and pay attention to certain other differences. We learn which ones to pay heed to as part of mastering the phonological system of our language. As speakers of English, for example, we pay attention to whether or not a stop is voiced. This difference is used to distinguish between [p] and [b], between [t] and [d], and between [k] and [g], which for us are functionally different sounds. By paying heed to the voicing of stops, we tell *pun* from *bun*, *tin* from *din*, and *come* from *gum*. On the other hand, we ignore the feature of labialization with stops. The difference between a plain [t] and [t] articulated with the lips rounded is not a functional one in English. There are no two morphemes of English that differ solely in that one has a plain [t] in the same position where the other has a labialized [t]. Functional differences, differences to which the speakers of a language pay heed in determining the identity of morphemes, are called **distinctive**. Voicing is thus distinctive in English with respect to the stops, but labialization is not.

The phonological system of a language imposes structure on the phonetic continuum. Just as the largely continuous speech stream is treated psychologically as a series of discrete sound segments, so the continuous articulatory dimensions are broken up into discrete ranges by a linguistic system. A sound may be voiced throughout its articulation, voiceless throughout, voiced at the beginning then voiceless, voiceless until the last hundredth of a second—the possibilities are endless; but for speakers of a language in which voicing is distinctive, a segment is treated as either voiced or voiceless, with no middle ground. From the alveolar ridge to the velum, there are an unlimited number of places where the tongue can make contact with the roof of the mouth in articulating a stop. As speakers of English, however, we treat this continuum as if it were divided into two discrete regions. A voiceless stop articulated with the tongue is judged to be either a [t] or a [k]. There are no other possibilities; a stop pronounced with the tongue in an intermediate position is forced into one of the two categories.

The functionally different sounds of a language are opposed to one another in a network of distinctive differences. In English, for example, [s] is opposed to [z] by the distinctive difference between voiceless and voiced segments; to [f], [θ], and [š] by the distinctive opposition among alveolar, labiodental, dental, and palatal articulations; to [t] on the feature of nonclosure versus closure (that is, fricative versus stop); to [d] on the features of closure and voicing; and to the other sounds of English by these and other distinctive differences. A small number of distinctive differences are sufficient to distinguish all of the functionally different segment types of a language. The other, nondistinctive differences are ignored.

Languages vary with respect to which differences are treated as distinctive and used to tell morphemes apart. In English, we pay attention to whether or not a stop or fricative is voiced. It matters, since some morphemes are distinguished from one another solely on this basis (for example, *pig/big*, *fan/van*, *vat/fad*). In many languages, however, the voiced-voiceless distinction is not exploited at all; there are no morphemes that are differentiated on the basis of this feature alone. In some languages, the difference between aspirated and unaspirated stops is distinctive, but it is not in English. In others, both voicing and aspiration are distinctive. Similar observations hold for labialization, glottalization, and pharyngealization. The feature of voicing is not distinctive in English with respect to the liquids. There is only one distinctive [l] sound in English, and only one [r]; no two morphemes are distinguished just by virtue of the difference between a voiced and a voiceless liquid. Some languages, though, rely on the contrast between, say, a voiced and voiceless [l] to differentiate morphemes. We have to recognize several functional vowel heights for English, to distinguish, for example, among *bit, bet,* and *bat.* In various other languages, however, a simple dichotomy between high and low vowels suffices.

Part of learning a language consists of mastering the system of distinctive oppositions that the language uses to differentiate morphemes. Beyond this, a speaker must assimilate the phonological representations of all the individual morphemes of the language. These are not separate tasks; they are closely connected. The system of distinctive oppositions determines what phonological information has to be learned individually for each morpheme and what information can be supplied by general phonological rules that hold for all the morphemes of the language.

The phonological properties of a morpheme that have to be learned individually for that morpheme are precisely those properties that are distinctive. Phonological properties that can be supplied by general rules cannot serve as distinctive properties.

Consider the initial sound of the English word *tin.* Phonetically, it is an aspirated voiceless alveolar stop. The information that it is a voiceless alveolar stop is distinctive and has to be learned individually for this morpheme. The information that it is aspirated, however, can be predicted by a general phonological rule of English. The property of being aspirated or unaspirated is not distinctive.

There is no way to predict that the English word for this kind of metal begins with a voiceless alveolar stop as opposed to a voiced one. Both voiced and voiceless alveolar stops occur in initial position; it is just an arbitrary fact that the form happens to be *tin* and not *din.* The feature of voicelessness is therefore distinctive in this position, serving to specify which of the two potential forms is the correct one. In the same way, the information that this segment is alveolar and not bilabial or velar is distinctive information. It is an idiosyncratic property of this one morpheme and distinguishes it from the possible English forms *pin* and *kin.* Finally, it is necessary to learn individually for this morpheme that the first sound is a stop and not, say, a fricative. This phonological property differentiates the morphemes *tin* and *sin*.

However, the fact that the stop sound of *tin* is aspirated does not distinguish this form from any other possible form of English. This information has no contrastive value, since initial voiceless stops in English are always aspirated when the following vowel is stressed. Because this property is characteristic of all morphemes that begin with a voiceless stop, it cannot be used to tell them apart. It is redundant phonetic detail that is filled in by a general rule of English on the basis of other phonological information. When a speaker learns how the word *tin* is pronounced, he does not have to learn individually for this form that the initial stop is aspirated. He aspirates it automatically in accordance with a phonological principle that holds across the board for English.

A couple of additional examples may prove helpful. It is a general phonological principle of English that nonlow back vowels (that is, [u ʊ o ɔ]) are rounded while all other vowels are unrounded. The rounded or unrounded character of vowels therefore does not have to be learned individually, over and over again, for each of the thousands of morphemes of the language. In learning to pronounce *pen*, for example, a speaker must learn the distinctive information that its vowel is a front vowel (to distinguish it from *pawn*), and he must learn its height (to distinguish it from *pin, pan*, and so on), but he does not have to learn that it is unrounded. This nondistinctive phonetic detail is supplied by a phonological principle of English that applies to thousands of other morphemes as well. It is much less of a burden to master this one simple rule than to learn, individually for each morpheme, the thousands of phonetic facts that it accounts for.

As a final example, consider the second segment of the word *spin*. Phonetically, it is an unaspirated voiceless bilabial stop. Of these four traits, only the last two are distinctive. The information that it is a bilabial stop, and not velar or alveolar, distinguishes this morpheme from the morpheme *skin* and from *stin*, which is a possible English form that does not happen to occur. The distinctive property of being a stop distinguishes the second segment from [w l m n] and the vowels, which can also occur after initial [s]. But stops in English are always unaspirated after initial [s]; this is a general phonological rule and not an idiosyncratic property of *spin*. Therefore, the unaspirated character of [p] after initial [s] is not distinctive. There could be no two morphemes of English that were identical except that one had an unaspirated stop in this position whereas the other had an aspirated stop.

The feature of voicing is for the most part distinctive in English with respect to the stops, but it is not after initial [s]. In this phonological environment, stops are always voiceless. A speaker does not have to learn this information for every morpheme beginning with [s] plus a stop; he masters a single rule which specifies that all stops in this environment are voiceless. There could thus be no morphemes of English distinguished solely by the different initial sequences [sp] versus [sb]; [st] versus [sd]; or [sk] versus [sg]. The contrast between the pairs [p b], [t d], and [k g] is said to be **neutralized** in this environment. The difference between them is systematically exploited for purposes of communication in other phonological environments, but not after initial [s].

The phonological representation of a morpheme, therefore, is the information that a speaker has to learn individually for that morpheme in order for him to know how it is pronounced. A morpheme is represented phonologically as an ordered series of segments. Each segment is specified by all and only those properties that are distinctive for segments in that position.

phonological rules

The function of phonological rules, as we saw in Chapter Four, is to connect surface structures with their phonetic manifestations (see Figure 4.4, page 95). A surface structure, you will recall, is a tree structure that terminates in a linear string of morphemes. Each morpheme in the string has a phonological representation, a specification of the distinctive properties that determine its pronunciation. Phonological rules relate a sentence and its phonetic manifestation on the basis of these specifications.

the specification of nondistinctive features

Phonological systems are anything but simple. The relation between surface structures and their phonetic manifestations is an indirect one, mediated by long and sometimes very intricate series of phonological rules. We will begin to illustrate this process by examining the derivation of the English morpheme *stack*.

Phonetically, *stack* consists of a sequence of four segments: [stæk]. [s] is a voiceless alveolar fricative; [t] is an unaspirated voiceless alveolar stop; [æ] is a low front unrounded nonnasal vowel; and [k] is an unaspi-

UNDERLYING PHONOLOGICAL REPRESENTATION

PHONETIC MANIFESTATION

figure 6.5

rated voiceless velar stop. If we wanted to make our description complete, we would have to add many more nondistinctive phonetic details. We would have to note that none of the segments, for example, is labialized, pharyngealized, or glottalized. We would have to indicate the precise spot of the velar closure for the articulation of [k]. Somewhere we would have to specify that [s] and [t] are not articulated with the very tip of the tongue, but with a part of the tongue slightly behind it. The full series of rules responsible for the phonetic manifestation of *stack* therefore contains many rules in addition to those that we will explicitly consider.

Not all of the phonological properties listed above are distinctive. The unaspirated quality of [t], for instance, can be predicted by a general rule of English, as can the lack of rounding for [æ] and several other features. As indicated in Figure 6.5, the distinctive phonological properties of *stack* —the features that have to be learned individually for this morpheme— constitute its phonological representation, which underlies its full phonetic manifestation. In both the underlying and phonetic representations, a segment can be viewed as comprising a bundle of phonological properties. In Figure 6.5, each bundle is enclosed in square brackets. The nondistinctive phonetic properties of *stack* are in bold type. These are specified by the phonological rules that connect the underlying phonological representation with its phonetic manifestation.

By comparing the two representations of *stack* in Figure 6.5, we find that phonological rules are responsible for specifying the voiceless and alveolar features of [s]; the unaspirated and voiceless features of [t]; the unrounded and nonnasal features of [æ]; and the unaspirated feature of [k]. The addition of all this phonetic detail is the cumulative effect of a number of individual rules, each of which holds for all the morphemes of English.

Let us start with the vowel. The information that the third segment is a low front vowel is distinctive; these features distinguish [æ] from non-low and nonfront vowels, as well as from the liquid [r], all of which can occur after initial [st] (for example, *stick, stool, strip*). The information that it is nonnasal, however, is not distinctive. There is a general phono-logical principle of English that specifies all vowels as being nonnasal. This is not an idiosyncratic property of any individual morpheme. None of the English vowels shown in Figure 6.3 is nasal, so the lack of nasality cannot be used to tell them (or morphemes) apart. We have already noted the existence of another rule of English to the effect that nonlow back vowels are rounded while all other vowels are not. Since [æ] is a front vowel, this rule fills in the nondistinctive detail that it is unrounded. Thus two rules combine to connect an underlying segment specified as a low front vowel with its phonetic manifestation as a low front unrounded nonnasal vowel.

We turn next to the initial segment. Normally, the voiceless and alveolar features are distinctive for the fricative [s]. At the beginning of a morpheme before a stop, however, they are not distinctive. [s] is the only fricative that can occur in this position; there are no English forms like *zdack* or *ftack*, where a voiced or nonalveolar fricative precedes a stop. The information that the first segment is a fricative, as opposed to a vowel, is therefore sufficient to identify it. (In fact, the information that it is a consonant suffices.) The other features can be specified as redundant pho-netic detail by the rule that a fricative is voiceless and alveolar in initial position before a stop. This is a general characteristic of English, not a property of individual morphemes.

We saw previously that the voiceless unaspirated character of stops after initial [s] is nondistinctive. These two features should probably be attributed to different rules. One rule specifies a stop as being unaspirated when it follows a fricative. The other pertains to consonant sequences— or **clusters**—composed of stops, fricatives, and affricates. It is a general principle of English that, when two or more of these sounds occur adjacent to one another in a string, particularly in the same syllable, either they are all voiced or they are all voiceless. For instance, *eggs* is pronounced [ɛgz] and *x* is pronounced [ɛks], but there are no English words pronounced [ɛkz] or [ɛgs]. The stop-fricative cluster can be completely voiceless, or com-pletely voiced, but not mixed. The voicing feature of the stop determines that of the following fricative, ruling out combinations such as [kz] or [gs]. The plural morpheme, for another illustration, is usually an alveolar fricative, as in **books** and **beds**. However, it is pronounced as [s] in the first of these words and as [z] in the second. Evidently, the voiceless [s] of [bʊks] and the voiced [z] of [bɛdz] agree in voicing with the preceding stop. As a final example, take the past-tense morpheme, which is an alveolar stop (for regular verbs). **Judged** and **reached** are phonetically [jʌjd] and [riĉt]. The past-tense morpheme is manifested as the voiced [d] after **judge**, since this ends in a voiced affricate, and as [t] after the voiceless affricate of **reach**. This general rule, then, which has to be posited for the phonological system of English to handle many other cases, specifies the second segment of **stack** as voiceless to agree with the initial [s].

We described the final segment of **stack** as being phonetically unaspirated. This is indeed one possibility, but it does not happen to be the only possibility. The articulation of final stops is an area in which English speakers have some latitude. Final stops may be either aspirated or unaspirated, and there is even the third option of moving the tongue up to the roof of the mouth for the stop closure but omitting the stop burst. This is done by simply not releasing the closure. Thus the rules that serve to fill out the phonetic detail for final stops must provide for all three of these possibilities.

We have examined the derivation of the phonetic manifestation of **stack** by phonological rules from its underlying representation. Even ignoring minute phonetic specifications, we found at least six rules to be involved in connecting the two levels. Each of these rules specifies one or more nondistinctive features for some segment, putting phonetic flesh on the skeletal representations in terms of distinctive properties alone.

other kinds of phonological rules

It would be wrong to conclude from the above example that phonological rules do nothing more than to specify nondistinctive features. It would also be wrong to conclude that underlying phonological representations and their phonetic manifestations differ only in that the latter are fleshed out, more detailed versions of the former; the relation between the two levels can be extremely distant and abstract. Phonological rules insert segments, delete segments, and change the identity and even the order of segments. In addition, they introduce and modify suprasegmental features.

A hypothetical example will allow us to illustrate these remarks simply and coherently. Consider the phonetic data in the table below, which could perfectly well be found in some real language. (An accent mark over a vowel indicates that the vowel is stressed.)

[béb]	'bird'	[bébib]	'birds'
[lót]	'tree'	[lódib]	'trees'
[mék]	'dog'	[mégib]	'dogs'
[rába]	'fire'	[rábib]	'fires'
[sónob]	'rock'	[sómbib]	'rocks'
[íf]	'run'	[ífa]	'ran'
[tíf]	'not run'	[tífa]	'did not run'
[éso]	'swim'	[ésa]	'swam'
[téso]	'not swim'	[tésa]	'did not swim'
[kínap]	'eat'	[kímba]	'ate'
[etkínap]	'not eat'	[etkímba]	'did not eat'
[síme]	'walk'	[síma]	'walked'
[estíme]	'not walk'	[estíma]	'did not walk'
[sárot]	'sleep'	[sárda]	'slept'
[estárot]	'not sleep'	[estárda]	'did not sleep'

Let us start by comparing the forms for 'bird' and 'birds,' [béb] and [bébib] respectively. [bébib] evidently consists of the morpheme [béb] 'bird' followed by the suffix [ib], which marks the plural. It seems, then, that the plural is marked in this language by the addition of [ib] as a suffix to the noun root.

The noun meaning 'tree' is [lót], and on the basis of the pair [béb] and [bébib], we would expect the form for 'trees' to be [lótib], which is what we obtain by adding [ib] to [lót] as a suffix. In fact, however, the form is not [lótib] but [lódib]. At first glance, therefore, the noun meaning 'tree' seems to be irregular with respect to plural formation; this root has two alternate forms, [lót] and [lód], depending on whether or not it is followed by the plural suffix. When we look at the words for 'dog' and 'dogs,' though, we find a similar alternation, suggesting that [lót] may not be irregular after all. The morpheme meaning 'dog' is [mék], but the plural form 'dogs' is [mégib] rather than [mékib]. [lót] and [mék] thus behave alike with respect to the formation of plurals; when the suffix [ib] is added, the underlying voiceless stop is manifested instead as a voiced stop.

In the phonetic data at hand, there is no instance of a voiceless stop that occurs between two vowels. It seems to be a general phonological principle of this language that a stop is always voiced when it is flanked by vowels; let us call this principle the Stop Voicing rule. According to

the Stop Voicing rule, then, [rába], [lódib], and [mégib] are possible phonetic sequences, but [rápa], [lótib], and [mékib], with voiceless stops occurring intervocalically, are not. In light of the general Stop Voicing rule, the
forms [lódib] 'trees' and [mégib] 'dogs' are seen to be completely regular.
Like [bébib] 'birds,' they are formed simply by adding [ib] as a suffix to
the noun root. The underlying representations so obtained are [lótib] and
[mékib], for 'trees' and 'dogs' respectively. The Stop Voicing rule applies
to these underlying representations and voices the intervocalic stops, producing the phonetic manifestations [lódib] and [mégib]. [béb], [lót], and
[mék] all form the plural in the same way, therefore, by the addition of
[ib] as a suffix. It is a general phonological rule of the language that
changes [t] to [d] and [k] to [g] between vowels. The surface irregularity
turns out, on examination, to reflect a deeper regularity.

The root for 'fire' is [rába], but the plural form is simply [rábib] instead
of the expected [rábaib]. Once again it seems that we are faced with a
phonological irregularity, until we look into the matter further. The
occurrence of [rábib] instead of [rábaib] is not at all surprising if we
examine the rest of the data; in no case do we find more than one vowel
after the stressed vowel of a word. This is apparently a phonological principle of the language. More specifically, let us postulate the existence of a
Vowel Deletion rule, which applies within a word and deletes a vowel
that follows a stressed syllable and precedes another syllable. Vowel Deletion thus applies to the regularly formed underlying representation [rábaib]
and deletes [a] to yield the phonetic sequence [rábib]. [a] can be deleted
because it follows a stressed syllable ([rá]) and precedes another syllable
([ib]).

We find further illustration of Vowel Deletion when we examine the
noun [sónob] 'rock' and its plural [sómbib]. If the noun [sónob] is regular
with respect to plural formation, then the phonetic sequence [sómbib]
must manifest a more abstract phonological representation of the form
[sónobib]. [sómbib] differs from this underlying representation in two
ways. First, the unstressed [o] of [sónobib] is lacking. Second, the underlying segment [n] shows up phonetically as [m]. Both of these differences
can be traced to the operation of general phonological rules. The Vowel
Deletion rule specifies that an unstressed vowel is deleted when it follows
a syllable containing a stressed vowel and precedes another syllable (in the
same word). Since [o] follows a stressed syllable in [sónobib], and since
another syllable follows [o], Vowel Deletion applies and reduces [sónobib]
to [sónbib]. From the representation [sónbib] produced by Vowel Deletion, a rule that we will call Nasal Assimilation derives [sómbib]. This rule
specifies that a nasal consonant is manifested as a bilabial when it precedes

a bilabial stop, [b] in this instance. **Assimilation,** a very common phonological phenomenon, is the modification of a sound to make it more similar to neighboring sounds. In this case, the underlying segment [n] is assimilated to the following [b], so that both are manifested phonetically as bilabials. Nowhere in the data will one find the phonetic sequence [nb], where an alveolar precedes a bilabial stop; Nasal Assimilation thus appears to be a general principle of the language.

If the data contained only the above nouns and their plurals, one might reasonably doubt the existence of certain of the rules we have posited. It could perfectly well be the case, for instance, that [sónob], like the English morpheme *child,* has a special form used only with the plural morpheme and that we were wrong in attributing the variant [sómb] to the operation of general phonological rules. When we turn to the verb forms, however, we find further justification for the rules in question.

The verb meaning 'run,' when unspecified with respect to tense, has the form [íf]. By comparing this with the past-tense form [ífa] 'ran,' we see that past tense is indicated by the addition of the suffix [a]. The negative forms [tíf] 'not run' and [tífa] 'did not run' support this analysis and at the same time show that negation is marked on the verb by the prefix [t].

Since 'swim' is pronounced [éso], we would expect the form for 'not swim' to be [téso], and this is indeed what the data shows. By the same token, we would expect the forms for 'swam' and 'did not swim' to be [ésoa] and [tésoa] respectively, for these result directly from the addition of the suffix [a] to indicate past tense. In fact, however, the forms are [ésa] and [tésa], not [ésoa] and [tésoa]. [ésa] and [tésa] thus seem irregular at first glance, but only until we recall the Vowel Deletion rule. In order to account for the occurrence of [rábib] 'fires' as the plural of [rába], and [sómbib] 'rocks' as the plural of [sónob], we posited the existence of this rule, which deletes a vowel that follows a stressed syllable and precedes another syllable in the same word. [éso] is seen to be perfectly regular with regard to past-tense formation when viewed in light of the Vowel Deletion rule. The addition of the past-tense suffix [a] to [éso] and [téso] yields the underlying representations [ésoa] and [tésoa]. Vowel Deletion applies automatically to these underlying representations and deletes [o] to produce the phonetic sequences [ésa] and [tésa]. The same phonological principle that accounts for the plural of the nouns [rába] and [sónob] therefore accounts as well for the past tense of the verb [éso].

[kínap] 'eat' and [kímba] 'ate' provide additional justification for Stop Voicing, Vowel Deletion, and Nasal Assimilation in similar fashion. Suffixing [a] to [kínap] produces the underlying representation [kínapa], whose phonetic manifestation, [kímba], results from it automatically by the application of these three rules. Stop Voicing specifies that a stop is

UNDERLYING REPRESENTATION

	[tkínapa]
Stop Voicing:	[tkínaba]
Vowel Deletion:	[tkínba]
Nasal Assimilation:	[tkímba]
Vowel Insertion:	[etkímba]

PHONETIC MANIFESTATION

figure 6.6

voiced when it occurs between two vowels; the application of this rule to
[kínapa] yields [kínaba]. Vowel Deletion requires the loss of a vowel that
follows a stressed syllable and precedes another syllable, and from [kínaba]
it produces [kínba]. Nasal Assimilation makes a nasal bilabial when it
occurs directly before a bilabial stop, as [n] does in [kínba]. Nasal Assimilation thus connects [kínba] with the phonetic sequence [kímba].

The other affirmative forms, [síme] 'walk,' [síma] 'walked,' [sárot]
'sleep,' and [sárda] 'slept,' confirm our analysis. [síma] 'walked' results
directly from the addition to [síme] 'walk' of the suffix [a], coupled with
the principle of Vowel Deletion. The suffixation of [a] to [sárot] 'sleep'
gives [sárota] as the underlying representation of [sárda] 'slept.' From this
underlying representation, Stop Voicing produces [sároda], which Vowel
Deletion reduces to [sárda].

On the basis of [tíf] 'not run' and [téso] 'not swim,' it is evident that
negation is marked on the verb by the prefix [t]. Adding this prefix to
[kínap] 'eat' yields for 'not eat' the underlying representation [tkínap],
whose phonetic realization is [etkínap]. Other negative forms such as
[estíme] 'not walk' and [estárot] 'not sleep' show that the appearance of
[e] is a general phenomenon, not an idiosyncratic property of [kínap].
Consequently, we are justified in positing the existence of a Vowel Insertion rule, which inserts [e] before a cluster of two consonants that would
otherwise begin a word. Vowel Insertion thus applies to the underlying
representation [tkínap] and connects it with the phonetic sequence
[etkínap]. [etkímba] 'did not eat,' the negative past-tense form of [kínap]
'eat,' must have the underlying representation [tkínapa], from which it is
derived by several rules, including Vowel Insertion. This derivation is outlined in Figure 6.6.

Since 'walk' is [síme], the underlying representation of 'not walk' must
be [tsíme] if this verb is regular. Vowel Insertion naturally applies to
[tsíme], the result being [etsíme]. The form meaning 'not walk' that is

UNDERLYING PHONOLOGICAL REPRESENTATION

	[tsimea]	[tsarota]
Stress Placement:	[tsímea]	[tsárota]
Stop Voicing:	(inapplicable)	[tsároda]
Vowel Deletion:	[tsíma]	[tsárda]
Nasal Assimilation:	(inapplicable)	(inapplicable)
Vowel Insertion:	[etsíma]	[etsárda]
Metathesis:	[estíma]	[estárda]

PHONETIC MANIFESTATION

figure 6.7

given in the data, however, is [estíme] rather than [etsíme]. [estárot] 'not sleep,' the negative of [sárot] 'sleep,' similarly displays the cluster [st] where we would expect instead [ts]. Apparently, then, this language contains a rule that reverses the order of the segments [ts] under certain conditions. We will call this the Metathesis rule; **metathesis** is the term used to indicate a change in the order of sound segments. Metathesis derives [estíme] 'not walk' and [estárot] 'not sleep' from [etsíme] and [etsárot] respectively.

We have now established five rules, including rules that insert and delete segments, modify segments, and change the order of segments. The data testifies to the existence of yet another rule, one that determines the placement of stress. The location of stress is not an idiosyncratic property of individual words or morphemes; it is completely regular. The stress always falls on the first vowel of the root, never on the second vowel of the root or on an affix. Thus we find forms like [béb], [sómbib], and [etkínap], but none like [sombíb], [etkináp], or [étkinap]. Stress is therefore not marked in the most abstract underlying phonological representations, since it is not distinctive. Rather, it is inserted by the general rule of Stress Placement. The derivations of [estíma] 'did not walk' and [estárda] 'did not sleep,' outlined in Figure 6.7, provide further illustration of the rules we have examined.

the abstractness of phonological systems

The preceding examples should give some indication of how abstract the relation between underlying phonological representations and their phonetic manifestations can be. The derivation of a phonetic sequence from its underlying representation is the cumulative result of the application of a long series of phonological rules. Very often, in fact, such derivations involve much longer series of rules than the rather simple cases we have examined. We see also that what appear to be idiosyncrasies and irregularities quite often turn out to result from perfectly regular phonological processes. To uncover these regularities, we must view the phonological system of a language as a system of rules that derive phonetic manifestations from relatively abstract underlying representations. Quite commonly there are regularities in the underlying representations that are obscured at the phonetic level by the application of phonological rules. We learned similar lessons in our examination of syntactic systems.

Phonological systems further resemble syntactic systems in that their rules must sometimes apply in a particular order. In the derivation of [kímba] from the underlying representation [kínapa], for example, Vowel Deletion applies before Nasal Assimilation. This is because it is only after Stress Placement, Stop Voicing, and especially Vowel Deletion have applied to produce [kínba] that the nasal [n] and the bilabial stop [b] are adjacent, causing the nasal to be assimilated.

Because phonological rules can change the identity of segments, as well as insert and delete them, the inventory of sounds used in a language may be different for the underlying representations and phonetic manifestations. That is, some segment types may occur in underlying phonological representations even though they are never manifested overtly at the phonetic level, and vice versa. In speaking of the sounds of a language, therefore, we may be referring either to overtly occurring phonetic entities or to the abstract entities of underlying representations, and it is of course necessary to be clear as to which we mean. When we listed the sounds of English as part of our examination of articulatory phonetics, we were referring to the sounds that occur on the phonetic level (with certain minor phonetic variations being ignored).

morphology

We observed in Chapter Four that a morpheme may have a number of different phonetic manifestations. The plural morpheme of English, for example, appears variously as [z], [s], and [əz], and it has other phonetic shapes as well (in *children, sheep, men,* and so on). The term **morphology** is applied to those aspects of phonological systems that account for variations in the phonetic manifestations of morphemes, though there is no neat dividing line between morphology and the rest of phonology.

The area of morphology is one in which languages tend to display a considerable amount of irregularity, especially if one does not pry beneath the surface. Why, for instance, should the plural of *child* be *children*, and not the expected *childs*? Why *women* and *sheep* instead of *womans* and *sheeps*? Why should the past tense of *eat* be the irregular *ate* and not the regular *eated*? There would seem to be no principled reason for our using *went* instead of *goed*.

For those forms that are truly irregular, special rules are required. Some rule of English, for example, must say that the sequence *eat+P'AST* is manifested as *ate*. As the statement of an irregularity, this rule does not hold for all the morphemes of English; it is a special rule that applies just to one morpheme and has to be learned individually for that morpheme. Similarly, a speaker of English has to learn as an arbitrary fact about the morpheme *woman* that *woman+PLURAL* is manifested as *women*; the rule that is required will be of no use to the speaker in predicting the plural form of other morphemes. (The plural of *man* is formed differently—do not confuse spelling and pronunciation!)

Phonological rules that apply to just one morpheme or morpheme sequence are at one extreme of the continuum which has at the other extreme general phonological rules that hold for all morphemes of the language. Between the extremes are rules specifying morphological alternations that are neither wholly idiosyncratic nor wholly regular. These rules apply to classes of morphemes, but not to all morphemes of the language. A number of English verbs, for instance, are put into the past tense by changing the vowel from [ɪ] to [æ]. The rule that manifests **PAST** in this way does not apply to all verbs of the language, but neither is it restricted to a single verb. The same rule accounts for the past-tense forms *sat, spat, rang, sang, swam, began, drank, shrank, stank*, and *sprang*. A number of verbs are put into the past tense by substituting [ɔt] for everything after the initial consonant cluster: *brought, bought, caught, fought, sought, thought*, and *taught*. The past-tense formation of this handful of verbs constitutes a subregularity of English morphology and can be expressed by a single rule that applies to them all. If these verbs were completely irregular, each would form the past tense in a separate, idiosyncratic manner, and each individual verb would require a special rule, as do *eat* and *go*.

It is very often the case, however, that apparent morphological irregularities turn out to be completely regular phenomena when examined carefully in relation to the entire phonological system. Consider, for instance, the English plurals formed with [əz], [s], and [z]. [əz] marks the plural in words like *glasses, sizes, bunches, judges, bushes*, and *rouges*. [s] occurs in plural words such as *hips, bits, books, fifes*, and *births*. [z] indicates the plural in words like *ribs, beds, eggs, elms, bins, bars, pills, loves, ways*, and *bras*. The choice of [əz], [s], or [z] to mark the plural is anything but random in this set of words. Notice that [əz] is used only when the last sound of the noun root is [s], [z], [č], [ǰ], [š], or [ž]. When the noun ends in some other sound, the form of the plural is determined by voicing; [s] occurs only after voiceless segments, and [z] occurs only after voiced segments.

For all these words, we may take the underlying phonological representation of the plural morpheme to be [z]. *Glasses, bunches, hips*, and *books*, for example, have the underlying representations [glæsz], [bʌnčz], [hɪpz], and [bʊkz], exactly parallel to those of *ribs* and *bras*, namely [rɪbz] and [braz]. The variants [əz] and [s] are derived from the underlying [z] by general phonological rules of English, rules that account for various other phonological phenomena as well.

Glasses and *bunches* are manifested phonetically as [glæsəz] and [bʌnčəz]. These phonetic forms are derived from the underlying representations [glæsz] and [bʌnčz] by a rule that inserts the vowel [ə] between the last segment of the noun and the suffix [z]. This rule is a general one; it inserts [ə] between a root and a suffix whenever the suffix consists of a single **obstruent** and the root ends in an obstruent of basically the same type. (An obstruent is a stop, fricative, or affricate—sounds formed by obstructing the flow of air.) In the relevant sense, [s z č ǰ š ž] are obstruents of basically the same type as [z]. They are fricatives articulated in the alveolar or palatal region (affricates such as [č ǰ], remember, end as fricatives after an initial stop-like closure). The sequences [sz zz čz ǰz šz žz] are thus changed respectively to [səz zəz čəz ǰəz šəz žəz] by the [ə] Insertion rule in determining the phonetic manifestations of *glasses, sizes, bunches, judges, bushes*, and *rouges*.

The possessive morpheme and the third person singular verb ending are also suffixes whose basic form is [z], as shown by words like *Bill's, Ed's, goes*, and *stabs*, phonetically [bɪlz], [ɛdz], [gowz], and [stæbz]. The underlying representations of *Chris's* and *reaches* are thus [krɪsz] and [ričz], parallel to the above forms. The rule that inserts [ə], being a general rule not restricted just to the plural morpheme, applies automatically to these underlying representations to yield the correct phonetic manifestations, [krɪsəz] and [ričəz]. Further evidence for the existence of the [ə] Insertion rule is provided by alternate forms of the past-tense morpheme. Its underlying form is [d], showing up overtly as [d] in words such as *bribed* [braybd] and *freed* [frid]. The underlying representations of *rotted* and *raided* are therefore [ratd] and [reydd], which are modified to [ratəd] and [reydəd]. The [ə] Insertion rule applies to produce these sequences because the final segment of the root is an obstruent of basically the same type (an alveolar stop) as the suffix.

The [əz] variant of the plural morpheme is therefore derived from the underlying form [z] by a general phonological rule of English, one that accounts for numerous other phenomena as well. The same is true of the [s] variant, which occurs after voiceless consonants other than [s č š]. We saw earlier that all of the consonants in a consonant cluster are voiceless if the first one is voiceless. Thus, while *box* [baks] is a possible English word, [bakz] or [bags] is not. This principle also specifies that the second segment of *stack* is voiceless, since it follows the voiceless fricative [s]. It is apparent that this same rule will apply to the underlying representations of *hips* and *books*, namely [hɪpz] and [bʊkz], to produce the phonetic manifestations [hɪps] and [bʊks].

This rule also accounts for variants of the possessive morpheme, the third person singular verb ending, and the past-tense morpheme. Since these have the respective basic forms [z], [z], and [d], the underlying representations of *Nat's, kicks,* and *kicked* must be [nætz], [kɪkz], and [kɪkd]. The final voiceless consonants of the roots cause the endings to be voiceless as well, accounting for the phonetic manifestations [næts], [kɪks], and [kɪkt].

The three plural endings [əz s z] all derive, therefore, from the same underlying representation. General phonological rules apply to this abstract representation to produce the superficial phonetic diversity. Notice that the [ə] Insertion rule must apply before the rule that specifies voicelessness; if the two rules were not ordered in this way, they would give the wrong results. *Glasses,* for instance, would be assigned the phonetic shape [glæsəs] instead of [glæsəz], since the underlying representation [glæsz] would be modified to [glæss] before the [ə] Insertion rule applied.

The hypothetical data we examined in the section on "Other Kinds of Phonological Rules" provides further illustration of how apparent morphological irregularities sometimes turn out to be completely regular phenomena when viewed in relation to the entire phonological system. If we examined only the phonetic data, for example, we would observe very little regularity in the formation of the past tense of verbs:

[íf]	'run'	[ífa]	'ran'
[éso]	'swim'	[ésa]	'swam'
[kínap]	'eat'	[kímba]	'ate'
[síme]	'walk'	[síma]	'walked'
[sárot]	'sleep'	[sárda]	'slept'

[íf] forms the past tense by the addition of [a]; [éso] by the substitution of [a] for the final [o]; [kínap] by the addition of [a] and the modification of [nap] to [mb]; [síme] by the substitution of [a] for the final [e]; and [sárot] by the addition of [a] and the modification of [ot] to [d]. On deeper examination, however, we found that all of these verbs form the past tense in exactly the same way—by the suffixation of [a]. The inter-action of the abstract underlying representations so obtained with general phonological rules produces the surface diversity that is observed in the phonetic data.

To understand the morphological patterns of a language, therefore, it is not sufficient to examine the phonetic data alone. The phonological mechanisms involved can be uncovered only if we look beneath the pho-netic surface and regard the phonological system as an integrated series of rules that apply to abstract underlying representations. When we do, we find that surface disparity very often results in a completely regular fashion from underlying uniformity.

suggestions for study and discussion

1. Malmberg's *Phonetics* and Ladefoged's *Elements of Acoustic Phonetics* are good basic introductions to general and acoustic phonetics, respectively. Heffner's *General Phonetics* is much more advanced and comprehensive, while Smalley's *A Manual of Articulatory Phonetics* is a manual for practical training in the production and transcription of speech sounds. For an introduc-tion to modern phonological theory and description, see Schane's *Generative Phonology*.

2. The symbol [ḵ] stands for a sound that is just like [k] except that it is articulated farther toward the front of the mouth. Both [k] and [ḵ] occur phonetically in English, but the difference between them is not distinctive, since it is possible to predict when [ḵ] will occur instead of [k]. Examine the data below and find the principle that determines when [ḵ] is used.

kʌt	*cut*	klɪp	*clip*
kul	*cool*	ḵeyp	*cape*
ḵip	*keep*	kat	*cot*
ḵɛn	*Ken*	kɪn	*kin*
kɔt	*caught*	kowl	*coal*
bæk	*back*	ḵæt	*cat*

3. In many dialects of English, the diphthong [ay] is rendered phonetically as [ʌy] under certain conditions. The alternation between [ay] and [ʌy] follows

a general rule, and hence the difference between them is not distinctive. Formulate this rule on the basis of the data given below.

bʌyt	*bite*	tay	*tie*	rayd	*ride*
fayl	*file*	lʌyf	*life*	taym	*time*
rayz	*rise*	rʌyt	*write*	fʌyt	*fight*
bay	*buy*	rʌys	*rice*	tʌyp	*type*
naynθ	*ninth*	fayr	*fire*	bʌyk	*bike*

4. The difference between [č] and [š] is distinctive in English, since it is used to distinguish morphemes; the morphemes *chip* [čɪp] and *ship* [šɪp], for example, are distinguished solely by the choice between [č] and [š] for the first sound. In Luiseño, on the other hand, [č] and [š] do not contrast; there is no pair of lexical items which differ solely in that one has [č] in the same position in which the other has [š]. Examine the words below and find the rule that determines whether [č] or [š] will occur in a given position.

čuŋi	'kiss'	hakmawiš	'hungry'
hiča	'something'	pešliš	'bowl'
čoraat	'round'	neči	'pay'
tapašmal	'mouse'	yawaywiš	'pretty'

5. In Swahili, the placement of stress within a word is regular. Formulate a rule to account for stress placement in the words listed below.

asubúhi	'morning'	fuatíša	'copy'
wokóvu	'salvation'	ušínde	'defeat'
utóto	'childhood'	karatási	'paper'
hurúma	'mercy'	edašára	'eleven'
dámu	'blood'	fikíre	'consider'

6. The forms below are from Araucanian, a language spoken in Chile and Argentina (data from Max S. Echeverría and Heles Contreras, 'Araucanian Phonemics,' *International Journal of American Linguistics* 35:2 [1965], pp. 132–35). [ɨ] stands for a high back unrounded vowel (the unrounded counterpart of [u]); [ṭ] stands for a stop like [t] except that it is articulated farther back in the mouth; and [ñ] stands for a palatal nasal. Stressed vowels may bear either primary stress, indicated by the superscript ['], or stress of a secondary degree of intensity, marked by [`]. Determine whether stress in Araucanian is regular, in which case it follows a general rule, or whether it is idiosyncratic and hence distinctive. If it is regular, formulate the appropriate stress rule; if not, explain why.

ñuké	'mother'	ṭipánto	'year'
ɨlmén	'rich, noble'	elwáfimì	'you will give him'
ɨnáy	'he scratches himself'	elúmuyù	'give us'
wulé	'tomorrow'	elúaènew	'he will give me'
akúle	'if he comes'	kimúfalùwulày	'he pretended not to know'

7. Reduplication is a common phonological process in which part or all of a lexical item is duplicated, usually to express some notion such as plurality, repetition, duration, or intensity. Reduplication is one of the processes involved in marking nouns plural in Papago, a Uto-Aztecan language spoken in Arizona and northern Mexico (data from Kenneth Hale, 'On Papago Laryngeals,' in Earl H. Swanson, Jr., ed., *Languages and Cultures of Western North America: Essays in Honor of Sven S. Liljeblad* [Pocatello: Idaho State University Press, 1970], pp. 54–60). Examine the data below and state the rules for deriving plural nouns from the corresponding singular forms. A long vowel is written with two occurrences of the vowel symbol; thus [aa] stands for a long [a], [oo] for a long [o], and so on.

SINGULAR	PLURAL	
bana	baabana	'coyote'
tɨɨma	tɨɨtɨma	'heel'
kuna	kuukuna	'husband'
paga	paapaga	'hole'
tɨho	tɨɨthɨo	'cave'
bahi	baabhai	'tail'
sona	soosona	'base'
tini	tiitini	'mouth'
naaka	naanaka	'ear'
piha	piiphia	'penis'
toona	tootona	'knee'

8. Piro is an Arawakan language spoken in Peru (data from Charles W. Kisseberth, 'The Treatment of Exceptions,' *Papers in Linguistics* 2:1 [1970], pp. 44–58). Given below in column I are Piro lexical items as they appear when they occur alone as independent words. In column II are listed forms derived from these lexical items by affixation. The data reveals the operation of a general phonological rule; formulate this rule. (Assume that every lexical item has a single underlying phonological representation.)

	I		II
yimaka	'teach'	yimaklu	'teaching'
xipalu	'sweet potato'	nxipalne	'my sweet potato'
čalu	'fish net'	nčalne	'my fish net'
čokoruha	'harpoon'	čokoruhkaka	'cause to harpoon'
yohima	'hide'	yohimlewa	'hide habitually'
kakonu	'build hunting shelter'	kakonru	'hunting shelter'

9. The words below are from Tonkawa, an American Indian language of Texas (data from Charles W. Kisseberth, 'Vowel Elision in Tonkawa and Derivational Constraints,' in Jerrold M. Sadock and Anthony L. Vanek, eds., *Studies Presented to Robert B. Lees by His Students*, Papers in Linguistics Monograph Series 1, 1970, pp. 109–37). The words in each of the three sets are formed from the same root by affixation, and each of the three roots has a single underlying phonological representation. Three phonological rules

function in determining the phonetic shape of the words represented; one rule deletes a word-final vowel, and a second deletes the first of two vowels that are directly adjacent to each other. Isolate the morphemes in the data below and state the meaning of each. Posit a uniform underlying representation for each root. Formulate the third rule needed to account for the phonetic output. Finally, show how the three rules derive the correct phonetic form of each word from its underlying representation. [ʔ] stands for a glottal stop, and [x] for a voiceless velar fricative.

	I		II
notox	'hoe'	picen	'castrated one, steer'
notxoʔ	'he hoes (it)'	picnoʔ	'he cuts (it)'
wentoxoʔ	'he hoes them'	wepcenoʔ	'he cuts them'
notxonoʔ	'he is hoeing (it)'	picnanoʔ	'he is cutting (it)'
wentoxonoʔ	'he is hoeing them'	wepcenanoʔ	'he is cutting them'

	III
netloʔ	'he licks (it)'
wentaloʔ	'he licks them'
netlenoʔ	'he is licking (it)'
wentalenoʔ	'he is licking them'

PART

3

linguistic
relationships

language change

borrowing

lexical borrowing

Living languages never hold still. Every language is the product of change and continues to change as long as it is spoken. For the most part, these changes escape our attention as they occur. They are minor enough or gradual enough to be imperceptible. Over a span of centuries, however, their cumulative effect is appreciable. Shakespeare's English is difficult for modern readers, and Chaucer's is almost incomprehensible without formal instruction.

One way languages change is through the influence of other languages. At one time the English word *patio*, for example, was not part of the English vocabulary. Now it is. The addition of this word to our lexicon thus constitutes a change in our linguistic system, albeit a minor one. Moreover, the word *patio* was not created out of thin air by English speakers. Prior to its use as an English word, it was a Spanish word with

179

comparable meaning (and still is). The addition of *patio* to our vocabulary clearly results from the influence of Spanish. Speakers familiar with the Spanish term started using it in English. Its use spread, and now it is a well-established word of our language. If this word had not existed in Spanish, or if English speakers had never had contact with it, it would not have become part of English. *Patio*, in short, was **borrowed** into English from Spanish.

Borrowing is a very common linguistic phenomenon. In all probability, no language is completely free of borrowed forms. Languages differ radically, however, with respect to the proportion of lexical items in their vocabularies that can be attributed to borrowing. In Albanian, for instance, all but a few hundred words are thought to have entered the lexicon through borrowing. English, although it has borrowed much less than Albanian, is often cited as a language that has borrowed heavily, since over half of the English lexicon is of foreign origin. In contrast, American Indian languages of the Athabaskan family tend to borrow relatively little. The reasons why languages differ in this regard are no doubt more historical and cultural than linguistic. Borrowing is never a linguistic necessity, since it is always possible to extend and modify the use of existing lexical items to meet new communicative needs.

An interesting variant of lexical borrowing is a phenomenon known as **loan translation**. The English expression *That goes without saying*, for example, is a literal translation from the French *Ça va sans dire*. What English speakers borrowed, in this case, was not actual lexical items, but rather a pattern for combining them figuratively to express a certain notion. The word *skyscraper* provides another illustration. French, with the term *gratte-ciel*, and Spanish, with *rascacielos*, have borrowed from English the metaphor of 'scraping the sky' to convey the idea of a very tall building. The German *Wolkenkratzer* is different only in that the form for 'clouds' occurs instead of the one for 'sky.'

syntactic and phonological borrowing

Lexical items are borrowed relatively freely. This fact is not really surprising; one lexical item more or less matters little to a language, since the lexicon is for the most part simply a list of independent elements. Changes in the syntax or phonology of a language also result from borrowing, but somewhat less frequently. Perhaps this is because a syntactic or phonological system consists of an integrated series of rules, and the modification of one rule could have drastic consequences elsewhere in the system. The extent to which languages can affect one another with respect to syntax and phonology is not really known, but there are cases that demonstrate the existence of this kind of influence.

For a syntactic example, we may cite the languages of the Balkan peninsula, such as Albanian, Bulgarian, Greek, and Rumanian. They are alike syntactically in that infinitival clauses are highly restricted in their use. Indeed, some of the Balkan languages lack infinitives entirely. Instead of *The children want to leave,* for instance, one would say something like *The children want that they leave.* The languages are related, but many of them only very indirectly, and it is clear that this shared syntactic trait is due to mutual borrowing.

The American Indian languages of the Pacific Northwest provide an example of borrowing in the realm of phonology. Many languages of this area have glottalized consonants; the percentage is much higher than it is in the languages of the world generally, and yet the languages displaying glottalized consonants are not all related. The explanation seems to be that glottalization spread among the tribes in the area through borrowing. Another example of phonological borrowing is seen in the many Indo-European languages of India that have **retroflex** consonants, consonants articulated with the tip of the tongue against the palate. It is fairly certain that these sounds developed in the Indo-European languages under the influence of the Dravidian family of languages, which are also spoken in India and which employ retroflex consonants.

causes of borrowing

A common cause of lexical borrowing is the need to find words for new objects, concepts, and places. It is easier to borrow an existing term from another language than to make one up. Many place names on the North American continent, for instance, were taken from Indian languages: *Mississippi, Michigan, Chicago, Dakota, Oklahoma, Kentucky, Manhattan,* and *Waukegan,* to cite just a few. From the American Indians we also received—along with the items themselves—the words *totem, wampum, moccasin, toboggan,* and *tomahawk.* From the aboriginal languages of Australia we get the words *kangaroo* and *wombat.* The word *gnu,* referring to an African antelope, is borrowed from the Bantu languages of that continent.

The paths of lexical borrowing reflect to a certain extent the paths of cultural influence. For example, a large proportion of the Arabic words in English pertain to the realm of science: *zero, cipher, zenith, alchemy, algebra, nadir, alcohol, bismuth,* and *alkali.* These borrowings, which came to English through Spanish, attest to Arabic influence in science and mathematics during the early medieval period. The importance of Italian influence in music and the other arts is apparent from the long list of Italian loan words that belong to this domain, such as *opera, tempo, adagio, soprano, piano, sonata, scherzo, virtuoso, sonnet, fresco, miniature, dilettante, balcony, cornice, corridor, colonnade, mezzanine, parapet,* and *niche.*

After the Norman conquest of England, great numbers of loan words came into English from French. Included among these borrowed words are scores of terms in such areas as government, the military, law, and religion, reflecting the fact that the Norman French, as the conquerors, exerted predominant influence in these areas. Governmental terms that came to English from French include *crown, power, state, reign, country, peer, court, duke, duchess, prince, realm, sovereign, minister, chancellor, council, authority, parliament, baron,* and *nation.* Borrowed terms pertaining to military matters are *battle, army, war, peace, lance, banner, ensign, officer, lieutenant, vessel, navy, admiral, soldier, sergeant, troops, arms, armor, assault, siege, enemy, challenge, gallant, march, company, guard, force,* and *danger.* Our legal vocabulary has been enriched by such words as *jury, judge, plaintiff, accuse, crime, justice, privilege, damage, traitor, felony, summon, defendant, sue, attorney, session, fee, plead, suit,* and *property.* Terms of religious and moral significance include *mercy, cruel, vice, nature, blame, save, pray, preach, angel, religion, virgin, saint, tempt, grace, pity, trinity, service, savior, relic, abbey, cloister, clergy, parish, baptism, friar, altar, miracle, sermon, sacrifice, virtue, charity, chaste, covet,* and *lechery.*

The influx of French borrowings into English during that Norman period was not matched by any comparable flow of loan words from English into French. The prestige factor, which was touched on in Chapter Three, is no doubt largely responsible. Since the French constituted an upper class, English speakers who desired social advancement were naturally led to learn French. The use of French words in English conversations became a common practice because of the air of prestige that accompanied them. The French, on the other hand, felt no corresponding pressure to master English, which was, after all, only the tongue of the masses.

The great prestige of French culture was also strongly felt among the upper classes of Czarist Russia. It was commonplace for the members of high society to speak French instead of Russian, and French expressions of course found their way into Russian conversations. Consequently, modern

Russian contains a great many French borrowings. American power and importance in today's world has brought on a trend of borrowing opposite to the one in Norman England. The number of English loan words in modern French is rising so rapidly that it is becoming a cause for alarm in some quarters (although it is hard to see why such a natural phenomenon as lexical borrowing should be considered alarming). Symptomatic of this modern French "Anglomania" are scores of expressions such as *snack bar, self-service, parking* 'parking lot,' *check list, deep freeze, pullover, living* 'living room,' *expressway, pinup, whisky, sandwich, weekend,* and *dancing* 'night club.' In a singing commercial for soft drinks that was once frequently aired on a Tijuana radio station, the line *a cada gusto,* which means 'for every taste,' was followed immediately by the line *a cada taste.* It was evidently felt that the prestige of an English word would induce Mexicans who desired to be modern and sophisticated to purchase these products.

Latin and Greek had great prestige in the world of scholarship during the Middle Ages. Consequently, words from Latin and Greek have been finding their way into English (often through French) and into other European languages ever since the Renaissance. By no means have all of them been taken from classical texts. A great many have been formed by combining Latin or Greek morphemes after the model of words of these languages, or just combining them in any way at all to make the result look scholarly. Words obtained from classical sources in these ways are sometimes called **learnèd words** (French *mots savants*); many thousands of them can be found in any large English dictionary.

The greatest concentration of learned words is probably to be found in the vocabulary of the sciences and other scholarly disciplines. Even the names of many of these disciplines are borrowed from the classical languages: *sociology, psychology, anthropology, philosophy, philology, biology.* Learned words are most certainly not limited to this domain, however. Hundreds of words in everyday use can be traced back to Latin and Greek. To take just one class of examples, consider these common English words starting with the Latin morpheme *ex* 'out of, from': *exact, exaggerate, exalt, exasperate, excerpt, exclude, excrete, excursion, execute, exempt, exert, exhaust, exhibit, expand, expect, expel, explain, explicit, explode, explore, export, extend, exterminate, extinct, extort, exude.* So prevalent are learned words in English that a number of Latin and Greek morphemes have come to be used productively. They can be combined with roots of any origin, not just those taken from the classical languages. *Ex-husband* and *ex-wife,* for instance, reveal the Latin *ex* prefixed to Germanic forms. The *able/ible* suffix, of Latin origin, combines with native roots in words such as *answerable, eatable, bearable, laughable,* and *salable.*

effects of borrowing

Normally, when a word is borrowed it is made to fit the phonological system of the borrowing language. The English word **rendezvous,** for example, was taken from French, but it obeys the phonological principles of English. It is pronounced with the English [r], not the French one; the first vowel is nonnasal, although it is nasalized in French; and so on. The reason is obvious—English speakers know English, but they do not, for the most part, know French.

Loan words are not always completely assimilated to the phonological system of the borrowing language, however. The same people who sprinkle their speech with French words for purposes of prestige may very well, for the same reason, attempt to preserve the French pronunciation. If enough people are familiar with the donor language, or if a great number of words are borrowed, the loan words may function as a phonological Trojan horse, sneaking new sounds into the inventory of sounds used in the borrowing language. As a matter of fact, the voiced fricatives [v z] worked their way into English from French in just this manner. They had occurred previously as variant phonetic manifestations of other sound types, but not as distinctive sounds. Loan words such as **very, veal, zeal,** and **zest** were responsible for their introduction.

Another result of heavy lexical borrowing can be the partitioning of the vocabulary with respect to the operation of phonological rules. Turkish, for example, has hundreds of loan words from Arabic, most of which do not follow the phonological rules of **vowel harmony** that apply to native Turkish words. (Vowel harmony means, roughly, that the vowels of a word are similar in a certain way. In the case of Turkish, all the vowels in a word must agree in being either front or back—front vowels and back vowels cannot occur in the same word.) Thus, the Arabic loan words behave in one way with respect to the phonological rules of Turkish, and the native Turkish words behave in another. The child who masters Turkish must learn, for every word he picks up, which class it falls into, because this information determines the word's behavior with respect to phonological rules and is therefore partly responsible for determining its pronunciation. A similar partitioning of the vocabulary exists in numerous other languages.

The borrowing of lexical items, then, can have an important impact on the phonological system of a language. One can hypothesize, in fact, that this is the basic mechanism by which languages influence one another phonologically.

internal change

lexical changes

Not all changes in linguistic systems are brought about by the influence of other languages. Borrowing, in all its forms, can be called **external change**, since it results from external linguistic influence. Without pretending that any neat dichotomy exists, we can label changes that do not come about through borrowing as instances of **internal change**.

Internal change can be discerned at all levels of linguistic structure. It affects individual lexical items as well as general rules, and it occurs in the semantic, syntactic, and phonological systems of a language alike.

The simplest form of internal change is probably the addition and loss of lexical items. There used to be an English verb *cere*, meaning 'wax,' but it is now obsolete. In order to express the notion 'idol,' few contemporary speakers would think of the word *maumet*, but there was a time when this word was current. *Congree* 'agree' is no longer used, and the same is true of the word *neat* 'cattle' (a native word, not to be confused with the modern English word *neat*, which is borrowed from French). What these examples show, of course, is that words can drop out of common use into oblivion. Were it not for written records, we would have no knowledge at all of words like *maumet* and *cere*.

The loss of lexical items seldom comes to our attention. They do not suddenly go into hiding, causing us to wonder what ever became of them; the process of obsolescence is a gradual one. For one reason or another, certain words fall into disfavor and disuse, dropping from sight little by little until, over a period of decades or centuries, they disappear completely. We can, however, put our finger on many lexical items that seem to be on their way toward oblivion. *Lo* is no longer a common word, for instance. Some speakers may not even recognize it without its caboose, *and behold. Fro* is reduced in its occurrence to the fixed phrase *to and fro. Verily* has a distinct biblical flavor. Not even proper names and oaths are immune to the ebb and flow of linguistic fashion. Contemporary American parents do not often name a child *Egbert, Bertha,* or *Percival.* We never use

Zounds! or *Egad!* without humorous intent. Some of these expressions may make a comeback in popularity, of course, but the odds would seem to be against it.

In a highly technical and complex society such as ours, there is a constant need for new lexical items. Where borrowing does not suggest itself as a way of obtaining a new term, alternative methods are available. A new term can be made up from scratch, coined just to meet the new need. Another possibility is to combine existing lexical items to form a more complex one that is in some way descriptive or appropriate. Still a third way to obtain a new term is to extend the use of an old one, making it applicable to new situations.

Of these three methods, the first is by far the least frequent. For the most part, people tend to readapt existing lexical material rather than to create entirely new material. Trade names for new products might be considered one area in which new coinages are frequent, but even here most terms have some relation to existing lexical items. Most trade names are taken either from proper names (*Plymouth, Lincoln, Ford, Edsel*) or from other already existing morphemes (*Rambler, Thunderbird, Mustang, Pinto, Colt, Dart, Caprice*). Of those that are not, the vast majority are clearly modeled after existing morphemes in a fairly transparent manner. *Vel, Lux, Jello, Brillo,* and *Fab,* for example, bear strong resemblances to *velvet, luxury, gelatin, brilliant,* and *fabulous*; the similarities are anything but accidental. Slang would seem to be an important source of linguistic inventions, such as *hip/hep, mooch, fink, moola,* and *barf.* Even slang expressions, however, most often consist of old lexical items in new semantic garb.

The creation of complex lexical items is such a frequent means of obtaining new terms that it is perhaps sufficient to give a few examples. When linguists started talking about *tree structure, spelling pronunciation, hypercorrection, loan translation, surface structure,* and *idiolects,* they combined previously existing lexical items into more complex ones for use as technical terms. When the word *hippie* was first coined, it was not pulled out of thin air; it consists of the diminutive suffix *y/ie* (as in *sonny, birdie*) added to the older morpheme *hip.* Similarly, such words as *beatnik, peacenik,* and *Vietnik* were formed by adding to an existing word the morpheme *nik,* which entered the language through the Russian loan word *sputnik* and the Yiddish *nudnik.* The word *hamburger,* originally from the place name *Hamburg,* was evidently analyzed as *ham+burger* by English speakers. The resulting lexical item *burger* has been the source of an endless stream of creations, among them *cheeseburger, pizzaburger, chiliburger, tomatoburger, mushroomburger, tunaburger, beefburger, doubleburger, steakburger,* and **Burger Chef**. The list of new creations from old lexical material could be lengthened *ad nauseam.*

The extension of existing lexical items to new situations involves both the metaphorical side of language and semantic change. Metaphorical extensions occur in such diverse domains as scientific terminology (electromagnetic **wave**, radiation **belt**, solar **storm**); marketing (**Salvo** laundry detergent, Plymouth **Fury**, **Spring** cigarettes); and slang (LSD **trip**, to **snow** a professor, to **squeal** to the cops). Not all extensions involve metaphor, of course. It is a common practice, for instance, to use a proper name to designate a new product, as in **Kent, Newport, Salem, Chesterfield, Marlboro, Winston,** and so on. In other cases, a label is adopted simply because it has a favorable or unfavorable connotation, or just for the sake of finding a label. **True** and **Lucky Strike** were no doubt chosen as names for cigarettes because of their favorable connotations. **Fuzz** was adopted to designate police for the opposite reason. The trade name **Pure Oil** is transparently propagandistic, but **Shell** seems to represent an arbitrary choice.

Metaphorical extension is one way in which semantic change comes about, though certainly not the only way. **Squeal to the cops** was no doubt a very vivid expression when it was new, but metaphors fade with continued use. The figurative force of **squeal to the cops** is now lost on us, since the expression is so familiar. **Squeal,** in short, has acquired the sense 'inform,' which it did not have originally. This extension in its use constitutes a change in the semantic system of English.

Over a period of centuries, a great many of the lexical items of a language change in meaning. The French verb **traire**, for example, used to have the general meaning 'pull' or 'draw.' In modern French, it is restricted to the specialized sense 'milk.' **Cuisse** 'thigh' originally meant 'hip' (Latin *coxa*). In English, **nice** used to mean 'foolish.' **Silly** had the sense 'happy, blessed, innocent.' **Cheek** is the modern continuation of the Old English word for 'jaw.' The word **meat** once meant 'food,' but it has narrowed in scope and now designates only one kind of food. **Bird** has broadened in scope, since it used to mean 'birdling, young bird.' **Bead** used to mean 'prayer'; it came to assume its present sense because of the practice of keeping track of one's prayers on what we now call the **beads** of a rosary. It should be apparent that there is no neat formula to describe the relationship between the old and the new meaning of a lexical item that has undergone semantic change. The relationship is sometimes very indirect, and it is often mediated by nonlinguistic factors. If there had been no such thing as rosaries, for instance, **bead** would not now mean what it does.

A lexical item can be characterized as a bundle of semantic, syntactic, and phonological properties. We have just observed that it is not at all unusual for a lexical item to change with respect to its semantic representation. It may be somewhat less common for the syntactic or phonological representation of a lexical item to undergo change, but this also occurs.

A few English nouns, including *friend* for most speakers and *enemy* for some, have undergone a change in their syntactic representation, resulting in expressions like *Bill is friends with Harvey*. We find in English a systematic relation between sentences with conjoined subjects and sentences with a simple subject and a prepositional phrase. For example: *Paul and Mary came/Paul came with Mary*; *The car and the truck collided/ The car collided with the truck*; *The oil and the water mixed/The oil mixed with the water*. When the predicate following a conjoined subject consists of a plural noun, there is normally no corresponding locution with a prepositional phrase; thus we find *Bill and Harvey are colleagues, Bill and Harvey are (old) acquaintances*, and *Bill and Harvey are antagonists*, but the following are ungrammatical: *Bill is colleagues with Harvey, Bill is (old) acquaintances with Harvey*, and *Bill is antagonists with Harvey*. The pattern is apparently being extended, however, for we now find alongside such sentences as *Bill and Harvey are friends* and *Bill and Harvey are enemies* the acceptable variants *Bill is friends with Harvey* and *Bill is enemies with Harvey*. The syntactic representation of *friend* has changed, since *friends* (but not *colleagues, acquaintances, antagonists, scientists*, and so on) can now occur in the prepositional-phrase locution. For those dialects that tolerate *Bill is enemies with Harvey*, the change has affected *enemy* as well.

The change in the morpheme *friend* was a purely syntactic one, since *friend* means the same in *Bill and Harvey are friends* and *Bill is friends with Harvey*. Quite frequently, though, syntactic change and semantic change accompany one another. When a morpheme is extended to a new syntactic class, it acquires a new meaning. The preposition/adverb *up*, for instance, can now be used as a verb (*The manager upped the prices*). Its new syntactic use is accompanied by a new meaning, 'raise.' *Down* has also become a verb, with the meanings 'drink' and 'knock from the air' (*He downed the medicine, Snoopy downed the Red Baron's plane*). Hundreds of examples of dual change of this sort can be found in English. If we wish to count this as syntactic change, then lexical items can be said to change very frequently in their syntactic properties.

Individual lexical items are also susceptible to change in their phonological representations. Under the influence of its spelling, as we saw earlier, *often* is now pronounced with a [t] by many people. These idiolects reflect a change in the phonological representation of *often*, because the [t] was not pronounced at an earlier period of English. More often, the phonological changes that morphemes undergo are of a morphological nature. The plural of *brother* used to be *brethren*, but now it is *brothers*; *brethren* survives only as a religious archaism. For some speakers, the plural of *ox* is not *oxen* but *oxes*. For these speakers, the morpheme *ox* is no longer an exception to the general rules that account for the phonetic manifestation of the plural morpheme. Its phonological properties have changed, since it interacts differently with the phonological rules of English. The conjugation of the French verb *aimer* 'love' will be our final example. As a regular development from Latin, it had the present-tense forms *j'aime* 'I love,' *tu aimes* 'you love,' *il aime* 'he loves,' *nous amons* 'we love,' *vous amez* 'you (plural) love,' *ils aiment* 'they love.' Notice that the root vowel is *ai* [ɛ] in four forms, but simply *a* [a] in the other two. In modern French, *ai* has been extended to all the forms: *nous aimons* 'we love,' *vous aimez* 'you (plural) love.'

rule changes

   Changes in the properties of individual lexical items are for the most part sporadic and idiosyncratic. Being limited to single lexical units, their effect on the linguistic system is minimal. Of much greater importance are changes in the rules of a language. Since rules apply to whole classes of lexical items and to infinite sets of sentence structures, the surface effect of modifying a rule may be extensive. Changes occur in the rules of both the syntactic and phonological systems of languages. They may take the form of the addition or loss of rules or the modification of existing rules.

   In modern French, possessive expressions like *mon livre* 'my book' and *le mien* 'mine' are syntactically related. To take an example, the two sentences *Ce livre est mon livre* 'This book is my book' (which is awkward, but grammatical) and *Ce livre est le mien* 'This book is mine' manifest the same underlying structure. In particular, the two noun phrases *mon livre* and *le mien* manifest the same underlying structure, *le mien livre*, literally 'the mine book' (parallel to *le grand livre* 'the large book'). When *livre* duplicates a noun that occurs previously in the sentence, it can be deleted, leaving *le mien*; for example, the underlying structure *Ce livre est le mien livre* reduces to *Ce livre est le mien* 'This book is mine' in this way. If *livre* is not deleted, however, the article *le* must be; the resulting expression, *mien livre*, is manifested phonologically as *mon livre* 'my book.' This situation is depicted in Figure 7.1.

UNDERLYING STRUCTURE

le mien livre 'the mine book'

figure 7.1

It is the Article Deletion rule that interests us, since this rule has been modified during the history of French. In modern French, the article cannot be deleted if the noun has been, since *mien* by itself is ungrammatical. Moreover, if the noun is not deleted from *le mien livre*, the deletion of the article is obligatory, since *mon livre* 'my book' is grammatical to the exclusion of *le mien livre*. Thus Article Deletion is applicable only when the noun is present and is obligatory when applicable.

The Article Deletion rule was part of Old French, but it applied in slightly different circumstances. In Old French, around the twelfth century, the article could be deleted regardless of whether or not the noun was present, and the rule was optional rather than obligatory. Thus expressions such as *L'abaie est moie* 'The abbey is mine' and *li nostre deu* '(the) our God' were well formed, though their counterparts would not be in modern French. The Article Deletion rule has therefore been modified during the historical development of French, in that the conditions for its application have changed.

Let us turn to English for another example of historical change in syntactic rules. In modern English, the negative form *not* can come directly after certain verb words but not others. The modals (words like *can, may, will*, and *must*) can directly precede *not*, and so can *have, be*, and *do*. Sentences like *He cannot come, He has not come, He is not coming*, and *He does not come* are grammatical, in other words, while sentences like *He comes not* or *He likes not chicken* are ungrammatical. It used to be the case, however, that *not* could follow any verb, not just this handful. Some examples are *It aperteneth nat to a wys man* 'It is not suitable for a wise man' and *Yff the maters went not to my maister entent* 'If the matters did not go according to what my master had planned,' in which *not* follows the verb forms *aperteneth* and *went*. Thus, the syntactic rules responsible for the position of *not* in English sentences have changed.

For a final example, consider English possessive expressions such as

John's friend. There is good reason to believe that such noun phrases result from underlying structures of the form *the friend of John's* (parallel to *a friend of John's*). Syntactic rules serve to permute the possessor noun phrase *John's* with *friend* (and also to delete *of* and *the*), thus producing *John's friend* from the postulated underlying structure. In modern English, the entire possessor noun phrase can be permuted, even if it is quite complex. (One can even get away with monstrosities like *The woman who I went to the party with's husband.*) Formerly, however, the permutation rule was considerably more restricted, since clauses or phrases modifying the possessor noun phrase could not be moved. Instead of *the King of England's throne,* one said *the King's throne of England;* the modifying phrase *of England* was left behind after the noun. The rule effecting this permutation has consequently been liberalized as part of the historical development of English.

The study of phonological systems uncovers a multitude of instances in which change has occurred through the addition or loss of phonological rules. Consider, for example, the phonological rules that accounted for the morphological patterns of Old English. English was at one time a highly inflected language; it was characterized by variations in the endings of words to distinguish case, gender, number, person, tense, and so on, much as Latin, German, and Russian are. The word *scip* 'ship,' for instance, had various endings that depended on its grammatical function in the sentence (case) and on whether it was singular or plural (number). *Scip* was used as the nominative and accusative singular form; *scipes* was the genitive singular form; *scipe* was dative singular. The corresponding three forms in the plural were *scipu, scipa,* and *scipum.*

Even without a close examination of the phonological structure of Old English, it is apparent that there must have been a fair number of phonological rules whose prime function was to specify the forms of all these inflectional endings. In modern English, however, there is relatively little in the way of inflection. Nouns have only a plural and a genitive or possessive ending, both of which are [z] in most cases, as we have seen. The inflection of verbs and pronouns has been vastly simplified, and the inflection of adjectives has been eliminated completely, except for comparative and superlative forms (*stronger, strongest*). Many phonological rules of English have therefore been dropped from the language. Some syntactic rules marking case and agreement must have been lost as well.

Comparing Latin and French, we find an instance of a phonological rule that has been retained but modified over the centuries. The rule in question is the one that assigns stress. In Latin, stress falls on the second syllable from the end of a word if this syllable is "heavy"; otherwise the third syllable from the end is stressed. A heavy syllable is one that either has a long vowel or is followed by two or more consonants (if the second consonant is not a liquid). *Antepōnō* 'I prefer' is therefore stressed on the second syllable from the end; this is a heavy syllable because the vowel is long (a bar over a vowel indicates length). Similarly, *advérsus* 'opposite' is stressed on the second syllable from the end because the vowel *e* is followed by two consonants. *Difficilis* 'difficult,' on the other hand, is stressed on the third syllable from the end, since the second from the end is not heavy. To complete the statement of the rule, we must add that a word of less than three syllables is stressed on the first syllable (for example, *béne* 'well,' *rēs* 'thing').

The evolution of Latin into modern French has involved, along with many other changes, modification of the stress rule. The rule in modern French is simply that the last vowel of a word is stressed. For example, *ami* 'friend,' *cheval* 'horse,' *finira* 'he will finish,' and *examiner* 'examine' are represented phonetically with stress as [amí], [šəvál], [finirá], and [ɛgzaminé]. The only qualification is that a final [ə] is ignored in the determination of stress placement. *Femme* 'woman' may be pronounced as either [fámə] or [fám], for instance, but [a] bears the stress in either case.

A comparison of Latin and modern French also provides an example of phonological change through the addition of a new rule. French has a rule that changes stressed [a] to [ɛ] in a large class of morphemes, illustrated by the following words:

mer	[mér]	'sea'	*marine*	[marínə]	'marine'
sel	[sél]	'salt'	*saline*	[salínə]	'saline'
clair	[klér]	'clear'	*clarté*	[klarté]	'clarity'

Mer, sel, and *clair* have the underlying representations [mar], [sal], and [klar]. The vowel [a] shows up overtly in these morphemes when the ending *ine* or *té* is added to them, since the ending bears the stress. When these morphemes stand alone as full words, on the other hand, [a] is the final vowel and is consequently stressed, yielding [már], [sál], and [klár]. The rule changing stressed [a] to [ɛ] is applicable to these forms, and from them it derives the phonetic sequences [mér], [sél], and [klér]. This rule was not part of Latin phonology, as shown by the words *máre* 'sea,' *sāl* 'salt,' and *clārus* 'clear,' the respective sources of French *mer, sel,* and *clair*.

change and language acquisition

Changes in the structure of a language do not come about instantaneously. Within a single idiolect, the linguistic system of a single speaker, we may find that certain minor changes are effected in an instant, and not over a period of time; a speaker may open a dictionary and learn a new word, for example. This is not the case, though, when we regard a language as a system shared by many speakers, and it is probably not even typical of idiolectal changes.

Take the word *hippie*, for instance, which recently spread very rapidly through much of the English-speaking world. Someone must have used this word first, or maybe a small number of people created it independently. In either case, many weeks or months must have gone by between the time it was coined and the time it became an item of general use. It is safe to say that there are still many English speakers who are not familiar with it. Most new lexical items spread and come into general use much more slowly, if they ever do at all. Moreover, an individual speaker may master a new lexical item only gradually. Perhaps, as a visitor in San Francisco, a speaker first saw the word *hippie* in a newspaper headline; only much later, when its use was more widespread and he had encountered it on numerous occasions and in various contexts, did he come to realize just what it means.

Changes in the rules of a language spread even more slowly than do lexical changes. Consider the rule of some English dialects that [ɛ] is manifested phonetically as [ɪ] before nasals. For the speakers who have this rule, *pen* and *pin* are both pronounced [pɪn], and *hem* rhymes with *him*. This rule is fairly widespread. The speech of certain radio and television announcers is characterized by the manifestation of [ɛ] as [ɪ] before nasals, so virtually all speakers of American English have been exposed to this linguistic trait. But while most speakers who have repeatedly encountered the word *hippie* have picked it up, so that it belongs to their linguistic system, the same is not true of the phonological rule in question. Although virtually all Americans have encountered speech in which *pin* and *pen* are pronounced alike, most of them have not picked up the phonological rule that is responsible.

Idiolects that have this rule thus coexist with idiolects that lack it. This linguistic difference does not hinder communication (indeed, it is usually not even noticed), and communication has not as yet wiped out the difference. Maybe it never will. Suppose, though, that we came back to American English several centuries from now and found that all speakers possessed the rule for manifesting [ɛ] as [ɪ] before nasals. With this greater time perspective, we would say that English had undergone a phonological change; this rule had been added to the phonological system. It had taken decades or centuries to spread to all speakers, however, and was anything but instantaneous. Whenever we speak of changes that a language has undergone in its historical development, we understand that the widespread adoption of the innovations may have taken a very long time.

Adults are thought to have limited linguistic flexibility. An adult who learns a foreign language can achieve near-native competence in it only with great difficulty, and he will almost always speak it with an accent (in part because of interference from the phonological system he already possesses). Yet despite the linguistic rigidity of adults, innovations are indeed made in their speech. Even the oldest of codgers could pick up the word *hippie*, for example. Moreover, adults can modify their speech with respect to rules, consciously or unconsciously patterning it after the model of another dialect. An adult Texan who moves to the Midwest is quite likely to make adjustments in his pronunciation, minimizing the differences between it and that of the speakers around him. An adult who desires social or occupational advancement may, with some success, study to "improve" his grammar.

Although we can only speculate at present, it is quite possible that the rule innovations of an adult speaker tend to be but a thin veneer over the system of rules he mastered as a child. In moments of excitement, fine points of grammar and pronunciation that an adult has carefully cultivated may go out the window. Regardless of whether this assessment is accurate, however, it is important for our ultimate understanding of language change that we understand the child's acquisition of his native language.

A linguistic trait that constitutes an innovation for adult speakers will not be so regarded by children who learn the modified linguistic system as their native language. An adult who learns a recently coined lexical item will be able to recognize it as an innovation. For children of succeeding generations, on the other hand, this item will have no aura of newness at all, since it will belong to their idiolects right from the start. If its status with mature speakers is insecure, the insecurity will disappear as the form is learned on a par with older lexical items by new waves of native speakers.

The difference between the language learning of children and that of adults, such as it is, is no doubt more important with respect to innovations in linguistic rules, since even adults can pick up new lexical items quite easily. It has been hypothesized that new syntactic or phonological rules can achieve only secondary status in the linguistic systems of adults, that they remain peripheral to the system of rules acquired when the adults were first learning to talk. Consider, however, the child who is exposed to speech characterized by rule innovations. Since he has no previous linguistic experience in which the innovations were lacking, he will naturally consider the new speech traits to be on a par with all the other traits of the language he is trying to learn. Consequently, the child will learn the new rules as an integral part of the linguistic system he acquires, not as superficial appendages to it.

The linguistic system that the child constructs for himself when he learns to talk may actually be simpler than the corresponding system of adults, particularly when the adult system includes rule innovations. Suppose, for the sake of discussion, that an adult's phonological system is modified by the addition of several rules, and that these rules have only secondary, peripheral status for him. When a child learns the modified dialect, the new rules are accommodated as an integral part of his linguistic system, not as isolated additions to it. In the context of the entire phonological system, the innovations may be significantly simpler than when they are learned independently. Children thus take a fresh look at a language when they go about learning it, and their efforts may entail a **restructuring** of the system.

Let us take a hypothetical example by way of illustration. Suppose there is a language that contains a rule to the effect that [t] is aspirated at the end of a word. A morpheme with the underlying representation [kit] would thus be manifested phonetically as [kitʰ], where the raised h after a segment indicates that the segment is aspirated. Suppose further that an innovation occurs in this language; for some unknown reason, perhaps just because of its stylistic value, speakers start pronouncing words using [s] instead of [tʰ]. By virtue of this innovation, then, the morpheme whose underlying representation is [kit] will be pronounced [kis]. If we assume that adult speakers learn new rules as essentially independent entities, the innovation for them consists in the addition of a phonological rule, a rule that manifests [tʰ] as [s]. The translation of [kit] into the phonetic sequence [kis] is thereby accomplished in two steps. First, the previously existing rule modifies [kit] to [kitʰ], since [t] comes at the end of the word. Second, the new rule manifests [kitʰ] as [kis].

When children become native speakers of this hypothetical language, they take a fresh look at things. Let us assume that there is structural evidence for positing [kit] as the underlying form of the phonetic sequence [kis] (for example, perhaps this morpheme is a verb, and in the past tense it is manifested as [kita], with the underlying [t] showing up overtly). The learners of this language will thus be confronted with underlying representations like [kit] that are paired with phonetic sequences like [kis], and as part of mastering the phonological system of the language they must construct some rule which effects all such pairings. The rule they come up with will probably be this one: Manifest [t] as a fricative in word-final position. Unlike the adult speakers, they will have no structural reason to posit a stage [tʰ] intermediate between [t] and [s], and one rule will suffice instead of two. The only reason why [tʰ] mediates [t] and [s] in the adult system is that the adult speakers, previous to the innovation, had mastered a system in which [t] was manifested as [tʰ]; children first learning the language will of course lack this motivation. The restructured phonological system they arrive at will be simpler than the adult one, for it contains only one rule connecting [t] and [s], while the adult system contains two.

In this hypothetical but plausible example, the adult dialect with the innovation is equivalent to the dialect learned by new speakers. Both pronounce our sample verb [kis], though they differ as to the rules that produce [kis] from the underlying representation [kit]. The speakers will be conscious of no difference at all, since linguistic rules cannot be directly observed, introspectively or by other speakers. A structural change in the language has nevertheless occurred; the phonological system has been restructured, and this restructuring can be attributed directly to the process of native language acquisition.

This is not the only mechanism by means of which change can stem from the child's acquisition of his native language. Another obvious mechanism is that of **imperfect learning**. In the transmission of a linguistic system from one generation to the next, some modifications are bound to creep in; the system the child constructs will inevitably diverge in at least minor ways from that of his linguistic models. In this case, we would expect the newly acquired system and the adult system not to be fully equivalent. The differences between them will have overtly manifested consequences.

Take the learning of vocabulary, for instance. Since thousands of lexical items must be mastered, there are bound to be some that the child learns not at all or only imperfectly. There may be some lexical items that are used only rarely, so that they fail, purely by chance, to occur in the child's linguistic experience. If he never encounters them, he will of course never learn them. He may become familiar with other lexical items without fully realizing what they mean, perhaps because they are used too infrequently or because they happen not to occur in a context that will allow him to deduce their meaning. It is not unusual to discover that a word does not mean for other people what it means for us.

Irregular morphological phenomena are frequent victims of imperfect learning. With very common morphemes, morphological irregularities can be sustained indefinitely. The English verb **go** is quite irregular; the past-tense form is not **goed** but **went,** and the past participle is **gone,** whereas with regular verbs the past participle is the same as the past-tense form. Since **go** is such a frequently occurring verb, however, these irregular forms are easily learned and retained. On the other hand, take a less common irregular verb like *strive*. *Strive* is not a verb we have occasion to use every day, and particular forms of it, like the past participle, may occur only rarely in the linguistic experience of a given speaker. It is not surprising, therefore, that the irregular past-tense and past-participle forms, *strove* and *striven*, are commonly replaced by the regular form *strived*. A child who learns English may happen never to hear *strove* and *striven*, or he may hear them so infrequently that they do not register with him. In the absence of information to the contrary, he will treat *strive* as if it were a regular verb.

Imperfect learning must be a significant factor in the modification of general rules as well. The child must construct his linguistic system on the basis of the speech traits he observes in the linguistic performance of others. The data that he has at his disposal is thus haphazard, distorted, and fragmentary. It contains errors that his models commit while talking, and it is likely to contain important gaps, since the sentences the child has occasion to witness constitute only a minute portion of the unbounded set of sentences that a language comprises. If only because of the imperfect character of the data the child has to go on, therefore, the rules he formulates may well differ in minor respects from those of his models. The consequences of this divergence may be so subtle that it is never noticed or corrected.

One should by no means conclude from this discussion that language change is fully understood. Many of the remarks in this section are quite tentative, particularly those pertaining to language acquisition. Much remains to be discovered about linguistic and psychological organization before all our questions about language change can be answered.

dialects revisited

the underlying uniformity of dialects

In our discussion of linguistic diversity in Chapter Three, we noted that no two people possess precisely the same linguistic system. Idiolectal differences can be found between any two speakers, regardless of whether or not these differences are consciously perceived. They are not to be taken at face value, however. When viewed in relation to the system of rules and abstract underlying representations in which linguistic structure resides, surface differences quite often appear to be much less numerous and important than they do at first glance.

For illustration, let us return to the dialect divisions indicated in Figure 3.2, page 49. Dialect B_1, you may recall, was distinguished from the other varieties of language B because its speakers shared numerous speech traits that distinguished them from other speakers of B. Speakers of B_1 were said to pronounce [u] in words in which other speakers pronounced [ʊ]; they were said to pronounce [i] in forms pronounced with [ɪ] in other dialects; and a number of other traits combined with these to set B_1 apart from B_2 and B_3.

If one were to concentrate on the surface differences alone, they might seem impressive. It would be possible to list thousands of words pronounced differently by speakers of B_1 and by other speakers of B. The former, for instance, might say [tup], [kitane], [isu], [gilipumay], and [sumo], whereas the latter would say instead [tʊp], [kɪtane], [ɪsʊ], [gɪlɪpʊmay], and [sʊmo]. On the phonetic level, then, B_1 differs from B_2 and B_3 in thousands of individual details.

These differences all but disappear when we regard phonetic details as merely the surface manifestation of a system of phonological rules that apply to abstract underlying representations. Notice, first of all, that these phonetic differences are quite regular. Whenever a word in B_1 is pronounced with [i], the corresponding word in B_2 and B_3 is pronounced with [ɪ] in the same position. Whenever a word of B_1 is pronounced with [u], the corresponding word in B_2 and B_3 is pronounced with [ʊ] in the same position. In comparing B_1 and the other dialects, therefore, we find a systematic **correspondence** between [i] and [ɪ] and between [u] and [ʊ]. The phonetic differences are not random, sporadic, and peculiar to individual lexical items. Rather, they are regular, follow a constant pattern, and hold for all morphemes of B.

B_1, we may suppose, has five distinctive vowels, whose phonetic manifestations are [i u e o a]. The difference between high, mid, and low vowels is distinctive; it separates [i u] from [e o] from [a]. For the high and mid vowels, the difference between front and back is distinctive; it distinguishes [i] and [u], as well as [e] and [o]. In the underlying phonological representations of morphemes, then, the segment [i] will be listed as a high front vowel, to distinguish it from the mid and low vowels [e o a] and from the high back vowel [u]. Similarly, [u] will be listed simply as a high back vowel. The precise phonetic shape of these distinctive underlying vowel segments will be determined by rules that specify nondistinctive phonetic detail and are of relatively minor interest.

But B_2 and B_3 are characterized by exactly the same scheme. They too have five distinctive vowels, which include a low vowel, phonetically [a]; two mid vowels, phonetically [e o]; and two high vowels. The only difference resides in the phonetic manifestation of the two high vowels, which is [ɪ ʊ] instead of [i u]. The underlying representations will be identical, since [i ɪ] are both high front vowels and [u ʊ] are both high back vowels. The vowel segment of [tup] /[tʊp], for instance, would be listed simply as high and back in all dialects of B; so far as distinctive phonological information is concerned, the representations of morphemes are uniform for all dialects of B. Moreover, almost all of the relevant phonological rules will be identical for B_1 and for the other dialects. The rule that all vowels are nonnasal, for instance, is shared. So is the rule that front and low back vowels are unrounded while nonlow back vowels are rounded. The differences boil down to this: High vowels are articulated with the tongue slightly higher in dialect B_1 than in B_2 and B_3. That is, the rule specifying tongue height makes a slightly (but not radically) different phonetic specification for the speakers of B_1. Only one rule is involved, since [i u] differ from [ɪ ʊ] respectively in the same way. This one minute difference in a single phonological rule accounts for the thousands of differences in phonetic detail.

Naturally, not all dialect differences turn out to be as minor as this one. Two dialects of the same language may differ in very significant respects, even in terms of their rules. The important point to remember is that differences in speech traits should not be accepted at face value. When we look below the surface, we usually find that the dialects of a language are similar in many more respects than they are different. The differences, furthermore, are more often than not of a superficial nature.

divergence into distinct dialects

The dialect picture of a language is never a static one. Over a period of years, various isoglosses indicating the boundaries of linguistic traits will shift. If two speakers or communities of speakers have frequent linguistic contact with each other, the dialect differences between them may tend to diminish through borrowing. An innovation that occurs in one dialect is likely to spread to the other if there is communication between the two.

But language change also contains the seeds of increased dialect diversity. Suppose, for example, that a relatively homogeneous group of speakers is divided by some accident of history into two smaller groups between which there is little or no subsequent communication. This separation might come about through the migration of a portion of the community, through the imposition of political barriers, because of a feud—the cause is irrelevant. What will be the linguistic fate of the two groups, once communication between them has ceased?

The linguistic system of both groups will of course change with time, and over a period of centuries the cumulative effect of the many individual changes that occur will be substantial. If the linguistic evolution of the two groups remains independent, the result will be divergence into two distinct dialects. Changes in the dialect of one will have no effect on the development of the dialect of the other. An innovation that spreads throughout one group will not be able to bridge the gap in the network of communication and spread to the second. Isoglosses will pile up along this gap to form a bundle, and the isogloss bundle will grow thicker and thicker as time passes and more and more features come to separate the two dialects.

The phenomenon of language change will therefore bring about increased linguistic diversity in a community of speakers unless there is enough communication and mutual linguistic influence within the group to offset this tendency. As long as the bulk of changes that occur within a group eventually spread to all its members, it will remain relatively homogeneous from the linguistic point of view. The dialect in question may change radically over a period of centuries, but the changes will be uniform within the group itself. When the changes are not coordinated for all speakers of the group, however, they will lead to increased diversity. The linguistic system of each subgroup will develop independently away from the common point of origin.

This mechanism is of extreme importance for the historical study of languages, so let us represent it diagrammatically. In Figure 7.2, L represents the shared linguistic system of a group of speakers, and the arrow symbolizes the passage of time. If the group coheres and the speakers continue to influence one another linguistically, the result will be a modified but still relatively uniform linguistic system, L′.

Suppose, on the other hand, that half of the speakers of L migrate to a distant island and that the two subgroups no longer communicate with each other. As time passes, the linguistic systems of the two subgroups diverge more and more. This situation is depicted in Figure 7.3. As the bundle of isoglosses between the two systems grows thicker, the split of L into two dialects, L_1 and L_2, becomes more and more apparent. Over a period of many centuries, L_1 and L_2 may become so different from each other that we would be inclined to call them two different languages, rather than dialects of the same language. In this case, L_1 and L_2 are said to be **related** languages.

L
↓
L'

figure 7.2   figure 7.3

For two languages to be related, therefore, means that they are divergent continuations of the same, historically earlier language. The Romance languages are a good example. French, Spanish, Italian, Portuguese, Rumanian, Catalan, and several others are related languages in this sense. They are all divergent continuations of spoken Latin, which developed independently in the various regions to which spoken Latin was carried by the Roman conquerors. They remain similar enough so that their relationship is apparent, but at the same time they are different enough from one another to be considered separate languages. They could just as well be called dialects of the same language, however. It should be evident that the distinction between related languages and dialects of a single language is only a matter of degree.

suggestions for study and discussion

1. List a number of English words, other than those given in the text, that you know to be borrowed from other languages. Have they been modified semantically, syntactically, or phonologically in being borrowed? Do they conform more closely to the structural patterns of English because of these modifications?

Choose several common English words and trace their historical origin in a large dictionary, or in an etymological dictionary such as Eric Partridge, *Origins: A Short Etymological Dictionary of Modern English*, 3rd edition (London: Routledge & Kegan Paul, 1961).

2. Take a large sample of trade names and speculate on the factors that motivated their adoption. Consider such matters as connotative or propagandistic value, sound symbolism, descriptiveness, plays on words, and metaphor.

3. Complex lexical items in common use are often shortened for greater ease of expression. For example, the word *private* (in the military sense) derives historically by truncation of the longer expression *private soldier*; *automobile* has been shortened to *auto* (which in turn is losing ground to the unrelated but shorter word *car*); *bus* derives from *omnibus*; and the word *pram* in

British English abbreviates the much longer *perambulator*. Find as many other words as you can that seem to have come about in this way, and check your hypotheses with a dictionary. Can you identify expressions that are now in the process of being shortened (such as **good morning**, which often comes out as just **morning**)?

4. An analogy was drawn in Chapter Two between linguistic competence and a symphony. In particular, it was argued that performance errors do not cast doubt on the existence of the abstract linguistic system any more than the existence of a symphony as an abstract entity is called into question because of a poor performance. This analogy is not a perfect one, however, because the vicissitudes of language use do in fact have a cumulative effect that gradually leads to change in linguistic competence. The shortening of commonly used lexical items is a case in point. Closely related to this is phonetic simplification, as exemplified by the common rendering of *probably* as *probly*. Metathesis, a reversal in the order of two elements, is illustrated by the frequent use of *prevert* in lieu of *pervert*. Blending is the conflation of two expressions, resulting in a new expression incorporating aspects of both; **as far as NP**, for instance, represents a blend of the two expressions **as for NP** and **as far as NP is concerned**. Although phenomena such as these come about originally through performance errors, they often become established in the language, so that a change in linguistic competence results. Thus *probly* is the expected form in certain styles, *prevert* is used consistently instead of *pervert* by some speakers, and **as far as NP** is fully grammatical for a great many speakers (but not all). Find as many other examples as you can of change coming about through phonetic simplification, metathesis, blending, and similar processes.

5. In the first column below are given reconstructed forms from Proto Burmish, the ancestor of Burmese and a number of other modern languages. The modern Burmese equivalents of these forms are given in the second column. (Data from Robbins Burling, 'The Addition of Final Stops in the History of Maru (Tibeto-Burman),' *Language* 42:3 [1966], pp. 581–86; and Robbins Burling, *Proto Lolo-Burmese*, Bloomington, Indiana University Research Center in Anthropology, Folklore, and Linguistics, Publication 43, 1967, supplement to *International Journal of American Linguistics* 33:2.) Compare the forms in the two columns and state the sound changes illustrated here that have characterized the evolution of Burmese from Proto-Burmish. (The superscript [h] indicates that the preceding segment is aspirated. Tones have been omitted.)

Proto-Burmish	*Burmese*	
ca	sa	'eat'
yei	yei	'skin'
no	nou	'breast'
s̆ei	θei	'die'
cun	sun	'kite (bird)'
mo	mou	'sky'
yo	you	'bone'
c̆ʰo	c̆ʰou	'sweet'

6. Given in the column at the left below are several sentences of Old French. Compare these with the modern French sentences (some grammatical and some ungrammatical) in the right-hand column, and describe a syntactic rule change pertaining to pronouns that occurred in the evolution of this language. (Word-for-word translations are given as well as free translations.)

<table>
<tr><td>Old French</td><td>Modern French</td></tr>
<tr><td>Tenez moy pour vostre annemy?
take me for your enemy
'Do you take me for your enemy?'</td><td>Grammatical:
Vous avez des enfants?
you have of-the children
'Do you have children?'</td></tr>
<tr><td>Demanderoiz me vos plus rien?
would-ask me you more anything
'Would you ask anything more of me?'</td><td>Il est resté ici.
he is remained here
'He remained here.'</td></tr>
<tr><td>Une espee du fuerre a trete.
a sword from-the scabbard has drawn
'He drew a sword from the scabbard.'</td><td>Ungrammatical:
Avez une épée.
have a sword
'You have a sword.'</td></tr>
<tr><td>Il est chi pour eles remés.
he is here for her remained
'He remained here for her.'</td><td>A demandé beaucoup.
has asked much
'He asked for a lot.'</td></tr>
</table>

7. Data from three dialects of Papago is listed below (see Kenneth Hale, 'Some Preliminary Observations on Papago Morphophonemics,' *International Journal of American Linguistics* 31:4 [1965], pp. 295–305). [ḍ] and [ṣ] are slightly retroflexed consonants. Assume that the underlying phonological representations given at the left are the same for all three dialects. In dialect 1, the following two rules serve to derive the phonetic outputs from the phonological representations:

A. [ḍ] becomes [l], and [ṣ] becomes [s], when followed by [i].
B. A word-final [i] is deleted.

How must these rules be ordered in dialect 1? Formulate the rules necessary to account for dialects 2 and 3. How are these rules ordered? Precisely how do the three dialects differ?

Phonological Representations	*Dialect 1*	*Dialect 2*	*Dialect 3*	
ʔuuṣi	ʔuus	ʔuus	ʔuus	'stick'
tini	tin	čiñi	čiñ	'mouth'
hɨwɨdi	hɨwɨl	hɨwɨli	hɨwɨl	'wind'
ṣuudagi	ṣuudag	ṣuudagi	ṣuudagi	'water'
tɨhani	tɨhan	čɨhañi	čɨhañ	'hire'
naadi	naad	naaǰi	naaǰ	'something kindled'
duuki	duuk	ǰuuki	ǰuuki	'rain'

8. Listed below are a number of active and passive verb forms of Maori (see Kenneth Hale's review of *A Profile Generative Grammar of Maori* by Patrick Hohepa, in *Journal of the Polynesian Society* 77:1 [1967], pp. 83–99). At an earlier historical stage of the language, the passive suffix was simply [ia], and Maori had a phonological rule that deleted any word-final consonant. For example, the underlying representation of 'embrace' was [awhit], which was manifested phonetically as [awhi] by virtue of the consonant deletion rule. In the passive 'be embraced,' on the other hand, the [t] was retained phonetically, because the passive suffix [ia] kept the [t] from being in word-final position.

There is good evidence to suggest that restructuring has occurred in Maori, so that the passive suffix now consists of both [ia] and the preceding consonant. Assuming this to be the case, describe in detail how the grammar of Maori has been modified. That is, precisely what changes have occurred in the rules and phonological representations involved? Can you speculate on the causes of this restructuring?

Active	Passive	
awhi	awhitia	'embrace'
hopu	hopukia	'catch'
aru	arumia	'follow'
tohu	tohuŋia	'point out'
mau	mauria	'carry'
wero	werohia	'stab'

CHAPTER 8 genetic relationships

family trees

direct and indirect relationships

Two languages are said to be related if they are divergent continuations of the same earlier language. L_1 and L_2 were seen to be related languages in Figure 7.3, since both are later stages of L. A language that occupies the position of L in such a situation is called a **proto** language; L is the prototype of L_1 and L_2. Spoken Latin can therefore be referred to as Proto Romance, since it is the language from which the contemporary Romance languages have descended. The various Slavic languages are divergent continuations of Proto Slavic.

Linguists have always found irresistible the temptation to speak of linguistic relationships with kinship terminology. A proto language can also be called a **parent** language, and its divergent continuations referred to as **daughter** languages. L would thus be the parent of L_1 and L_2. L_1 and L_2, since they are daughters of the same parent, are **sister** languages.

A parent language and its daughters constitute a language **family**. Latin and French, Spanish, Italian, Portuguese, and their sisters make up a language family, and so do Proto Slavic and the modern Slavic languages. Relationships of this type are called **genetic** relationships.

A daughter language, with the passage of time, itself becomes a parent language. Its historical evolution may involve divergence into a number of distinct dialects, and if the divergence becomes marked enough, these dialects can be considered separate but related languages. The "family tree" representing genetic relationships can therefore be quite complex. Consider Figure 8.1, for example. B, C, D, and E are shown as daughters of A, the proto language. As the historical development of this language family continues, each of the daughters of A splits into a number of daughters of which it is the parent. F and G, for instance, are divergent continuations of B; B is thus a daughter of A but a parent of F and G. G in turn serves as the proto language from which Q and R descend. Proto Slavic, to take a real example, is one of the daughters of Proto Indo-European. The contemporary Slavic languages, such as Russian, Czech, and Polish, are in turn daughters of Proto Slavic. The continued historical development of this family may see Russian or Polish in the role of a parent language.

From Figure 8.1, we see that the connection between related languages can be either direct or indirect. Q and R are directly related, since they are continuations of G, which is the most immediate predecessor of both. S, T, and U are directly related in similar fashion. The relationship between Q and S, on the other hand, is quite indirect. They both descend from A, but this common ancestor is very far removed. Since Q and S have both diverged so far from A, they may be very different indeed. The sister languages Q and R will resemble each other much more closely than either will resemble S. English and German, for example, are very similar to one another, since they both descend from Proto Germanic. Likewise, Russian and Polish are quite similar, being directly related through Proto Slavic. English and Russian are also related, but only indirectly; Proto Germanic and Proto Slavic are both daughters of Proto Indo-European, and the latter mediates the genetic relationship of English and Russian. Because English and Russian are related only indirectly, they are much less similar to each other than they are to their respective sister tongues.

It is natural to ask whether all human languages are related, however indirectly. Are all human languages, in other words, linked in a single, vast family tree? This is something that we do not know at present, and we may never know. It has never been demonstrated that all languages are members of a single, giant family. On the other hand, the opposite has never been proved either, and in principle could not be proved. It is possible to prove that two languages are related, by demonstrating that they display extensive similarities in structure that can reasonably be accounted for only by assuming them to be divergent continuations of the same proto language. How, on the other hand, would it be possible to show that two languages are not related? If they are radically different, it is clear that they are not directly related, but differences in structure can never rule out the possibility that they may be related indirectly. The common ancestor that connects them may lie so far in the past that all the original structural similarities have been wiped out during their long, divergent courses of development. It is perfectly conceivable, then, that all human languages are in fact related but that proof of this universal genetic relationship will never be forthcoming. It is equally conceivable that human languages are not all related; in this event, proof is ruled out in principle.

the techniques of historical investigation

Establishing conclusively that a number of languages are related and identifying the genetic relationships that connect them is no simple matter. Languages do not carry signs saying "I belong to the X family of languages." Nor do family trees grow in linguists' back yards where they can be observed at leisure. We can today speak of the Indo-European family of languages and sketch the broad outlines of the genetic relationships among them only because of the genius of preceding generations of scholars. Discovering what languages are related, and how they are related, is a scholarly and analytical task of the first order.

For the most part, only descriptions of contemporary languages are available to work from in establishing genetic relationships. Sometimes, however, the investigator has at his disposal written records of earlier stages of a language, and these can be extremely valuable. We have written records of English covering more than a thousand years of its development; without them we would be very much in the dark concerning many aspects of its evolution. In some cases, written records preserve knowledge of a language that is no longer spoken and could not otherwise be taken into account. Our knowledge of Gothic, for example, has been a valuable resource in the historical investigation of the Germanic languages. Gothic has been extinct since the sixteenth century, but it is known from written documents. Of even greater significance for the study of genetic relationships is the preservation via writing of the proto language of a family.

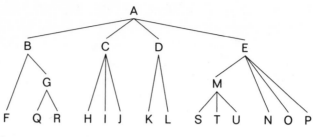

figure 8.1

Because we have extensive written records of Latin, including some reflecting spoken Latin, our knowledge of Proto Romance is reasonably complete. We are aware of many features of the proto language that could not be discovered just by examining the contemporary Romance languages.

Linguistic scholars are rarely fortunate enough to have direct knowledge of a proto language. Very often, in fact, historical investigation must proceed without any written records at all. Let us put ourselves in the shoes of a linguist who finds himself in this situation. Suppose he stumbles on the language family of Figure 8.1. Available to him as evidence are the contemporary languages F, Q, R, H, I, J, K, L, S, T, U, N, O, and P. He can observe that they are similar in various respects (other than those respects in which all languages are similar). Thus he is led to the hypothesis that these languages are genetically related. How, and to what extent, can he discover the nature of these genetic relationships without written records to guide him?

Clearly, there will be some things he will not be able to discover at all. He may posit the prior existence of M, for instance, the parent of S, T, and U (if he notices that these three are especially similar). He may even be able to ascertain some of the properties of M by comparing its three daughters. But he will never be able to reconstruct a picture of M that is as complete as his information about the daughter languages. Many important structural details are bound to have been lost in the historical shuffle. Suppose, to take a plausible example, that M was highly inflected, but that the three daughter languages have independently lost the original inflections. From S, T, and U alone, then, it will be impossible to determine completely the details of the inflectional processes of M.

To some extent, one can reconstruct certain features of earlier stages of the individual contemporary languages. This technique, in which earlier stages of a language are partially reconstructed on the basis of structural properties of its later stages, is known as **internal reconstruction**. Suppose, for example, that [č] occurs only before [i] in language S, and that [t] never occurs before [i]. S thus has morphemes like [čik] and [tak], but none like [čak] or [tik]. [č], it seems, is the variety of [t] that occurs before [i]. If we now find in S the morphemes [mač] and [kač], we are naturally led to the conclusion that these forms once ended phonetically in [i]. The final [i] conditioned the modification of [t] to [č] in these morphemes before being lost. On the basis of internal, nonhistorical evidence, we can reasonably posit the existence of final [i] in such morphemes at an earlier stage of the language. (In fact, they may still contain final [i] in their underlying phonological representations; this [i] causes [t] to become [č] but is later deleted by a phonological rule.)

The limitations of internal reconstruction are rather severe, however. An earlier structural feature of a language can be reconstructed only if evidence for positing it happens to have been retained, and this is by no means always the case. For an obvious example, consider the loss of a lexical item. If S used to have a word [tal] but no longer does, it is quite possible that no features of contemporary S will lead one to suspect this word's previous existence.

A much more powerful technique is available for investigating the historical origins and development of a group of languages that seem to be related. Instead of examining individual languages, as in internal reconstruction, one can compare two or more languages, with the object of figuring out what their common ancestor must have been like. If Q and R appear to be much more similar to each other than to other languages of the putative family, it is reasonable to hypothesize that Q and R constitute a subfamily, that they are divergent continuations of the same earlier language. By pooling and contrasting the evidence from two or more daughters, one can obtain a much clearer picture of the proto language than by examining just one.

The technique of comparing sister languages to arrive at a reconstruction of the proto language is known as the **comparative method** and was developed in the nineteenth century. In its classic form, the comparative method concerns primarily the sounds of a parent language and how these sounds are reflected in the daughters. It is a technique both for showing that several languages are related and for reconstructing the sounds of the parent.

Of course, we are not limited to the sounds alone when we compare two or more related languages. Extensive similarities in the morphology of two languages can be counted as evidence in favor of the claim that they are related; the same is true of syntactic similarities. Moreover, by comparing the morphological and syntactic properties of the daughters, conclusions can naturally be drawn regarding those of the proto language.

The linguist is therefore not at a total loss to trace the historical relationship and development of a group of languages when there are no written records to guide him. The close examination of an individual language will provide him with some clues concerning earlier stages of it. By comparing and contrasting two or more languages that seem to be related, he can ascertain various characteristics of the proto language; the proto language can be partially reconstructed by a process of triangulation.

Nevertheless, there are limitations. A proto language can never be reconstructed completely, no matter how many of its daughters are known. Since less can be ascertained about the structure of a proto language than about the structure of a living language, reconstructed parent languages are not always known in enough detail to be used for further reconstructions. The farther back we delve into the historical antecedents of a family of languages, the less data there is to work with.

Take the family of Figure 8.1 once again. Suppose it is correctly surmised that Q and R constitute a subfamily, and that F is more closely related to Q and R than to the other languages. From Q and R, it will be possible to partially reconstruct the proto language G, but G will be known much less completely than its daughters. Consequently, the usefulness of G in reconstructing B, the parent of G and F, will be diminished. The reconstruction of B will be more tentative and incomplete than that of G. The reconstructions of B, C, D, and E may not contain enough information to allow any reconstruction of A at all, since none of A's immediate daughters is known directly. Because of the increasing paucity of data as one digs farther and farther into the past, there is a point at which all known techniques of historical reconstruction cease to yield reliable results.

The situation is not basically different when written records are available. Written records allow us to pry a little deeper into the linguistic past, since they show earlier stages of languages in more detail, but they carry us back only a short distance. We have Gothic texts from as early as the sixth century, for example, but we have only scratched the historical surface even when we have gone back that far.

It should now be clear why no one has ever demonstrated that all human languages are related. The claim that they are related can be made, but it is an empty one. For the claim to be meaningful, one would have to show which established language families belong together in more comprehensive families, which of these belong together as members of still more inclusive families, and so on, until all human languages were accommodated. At each stage, it would be necessary to partially reconstruct a proto language and to demonstrate that its putative daughters were similar in ways that could best be explained by the hypothesis that they were divergent continuations of it. Even if all languages are in fact genetically related (which is a big assumption), it is simply not possible to reconstruct the family tree that links them all, thus establishing their relatedness. The time span is so great, and so many echelons of proto languages are involved, that the data supplied by contemporary languages will not take us back far enough.

the problem of borrowing

Complicating the whole picture of genetic relationship is the phenomenon of borrowing. When one language borrows a trait from another, the two are subsequently more similar to each other than they were before. If only one or a handful of traits are borrowed, the adjustment will of course be minute. It sometimes happens, however, that two languages influence each other on a grand scale. If the mutual influence is extensive enough, the languages involved may appear on cursory examination to be related when they really are not. In order to avoid false hypotheses of genetic relationship, one must be careful to distinguish similarities that are attributable to a common heritage from those that result from borrowing.

The problem that borrowing poses is usually much more subtle than this, however, and concerns the process of working out the genetic relationships of a group of languages that are in fact related. The problem, essentially, is that linguistic traits introduced through borrowing cannot be used for reconstructing a proto language; the amount of data that can validly be used for reconstruction is reduced significantly if one or more of the daughter languages has borrowed heavily. Suppose, for example, that two sister languages have been subjected to strong lexical influence from languages of other families, so that over half of the native lexical items have been replaced in each. Since the native lexical items are by definition those that descend from lexical items of the proto language, their loss inevitably diminishes the portion of the proto language that can be reconstructed.

The same is true when a language borrows from a related language. Such borrowing is very common, since speakers of divergent dialects usually continue to have some contact with one another during the historical evolution that leads to separate languages; it is an idealization to suppose that the speakers of a proto language suddenly split up into smaller speech communities between which there is absolutely no subsequent communication. (It is also an idealization to attribute complete linguistic homogeneity to speakers of the proto language.) If language Q has borrowed heavily from language R during their divergent evolution from the proto language G, the borrowed features of Q will add little information that cannot be provided by an examination of R. Moreover, the features of Q that have been dropped under the influence of R will not be available for establishing the relatedness of Q and R or for reconstructing the proto language. A good case in point is Albanian. Because it has borrowed so extensively from other languages, including Greek and the Slavic and Romance languages, only a few hundred native words remain. In addition, the inflectional endings have undergone considerable modification. As a result, the recognition of Albanian's place in the Indo-European family was relatively late.

the comparative method

We will examine the comparative method first in its classic form and then in light of more recent insights, taking into account the necessity of viewing the sounds of a language in relation to a system of phonological rules and abstract underlying representations. The clearest and easiest way to introduce the comparative method is by means of a concrete example of its application. We will use a hypothetical example in order to keep the data down to a manageable amount, but the phenomena that will be illustrated are typical of those found in the more complex cases of reality.

the data

Suppose that four new languages are discovered on a large island in the Pacific. For purposes of identification, we will call them L_1, L_2, L_3, and L_4. In addition to extensive syntactic and morphological congruence, these languages display striking similarities in their lexicons. A representative list of lexical items is given below with their meanings. (The symbol [x] stands for a voiceless velar fricative.)

From the very first glance, it is apparent that the four languages have lexical similarities that go far beyond the few that could be expected to occur by chance. In word after word, we find resemblances in both sound and meaning. The words for 'tree' in the four languages, [puxa], [buga], [puka], and [puk], differ from one another only in minor respects, and this similarity is typical of each set of words with the same meaning. Further-

L_1	L_2	L_3	L_4	Meaning
[puxa]	[buga]	[puka]	[puk]	'tree'
[lisu]	[lisu]	[risu]	[lis]	'bug'
[mani]	[mani]	[meni]	[man]	'sky'
[lana]	[lana]	[rena]	[rena]	'stone'
[kaxa]	[gaga]	[kaka]	[kak]	'hut'
[tupi]	[dubi]	[tupi]	[tup]	'thunder'
[palmufo]	[nili]	[niri]	[nil]	'spear'
[samu]	[samu]	[semu]	[sam]	'river'
[matu]	[madu]	[matu]	[mat]	'arrow'
[nipa]	[niba]	[nipa]	[nip]	'ocean'

more, the pervasiveness of the similarities is such that borrowing would not seem to be a likely explanation for them. We would not expect each of three languages to borrow in such a uniform and exceptionless manner from a fourth. Borrowing is a common phenomenon, but not a very regular one. Since chance and borrowing are both ruled out as reasonable explanations for the resemblance of the four languages, we are left with the hypothesis that they are genetically related, that they are similar because they are divergent continuations of the same, historically earlier language.

Before examining more carefully the regularities in the data, however, we must deal with two forms that are not at all what we would expect. The word for 'spear' in L_1 stands out from the rest; [palmufo] has virtually nothing in common with [nili], [niri], or [nil], the words for 'spear' in L_2, L_3, and L_4. Furthermore, [palmufo] seems to violate otherwise valid phonological principles of L_1. All the other words of L_1 contain precisely two syllables, each of the form consonant plus vowel; consonants do not occur adjacent to one another within a word. [palmufo] is odd on both counts, for it has three syllables, not two, and contains the consonant sequence [lm]. The most likely explanation for these peculiarities is that [palmufo] was borrowed into L_1 from some other, unrelated language. Coming from another language, it has certain phonological properties not shared by native words of L_1; it has probably been modified by the borrowing speakers in the direction of L_1, but not completely. Our hypothesis that [palmufo] represents a borrowing would of course be confirmed if we should find another language spoken on the island in which [palmufo], or something very similar, is the word for 'spear.'

The other suspicious form is [rena], the word for 'stone' in L_4. It is the only word in L_4 that ends in a vowel, and in addition it is the only one containing the vowel [e] or the consonant [r]. If it is a borrowed word, however, it must have been borrowed from a related language, since the words for 'stone' in L_1, L_2, and L_3 are so similar: [lana], [lana], [rena]. In fact, the most likely explanation is that L_4 borrowed the word for 'stone' from L_3. This accounts both for the identity of the words in the two languages and for the oddness of [rena] with respect to the phonological properties of L_4. [rena] is not at all unusual as a word of L_3. [r] and [e] occur in other words of L_3, and it is normal for words of L_3 to end in vowels.

Since [palmufo] and [rena] entered L_1 and L_4 by borrowing, they cannot properly be used in reconstructing the proto language. The reduced body of data from which we can work is given below.

L_1	L_2	L_3	L_4	Meaning
[puxa]	[buga]	[puka]	[puk]	'tree'
[lisu]	[lisu]	[risu]	[lis]	'bug'
[mani]	[mani]	[meni]	[man]	'sky'
[lana]	[lana]	[rena]		'stone'
[kaxa]	[gaga]	[kaka]	[kak]	'hut'
[tupi]	[dubi]	[tupi]	[tup]	'thunder'
	[nili]	[niri]	[nil]	'spear'
[samu]	[samu]	[semu]	[sam]	'river'
[matu]	[madu]	[matu]	[mat]	'arrow'
[nipa]	[niba]	[nipa]	[nip]	'ocean'

sound correspondences

The crucial observation to be made concerning this data is not that the words for each concept are similar in the four languages, but rather that their similarities and differences follow fixed patterns. The sounds of the four daughter languages **correspond** in a completely regular fashion.

Take the sound [m], for instance. [mani], the word for 'sky' in L_1, starts with [m], and so do the corresponding words in the other three languages: [mani], [meni], and [man]. The word for 'river' has [m] as the third segment, not in just one or two of the languages, but in all of them. All four words for 'arrow' have [m] in initial position. Without exception, an [m] in L₁ always corresponds to an [m] in L₂, L₃, and L₄. The corresponding sounds in the four languages are thus [m] - [m] - [m] - [m].

Another regular sound correspondence is [n] - [n] - [n] - [n], and a third is [s] - [s] - [s] - [s]. For every word in L₁ that contains [n], the corresponding words in the other three languages also contain [n], and in the same position. Thus we find [mani], [mani], [meni], and [man] for 'sky,' as well as [nipa], [niba], [nipa], and [nip] for 'ocean.' With regard to the words for 'stone' and 'spear,' we have data from only three languages to work with, but the available forms follow the same pattern: [lana], [lana], [rena]; [nili], [niri], [nil]. In the same way, [s] in one language corresponds to [s] in the other three. All four words for 'bug' have [s] as the third segment, and all four words for 'river' have [s] as the initial segment: [lisu], [lisu], [risu], [lis]; [samu], [samu], [semu], [sam]. These correspondences are therefore completely regular.

Still a fourth exceptionless correspondence is [l] - [l] - [r] - [l]. In every position where L₁ has [l], so do L₂ and L₄; in the corresponding position, L₃ always has [r]. Alongside [lisu] in L₁, we thus find [lisu], [risu], and [lis] in L₂, L₃, and L₄ respectively. The data for 'stone' and 'spear' is incomplete, but the available words conform to the pattern perfectly. Notice that a sound correspondence can be completely regular even though the members of the correspondence differ from language to language. L₃ is different from the other languages because it has [r] instead of [l], but this difference is an entirely systematic one. It is possible to give a formula ([l] - [l] - [r] - [l]) that will hold uniformly for all lexical items of the sister languages, and it is this regularity, rather than phonetic identity, that is of greatest interest for reconstructing the proto language.

Two other fully regular correspondences of this type are [p] - [b] - [p] - [p] and [t] - [d] - [t] - [t]. From the words for 'tree,' 'thunder,' and 'ocean,' we see that whenever a word of L₁ has [p], the corresponding word in L₂ has [b] in the same position; the parallel forms in L₃ and L₄ agree with L₁ in having [p]. 'Tree,' for example, is rendered as [puxa], [buga], [puka], and [puk], and 'thunder' as [tupi], [dubi], [tupi], and [tup]. The latter series also illustrates the [t] - [d] - [t] - [t] correspondence, as do the words for 'arrow,' [matu], [madu], [matu], and [mat].

We have now established six completely regular correspondences: [m] - [m] - [m] - [m]; [n] - [n] - [n] - [n]; [s] - [s] - [s] - [s]; [l] - [l] - [r] - [l]; [p] - [b] - [p] - [p]; and [t] - [d] - [t] - [t]. When we try to find others, however, there seem to be exceptions. Take the sound [k] in L₃, for example. On the basis of the word for 'tree,' it appears that [k] in L₃ corresponds to [x], [g], and [k] in L_1, L_2, and L_4 respectively: [puxa], [buga], [puka], [puk]. This would lead us to set up the correspondence [x] - [g] - [k] - [k]. On the basis of this formula and the L_3 word for 'hut,' [kaka], we would expect the parallel words in the other three languages to be [xaxa], [gaga], and [kak] (with respect to the consonants). Our expectations are not fully borne out, though, since the L_1 word is not [xaxa], but rather [kaxa]. The initial consonant violates the pattern.

What this means is that some (but not all) correspondences have to be stated relative to a specific phonological environment. In the case at hand, the [x] - [g] - [k] - [k] correspondence is valid, but only if we exclude initial consonants. The noninitial velar consonants of [kaxa], [gaga], [kaka], and [kak] conform perfectly to the pattern observed in the words for 'tree.' Another formula is needed for initial velar consonants, namely [k] - [g] - [k] - [k]. We would expect other lexical sets to confirm this environmentally conditioned correspondence; for instance, the four corresponding words [kili], [gili], [kiri], and [kil] would constitute evidence that the L_1 word for 'hut' is not exceptional.

The correspondences involving the vowels [u] and [i] are relative to specific phonological environments in the same way. From the words for 'tree' and 'ocean,' the correspondences would appear to be [u] - [u] - [u] - [u] and [i] - [i] - [i] - [i]: [puxa], [buga], [puka], [puk]; [nipa], [niba], [nipa], [nip]. In both sets of words, the vowel in question occurs in nonfinal position. A glance at the words of L_4, though, shows that special provisions have to be made for word-final vowels, since L_4 has none. The words for 'river'—[samu], [samu], [semu], and [sam]—show that the [u] series is [u] - [u] - [u] - [ ] at the end of a word (the empty brackets indicate the absence of a segment). The word-final [i] series, similarly, is [i] - [i] - [i] - [ ], as we can see from the words for 'sky': [mani], [mani], [meni], [man].

The [a] series in word-final position is comparable; from [nipa], [niba], [nipa], [nip] we see that it must be [a] - [a] - [a] - [ ]. This is confirmed by the words for 'tree' and 'hut.' In other cases, however, [a] in L_1, L_2, and L_4 corresponds sometimes to [a] in L_3 and sometimes to [e]. Thus we have [matu], [madu], [matu], and [mat] for 'arrow,' but [mani], [mani], [meni], and [man] for 'sky.' Is this then an irregularity in the system of correspondences, or is there a general principle that determines when L_3 has [a] and when it has [e]? If we examine the words of L_3, we find that [e] occurs only before a nasal consonant, and that [a] never occurs before a nasal: [puka], [meni], [rena], [kaka], [semu], [matu], [nipa]. The variation between [a] and [e] as the counterpart of [a] in the other languages is not an irregularity, therefore, but rather a subregularity. The correspondence is [a] - [a] - [e] - [a] before a nasal and [a] - [a] - [a] - [a] elsewhere.

The correspondences we have found are summarized in the table below.

(1)	[m] - [m] - [m] - [m]
(2)	[n] - [n] - [n] - [n]
(3)	[s] - [s] - [s] - [s]
(4)	[l] - [l] - [r] - [l]
(5)	[p] - [b] - [p] - [p]
(6)	[t] - [d] - [t] - [t]
(7a)	[k] - [g] - [k] - [k] (in word-initial position)
(7b)	[x] - [g] - [k] - [k] (elsewhere)
(8a)	[u] - [u] - [u] - [ ] (in word-final position)
(8b)	[u] - [u] - [u] - [u] (elsewhere)
(9a)	[i] - [i] - [i] - [ ] (in word-final position)
(9b)	[i] - [i] - [i] - [i] (elsewhere)
(10a)	[a] - [a] - [a] - [ ] (in word-final position)
(10b)	[a] - [a] - [e] - [a] (before a nasal)
(10c)	[a] - [a] - [a] - [a] (elsewhere)

The words of the four sister languages are locked together with respect to their phonetic shapes by these formulas. This tabulation of regularities allows us to predict the pronunciation of a word in one language if we know how it is pronounced in its sisters. The native L_1 word for 'spear,' for instance, was replaced by the borrowed word [palmufo], but from [nili], [niri], and [nil] (the corresponding words in the sister languages), and from the established correspondences, it is easy to figure out that the native L_1 word would have been [nili] had it survived. Similarly, we know from [lana], [lana], and [rena] that the native L_4 word for 'stone' would have been [lan] if the borrowed word [rena] had not replaced it.

the regularity of sound change

By the process of elimination, we concluded earlier that the similarities in the four languages were due to genetic relationship. More explicitly, we will now hypothesize that they are divergent continuations of the same proto language, which we will call PL, as shown in Figure 8.2. The observed regularities can be explained in part by this hypothesis; it is not surprising, for example, that the words for 'tree' in the daughter languages are similar, since they all descend from the same form, the word for 'tree' in PL.

Nevertheless, the hypothesis of genetic relationship does not in itself explain the existence of systematic sound correspondences. It would be perfectly conceivable for each set of four words to be similar but for the nature of the similarities to be different for each set. This would be the case if the historical development of each word of the proto language were

figure 8.2

idiosyncratic. Initial [m], for instance, might develop one way in the word for 'sky' and another way in the word for 'arrow.' If changes in the sounds of the proto language were idiosyncratic, or peculiar to individual lexical items, it would not be possible to find systematic sound correspondences linking the words of the daughters and holding across the board for all sets of words with the same origin.

In order to explain the existence of systematic sound correspondences, therefore, a double-barreled hypothesis is necessary. We must add to the hypothesis of genetic relationship the assumption that sound changes are basically regular. If initial [m] of PL is reflected as [m] in the L_1 word for 'sky,' it will be so reflected in all words of L_1. If an [a] of PL is reflected as [e] in L_3 when the next segment is a nasal, [a] will always be reflected as [e] in this environment. There may be sporadic exceptions, as there are to any rule, but sound change is envisaged as a fundamentally regular process. The common origin of each set of words, together with the assumption that sound change is regular, explains both the phonetic similarity of the words of each set and the fact that they are linked systematically by correspondence formulas that are valid for all words having a common origin.

A set of words that are genetically related in this way is said to constitute a **cognate set**, and the members of such a set are called **cognates**. The daughter words for 'tree,' to take one example, constitute a cognate set; [puxa], [buga], [puka], and [puk] are cognates. For each cognate set, there is by definition some proto form of which the members of the set are divergent continuations. The next step is to attempt the reconstruction of these proto forms and to state the sound changes that must have taken place in the development of each of the daughter languages.

reconstruction

The existence of cognate sets linked by systematic sound correspondences is very strong evidence that the four languages are genetically related. The next step of the comparative method—partially reconstructing the proto language and stating the sound changes that have taken place—

provides additional confirmation of the hypothesis. It demonstrates in detail the plausibility of explaining the observed regularities in terms of genetic relationship, since it shows that a real language could in fact have existed and diverged into the daughters by means of reasonable sound changes.

For each sound correspondence, we can set up a segment type of the proto language. If the correspondence is relative to a specific phonological environment, the reconstructed segment type will also be relative to that environment.

Take the correspondence [m] - [m] - [m] - [m], for instance. Whenever [m] occurs in some word of a daughter language, its cognates also contain [m], and in the same position. It is reasonable to suppose that this agreement comes about because the underlying word in the proto language also contained [m] in that position. The supposition, in other words, is that [mani], [mani], [meni], and [man] all start with [m] because the word for 'sky' in PL started with [m]; that the third segment of [samu], [samu], [semu], and [sam] is in each case [m] because the third segment of the PL word for 'river' was [m]; and so on. To underlie the segment [m] in the daughter languages, then, we reconstruct for PL the segment *[m]. (An asterisk is used to mark reconstructed entities that have not been observed directly.) The resulting situation is depicted in Figure 8.3. In this case, no sound changes affecting the reconstructed segment have occurred.

Similarly, we can reconstruct the segments *[n] and *[s] for PL. The former underlies the [n] - [n] - [n] - [n] correspondence observed in the daughter languages, and the latter underlies the series [s] - [s] - [s] - [s]. Once again it appears that no sound changes have affected the proto segments in question, since their **reflexes**—their manifestations in the daughter languages—are uniform.

This uniformity is lacking in the [l] - [l] - [r] - [l] correspondence. The reflex of the proto segment in L_3 does not match the reflexes in the other daughters. What segment should we then reconstruct to underlie this correspondence? The most important requirement is that the reconstructed segment be capable of developing historically to both [l] and [r], since we are claiming that such a development took place. On this basis alone, either [l] or [r] could be postulated as the proto segment, since the two sounds are very similar and the interchange of [l] and [r] is a frequent linguistic phenomenon. That is, [l] often changes to [r], and the opposite development also occurs.

We will reconstruct *[l] to underlie the series [l] - [l] - [r] - [l], as shown in Figure 8.4. In making this decision, we implicitly claim that the historical development of PL into L_3 involved, along with many other changes,

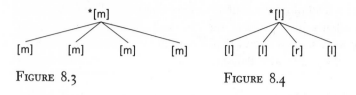

FIGURE 8.3   FIGURE 8.4

the change of [l] to [r]. This claim is somewhat more reasonable than the opposite one. If we were to reconstruct *[r] instead, we would be claiming that [r] changed to [l] independently in L_1, L_2, and L_4, being retained only in L_3. While this is not impossible, it is somewhat less likely than the single change of [l] to [r]. We see from this example that it is not always possible to conclude with certainty what the precise phonetic shape of a proto segment must have been. Clearly, a single segment type must have been present to underlie its observed reflexes in the daughter languages, but beyond a certain point we can only speculate as to its exact character.

The next two correspondences present a similar problem, and we will suggest a similar solution—the majority rules, unless there is evidence to the contrary. For [p] - [b] - [p] - [p] we will reconstruct *[p], and for [t] - [d] - [t] - [t] we will reconstruct *[t]. With each reconstruction, we are claiming that a sound change occurred in L_2; the claim is that [p] changed to [b] in L_2, and that [t] changed to [d]. It is simpler to assume that changes occurred in L_2 than to assume that [b] and [d] are historically basic. With the latter assumption, we would have to accept that parallel innovations took place in L_1, L_3, and L_4, which is somewhat less likely.

The correspondence [k] - [g] - [k] - [k] was limited to word-initial position. By the same reasoning used above, we can reconstruct *[k] for PL in this position, claiming at the same time that [k] changed to [g] in L_2. If we were correct in reconstructing *[p] and *[t], the third reconstructed stop almost has to be *[k] and not *[g]. The reason is that the inventory of sounds used in a language tends to display a certain symmetry, especially with regard to stops, fricatives, and nasals. It is very common for a language to have three voiceless stops, say [p t k], but it is much less common for a language to have two voiceless stops and a voiced one, say [p t g]. With our reconstructed stops *[p t k], we take this tendency toward symmetry into account.

If PL had the stop *[k] in initial position, the same stop probably occurred in noninitial position as well. Therefore, the same segment no doubt also underlies the correspondence [x] - [g] - [k] - [k]. Both correspondences are illustrated in the cognate set for 'hut': [kaxa], [gaga], [kaka], and [kak]. The proto word for 'hut' evidently contained two occurrences of *[k]. Both occurrences are retained in the L_3 and L_4 words; no

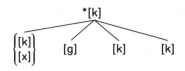

figure 8.5

sound changes affected [k] in these languages. The sound change that occurred in L₂ was not restricted to any special environment; [k] became [g] in all environments. Thus both instances of *[k] in the proto word are reflected as [g] in the L₂ word. In L₁, on the other hand, a sound change must have taken place that was relative to a specific environment: [k] became [x] when it occurred between two vowels. The word-initial [k] was retained, but the intervocalic [k] underwent this sound change to be reflected in L₁ as [x]. The situation is represented in Figure 8.5. The postulated sound change is a quite reasonable one, for it often happens that a stop becomes a fricative, especially when it occurs intervocalically. The opposite development, where a fricative becomes a stop, is less usual.

This brings us to the vowel correspondences. We found the correspondence [u] - [u] - [u] - [ ] to be valid in word-final position, while [u] - [u] - [u] - [u] held in other environments. The obvious solution is to postulate *[u] for all positions in PL, together with this sound change for L₄: [u] was lost in final position. The same solution is appropriate for the two correspondences with [i], namely [i] - [i] - [i] - [ ] in final position and [i] - [i] - [i] - [i] elsewhere. The proto segment was no doubt *[i], and L₄ underwent this change: [i] was lost in final position.

With respect to [a], we found three correspondences. In word-final position, the correspondence was [a] - [a] - [a] - [ ]; before nasals, it was [a] - [a] - [e] - [a]; and elsewhere, it was [a] - [a] - [a] - [a]. For each correspondence, we will set up the proto segment *[a]. The following two sound changes then account for the data: In L₃, [a] became [e] before a nasal; in L₄, [a] was lost in final position. It is readily seen that this solution is simpler and more reasonable than any obvious alternative.

In effect, we have now reconstructed the ten proto words underlying the data from which we started. Every segment in the data was accounted for by some correspondence, and for each correspondence we have reconstructed a proto segment. Reconstructing the proto words is only a matter of summarizing what we have already done. The reconstructed proto words are given in the table below with their cognate sets, and the postulated sound changes, which derive the cognate sets from the proto words, are recapitulated.

Let us go through a couple of examples for illustration. We will recon-

PL	L₁	L₂	L₃	L₄	Meaning
*[puka]	[puxa]	[buga]	[puka]	[puk]	'tree'
*[lisu]	[lisu]	[lisu]	[risu]	[lis]	'bug'
*[mani]	[mani]	[mani]	[meni]	[man]	'sky'
*[lana]	[lana]	[lana]	[rena]		'stone'
*[kaka]	[kaxa]	[gaga]	[kaka]	[kak]	'hut'
*[tupi]	[tupi]	[dubi]	[tupi]	[tup]	'thunder'
*[nili]		[nili]	[niri]	[nil]	'spear'
*[samu]	[samu]	[samu]	[semu]	[sam]	'river'
*[matu]	[matu]	[madu]	[matu]	[mat]	'arrow'
*[nipa]	[nipa]	[niba]	[nipa]	[nip]	'ocean'

In L₁ [k] became [x] between vowels.

In L₂ [p] became [b]; [t] became [d]; and [k] became [g].

In L₃, [l] became [r]; and [a] became [e] before a nasal.

In L₄, [u] was lost in final position; [i] was lost in final position; and [a] was lost in final position.

struct the PL words for 'tree' and 'stone' and then trace the reconstructed forms in their historical development.

The cognate set for 'tree' is [puxa], [buga], [puka], and [puk]. The initial segment of these forms represents the correspondence [p] - [b] - [p] - [p], for which we reconstructed *[p]. For the [u] - [u] - [u] - [u] correspondence, we reconstructed *[u]; the second segment of the proto word must therefore have been *[u]. The last two segments represent the correspondences [x] - [g] - [k] - [k] and [a] - [a] - [a] - [ ], for which we reconstructed *[k] and *[a] respectively. Putting the proto segments together, we find that the proto word for 'tree' must have been *[puka].

In its development from PL, L₁ underwent a sound change: [k] changed to [x] between vowels. One specific effect of this change was the manifestation of *[puka] as [puxa] in L₁. The change, we notice, was a regular one, affecting all morphemes containing intervocalic [k]. Thus *[kaka] developed to [kaxa] in L₁ in the same manner. Two of the sound changes of L₂ are applicable to *[puka]: [p] became [b] and [k] became [g]. The result of these two regular changes was the L₂ word [buga]. Neither of the sound changes characteristic of L₃ could affect *[puka], so the L₃ word for 'tree' is identical to the PL word. Finally, *[puka] became [puk] in L₄ by the loss of [a] in final position.

Only three cognates are available for 'stone,' [lana], [lana], and [rena], but this leads to no difficulty in setting up the proto form. The first segment exemplifies the correspondence [l] - [l] - [r] - [l]; the second, [a] - [a] - [e] - [a]; the third, [n] - [n] - [n] - [n]; and the fourth, [a] - [a] - [a] - [ ]. Respectively, we reconstructed for these the proto segments *[l], *[a], *[n], and *[a]. The PL word for 'stone' must therefore have been *[lana].

[lana] is retained as the form in both L_1 and L_2, because the sound changes that took place in these languages affected only stops. Both sound changes of L_3 were applicable to *[lana]: [l] became [r], and [a] became [e] before a nasal. Consequently, the L_3 word for 'stone' is [rena]. The L_4 term was replaced through borrowing, but the principles we have uncovered make it clear that it would have been [lan] had it survived, since final [a] was regularly lost in L_4.

In its classic form, then, the comparative method can be viewed as comprising several steps. First, apparent cognates are isolated. Second, the systematic sound correspondences linking the cognate sets are uncovered. Third, a proto segment is posited to underlie each observed correspondence. Fourth, words of the proto language are reconstructed on the basis of the cognate sets. Fifth, the sound changes that have occurred in the development of each daughter language from the parent are stated. These changes must account for the evolution of each set of cognates from their common proto form. Moreover, the proto language, insofar as it can be reconstructed, must look like a real language, and the postulated sound changes must be reasonable ones, changes of the kind that are known to occur. If all these steps are taken, and if all the conditions are met, two things have been accomplished: It has been demonstrated that the putative sister languages are in fact genetically related, and the parent language has been partially reconstructed.

Needless to say, historical reconstruction is not always as easy as our hypothetical example might indicate. Many more segment types are involved with real languages; seldom are there so few gaps in the data; it is normally not so easy to recognize borrowed forms; the sound changes responsible for deriving the daughters from the proto language are usually much more numerous; syntactic and morphological evidence has to be taken into account as well; there is no *a priori* way to determine whether or how the related languages cluster into subfamilies—this list of problems could be extended. Nevertheless, the principles illustrated here are fully applicable to the data provided by real languages. The comparative method is a valid instrument for establishing the genetic relationship of a group of languages and for reconstructing proto forms.

the interpretation of sound change

In our hypothetical example, we were able to establish genetic relationship, and to reconstruct proto forms, without ever scratching below the phonetic surface. We worked from the phonetic shapes of the daughter words alone, never taking into account their underlying representations or the phonological rules responsible for their manifestation. Proceeding in this manner, we uncovered a rather surprising fact: Sound change is regular. If [a] became [e] before a nasal in L_3, it did so in all words containing [a] before a nasal, not in just one or a handful. The modification of [a] to [e] was not peculiar to individual morphemes but held across the board for all morphemes of the language. The common proto forms, together with the regularity of sound change, account for the observed sound correspondences that relate cognates in the daughter languages and relate the members of each cognate set in the same way. Since their development from the common proto forms is regular, cognates are related to one another in phonological shape according to regular patterns.

But why should sound change be regular? The regular character of sound change was a revolutionary discovery for the nineteenth-century philologists who developed the comparative method, but they never gave a satisfactory explanation of why it should be so. For this we must reinterpret things in terms of the more recent view of phonological systems outlined in Chapter Six. When the phonetic data we were working with is treated as the manifestation by phonological rules of abstract underlying representations, the regularity of sound change becomes quite understandable.

Let us reexamine the data that illustrates the change of [a] to [e] before a nasal in L_3. The ten L_3 forms available to us are [puka], [risu], [meni], [rena], [kaka], [tupi], [niri], [semu], [matu], and [nipa]. Phonetically, L_3 has both [a] and [e]. We notice, however, that the difference between them is not distinctive. There are no two morphemes that are distinguished solely by the fact that one has [a] in the same position where the other has [e]. Moreover, this could not be the case (if we take our small lexical sample to be indicative of the whole language). Since [e] occurs only before nasals, and since [a] never occurs before nasals, the difference between [e] and [a] in some position could never be the sole trait differentiating morphemes.

In L_3, therefore, [e] is nothing but a variant manifestation of [a]. It is the form that [a] assumes overtly when the following segment is a nasal. In the underlying representations, [a] and [e] are not differentiated, since the difference between them is not distinctive. The first vowel of both

[semu] and [matu], for instance, would be listed simply as being low (to distinguish [a]/[e] from the high vowels [i u]). In most circumstances, a low vowel is ultimately specified as [a], as in [matu]. The [e] of [semu], however, results from the application of this rule of L₃: A low vowel is manifested as a mid front vowel before a nasal. If we use [a] to indicate a low vowel, we can say that the underlying representation is [samu], and that the above rule is responsible for its surface manifestation as [semu]. Similarly, [meni] and [rena] result from the more abstract representations [mani] and [rana].

In L₃, then, there is an underlying segment type [a] (that is, a low vowel) and a phonological rule to the effect that [a] is manifested as [e] before a nasal. Turning now to the proto language PL, we find that there is no [e] at all, only the reconstructed low vowel *[a], whose precise pronunciation cannot be surmised. By comparing L₃ with its earlier stage PL, we find that the difference between them, insofar as the vowels are concerned, is nothing more than the existence in L₃ of the rule manifesting [a] as [e]. The two stages are identical with respect to the underlying representation of the vowel segments in question; at both stages it is sufficient to specify the vowel as being low. In PL, an underlying low vowel was presumably always manifested phonetically as a low vowel (at least there is no evidence to the contrary); in L₃, a low vowel can be manifested as either a mid or a low vowel depending on its phonological environment.

We said earlier that L₃ underwent a sound change in its development from PL, namely [a] changed to [e] before a nasal. The nature of this sound change should now be quite evident; the rule that [a] is manifested as [e] before a nasal was added to the phonological system of L₃. The change was not a change in the sounds *per se*, but rather in the system of rules responsible for them. It should also be apparent why this sound change was regular, why it held for all morphemes of the language instead of being peculiar to individual morphemes. The change consisted in the addition of a general rule, and a general phonological rule is by definition a principle that holds across the board, not an idiosyncratic property of individual lexical items.

The regularity of the other sound changes we postulated can be explained in a similar manner. In L₁, [k] became [x] between vowels, giving us forms like [puxa] and [kaxa]. The difference between [k] and [x] is not distinctive, however, since [x] occurs only intervocalically and [k] never occurs in this position. In both PL and L₁, therefore, there is a single underlying velar consonant. The sound change consisted in the addition of this rule to the phonological system of L₁: [k] is manifested as a fricative between vowels. The change was regular because the phonological representations of individual morphemes were not affected; a rule was added instead.

Three sound changes were postulated for L_2: [p] became [b]; [t] became [d]; and [k] became [g]. In neither PL nor L_2 is the difference between voiced and voiceless stops distinctive. All stops were presumably voiceless in PL, and all stops are voiced in L_2. At both stages, then, the specification of voicing for stops is redundant phonetic detail, detail that is added by a phonological rule. The rule for PL is simply that stops are voiceless, while the rule for L_2 is simply that stops are voiced. The sound change consisted in the modification of this rule specifying voicing, so that stops were subsequently specified as being voiced rather than voiceless. Since a rule was modified, not individual phonological representations, the change was regular. Notice also that a single, general rule is involved. All stops are specified as voiceless in PL and as voiced in L_2; the rule in question applies to the class of all stops. There is no reason to adopt the more complex, less general, and less insightful analysis whereby three separate rules are postulated, one for each kind of stop. Three separate sound changes took place, so far as surface phonetic facts are concerned, but all three are consequences of the same minor rule modification.

The change of [l] to [r] in L_3 is parallel. In neither PL nor L_3 is the difference between [l] and [r] a distinctive one. At both stages, it is sufficient to specify the underlying segment as a liquid, with its precise phonetic shape being determined by phonological rules. The change of [l] to [r] was thus a minor rule modification similar to the one affecting stops in L_2.

Three changes occurred in L_4: [u] was lost in final position; [i] was lost in final position; and [a] was lost in final position. By now it should be obvious that these three changes are consequences of the same historical phenomenon, not isolated events. To know just what this historical phenomenon was, however, we have to know a little more about L_4.

One possibility is that the underlying phonological representations have not changed in the development of PL into L_4, but that a rule deleting final vowels has been added to the phonological system. If this is the case, the underlying representations [puka], [lisu], and [mani] are translated into the phonetic shapes [puk], [lis], and [man] by this deletion rule. For the underlying vowels to be retained in final position despite their phonetic absence, however, there must be nonhistorical structural evidence in the language to posit them. Suppose, for example, that [n] is added as a suffix to form the plural of nouns, and that the plurals of the above nouns are [pukan], [lisun], and [manin]. Since the underlying vowels show up overtly in the plural (where the [n] suffix keeps them from being in final position and hence blocks their deletion), there is structural evidence for their existence. When children learn L_4, they have a reason to learn phonological representations for these nouns that include the specification of final vowels.

Suppose, on the other hand, that there is no such evidence. Suppose that all words of L_4 have just one syllable, and that the child who learns this language has no structural reason whatever to set up abstract underlying representations containing final vowels. In this case, the difference between PL and L_4 does not reside in the phonological rules, but rather in the underlying representations, since morphemes do end in vowels in the underlying representations of PL. But if the representations of individual morphemes have been altered, and not rules, why was the change regular? Why do morphemes not vary idiosyncratically as to whether they retain the final vowel?

The answer is that this change originated as a rule change. At some point in the historical evolution of PL into L_4, speakers adopted a rule dropping vowels in final position. Perhaps this mode of pronunciation spread because of its stylistic value, or perhaps there was some other reason. In any event, speakers who had learned phonological representations with final vowels started omitting these vowels when they pronounced words. The phenomenon was essentially regular, for a rule was responsible.

Children who learned to talk under these conditions took a fresh look at things. Hearing no final vowels, and having no reason to postulate them, they learned phonological representations in which all of the final vowels were lacking. Consequently, they had no reason to learn the rule for deleting these vowels. The change in underlying representations thus came about through restructuring. After final vowels had disappeared phonetically, by virtue of a new rule added to the phonological systems of adult speakers, children who subsequently learned to talk arrived at a simpler system, one in which final vowels were lacking entirely.

Thus in all but one case, sound changes in the daughter languages turn out to be rule changes; there is only one possible instance of change in the underlying phonological representations, and even this presupposes a previous rule change. Our hypothetical example may not be completely representative, but rule changes do seem to preponderate in reality. The limited but growing amount of investigation in this area suggests that rule changes occur frequently in phonological systems, while underlying representations are fairly stable by comparison.

language families of the world

A note of caution is appropriate to preface this outline of the major language families of the world. When we leave the well-worn path of Indo-European and turn to languages that have been studied less thoroughly, genetic classifications are often more tentative. There are thousands of languages in the world, and many of them have been described very sketchily or not at all. When languages are known only poorly, of course, attempts to group them into families can easily go astray. Although we will concentrate on classifications that seem fairly well established, avoiding the more speculative ones, it should be kept in mind that not all of these putative families have been shown conclusively to be families by a rigorous application of the comparative method.

indo-european

There is least doubt of all about the Indo-European family. In fact, the genetic relationships of this family were established concurrently with the development of the comparative method. Proto Indo-European has been reconstructed, to the extent that such a distant language can be reconstructed, and the historical evolution of the Indo-European languages has been traced in considerable detail.

The Indo-European family comprises ten subfamilies, as shown in Figure 8.6. Attempts to combine these subfamilies into larger ones have been inconclusive. The exact relationship of Anatolian to the rest of Indo-European is still not agreed on; Anatolian is sometimes claimed to be a sister of Proto Indo-European rather than a daughter of it.

The Anatolian languages, long since extinct, were spoken in Asia Minor. They are known through inscriptions dating from around 1400 B.C. and spanning about a millennium. The Anatolian language known in most detail is Hittite, but records have also been preserved of Luwian, Palaic, and Lydian. Because it was spoken at such an early period, Hittite is quite important for the reconstruction of Proto Indo-European, which dates from before 3000 B.C.

Tocharian is also extinct and known only from records. These fragmentary records, which cover the sixth to the eighth centuries A.D., were found in Chinese Turkestan. Two dialects are evidently represented, called Tocharian A and B.

Albanian apparently belongs by itself as a subfamily, and the same is true of Armenian. The former is spoken in Albania and extends into Italy

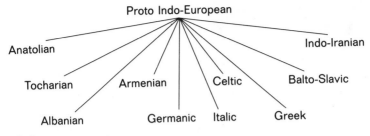

figure 8.6

and Greece. Armenian is spoken in the southern Caucasus as well as in parts of Turkey.

The first major subfamily we will treat is Germanic. Along with Gothic, which was last spoken in the Crimea in the sixteenth century, Scandinavian and West Germanic are usually considered to be subgroups of Germanic. Scandinavian includes Icelandic, Danish, Swedish, and Norwegian, the last three being quite similar.

English belongs to the West Germanic group. Its closest relative is Frisian, which is spoken along the coast of the Netherlands and on islands in the North Sea. The West Germanic languages of continental Europe are commonly divided into High German and Low German. High German, so called because it is spoken in the higher, more mountainous regions to the south, includes the dialects of Austria, southern Germany, and Switzerland. Low German includes Dutch, Flemish (spoken in Belgium), and the dialects of northern Germany. Yiddish, the language of Jews who settled in eastern Europe centuries ago, is High German. Afrikaans is a development of Dutch, spoken in South Africa.

The Italic subfamily comprises the languages that were spoken in ancient Italy, together with their descendants. Besides Latin, which eventually displaced all the others, they included Oscan, Umbrian, and Venetic, which have long been extinct. Latin of course survives in the modern Romance languages. In addition to French, Spanish, Italian, Portuguese, and Rumanian, which everyone has heard of, they include the less familiar Provençal, Catalan, Ladin, Sardinian, and Dalmatian. Provençal is a collective term for the dialects of southern France. During the early Middle Ages, it was a literary language and rivaled the Parisian dialect in prestige. Catalan is spoken in the eastern part of Spain, around Barcelona. Ladin, also known as Rhaeto-Romance and Romansch, coexists in Switzerland with French, Italian, and Swiss German, extending as well into northern Italy. Sardinian is spoken on the island of Sardinia, oddly enough, while Dalmatian, extinct since the death of its last speaker in 1898, was centered in what is now Yugoslavia.

The Celtic peoples were once an important force in Europe, spreading across the continent into Asia Minor. The Celtic languages have given ground steadily, however, and survive today only in the British Isles and in France. Breton is the tongue of Brittany, in the northwest of France. In the British Isles we find Welsh, Irish, Scots Gaelic, and Manx. Another Celtic language, Cornish, has been extinct since the eighteenth century.

Greek has a known history of more than three thousand years. Ancient Greek was composed of many local dialects, the most important of which was Attic Greek, the dialect of Athens. Attic Greek rose to prominence because of the cultural ascendancy of Athens and spread throughout the Greek empire. Virtually all the modern dialects descend from Attic Greek.

It is a matter of contention whether the Baltic and Slavic languages are similar because they constitute a subfamily or because of mutual influence. Instead of a Balto-Slavic subfamily, therefore, it may be proper to speak of two subfamilies, Baltic and Slavic. In any case, the Baltic group comprises Lithuanian and Latvian, as well as Old Prussian, extinct for several centuries. The Slavic languages are often divided into the South, East, and West Slavic groups. South Slavic includes Serbo-Croatian, Slovenian, and Bulgarian. In the East Slavic group are Russian, Ukrainian, and Byelorussian, which are very similar to one another. Czech and Slovak, which are dialects of one language, belong with Polish in the West Slavic group. The earliest written records of Slavic are from a ninth-century translation of the Bible. The language of this translation is known alternately as Old Church Slavonic, Old Church Slavic, and Old Bulgarian, and it has survived as a liturgical language.

The remaining subfamily is Indo-Iranian. Modern representatives of the Iranian group are Persian, spoken in Iran; Pashto, spoken in Afghanistan; Ossetic, spoken in the northern Caucasus; Kurdish, spoken in Iran, Iraq, and Turkey; as well as others. Two ancient Iranian languages are known through texts and inscriptions: Old Persian is known from as early as the sixth century B.C., while Avestan, the language of the Avesta (the Zoroastrian scriptures), dates from the same period but is preserved only in later manuscripts. The Indic group includes Sanskrit, which can be traced as far back as 1200 B.C., and many modern languages of northern India and Pakistan, among them Hindi, Urdu, Bengali, Panjabi, Gujerati, Marathi, Nepali, and Kashmiri.

the rest of eurasia

The Indo-European family includes almost all the languages of Europe; in addition, it covers parts of Asia and has been carried by colonizers to many other regions of the world. Two other families are represented in Europe. Basque, a language spoken in the Pyrenees, apparently constitutes a family in itself. It has no proven affiliations with any other known language. The remaining family of Europe is the Uralic family, the two main branches of which are Finno-Ugric and the Samoyed languages.

Of the large number of Finno-Ugric languages to be found in Europe and Asia, the most important are Finnish and Hungarian, the latter constituting a Finno-Ugric island surrounded by Indo-European languages. The other languages of this family extend eastward from Scandinavia into Siberia. They include Estonian, Lappish, Cheremiss, and Mordvin. The Samoyed languages are found in the far north of Russia.

The Altaic family is spread across much of central and northern Asia from the Mediterranean to the Pacific. Farthest to the west is the Turkic branch, which includes Turkish and a number of related languages, among them Azerbaijani, Uzbek, and Kirghiz. To the east lie the Mongol and Manchu branches. It is sometimes speculated that the Uralic and Altaic families should be joined in a larger family called Ural-Altaic. Korean and Japanese, which have been shown to be related to each other but not to any other major languages, are also contemplated as members of Ural-Altaic. If we wish to rely on something more than speculation, however, for the time being we must take Uralic, Altaic, and Japanese-Korean as constituting three separate families.

Two families are found in the Caucasus, the region between the Black Sea and the Caspian Sea. Among the better known members of the North Caucasian family are Kabardian, Avar, and Abkhasian. Georgian is the best known member of the South Caucasian family. To complete this survey of central and northern Asia, we might mention Ainu, a language of Japan, as well as a number of languages, among them Chukchi and Gilyak, that belong to other families and are found in the extreme northeast portion of the continent.

Most of the languages in the north of India are Indo-European. In southern India, the Dravidian family predominates. As far as the number of speakers is concerned, Telugu and Tamil are among the most important languages of India. Other important Dravidian languages are Kanarese, Malayalam, Brahui, Gondi, Kurukh, and Kui. Still a third language family of India is Munda. Munda is thought to be related to various languages found in Southeast Asia, the most notable being Mon, Khmer, and Vietnamese. This suggested family is called Austro-Asiatic.

The genetic relationships of the major languages of Southeast Asia are not completely clear, and there are conflicting proposals. The various dialects of Chinese constitute one family; Tibetan, Burmese, and many other lesser languages form another family, known as Tibeto-Burman; still another, called Tai or Kadai, has Laotian and Thai as its major members. The proposals conflict as to how these should be grouped into larger families, if at all. Under one proposal, they are all to be gathered into the inclusive Sino-Tibetan family. Another suggestion is that Tibeto-Burman and Chinese are related to each other, but not to Tai.

the pacific

The languages of the Pacific are generally grouped into four families. The numerous languages of the Australian aborigines are thought to form one family, and the same is true of the languages of Tasmania (an island just south of Australia), now extinct. The languages indigenous to New Guinea and adjacent islands are not known very well as yet; they are tentatively grouped under the label Papuan, but it is by no means certain that the Papuan languages constitute a single family.

The fourth Pacific family, Malayo-Polynesian (or Austronesian), is by far the largest. It stretches from Madagascar in the west, through the East Indies, to Hawaii and Easter Island in the east, also taking in New Zealand to the south. The Malayo-Polynesian family is commonly divided into three groups: Indonesian, Melanesian, and Polynesian. The Indonesian subfamily includes Malagasy, spoken on Madagascar, and the languages of Malaysia, Indonesia, Formosa, and the Philippines. Among the more important of the latter are Malay, Indonesian, Javanese, Sundanese, Dayak, Maduran, Balinese, Macassar, Formosan, Tagalog, Illocano, and Visayan. The Melanesian languages are spoken in the South Pacific; Fiji is the best known language of this group. Polynesian is the easternmost branch of Malayo-Polynesian. The most important of its languages are Samoan, Hawaiian, Tahitian, and Maori (spoken in New Zealand).

africa

The linguistic situation of Africa is a complex one. Much remains tentative, although the Afro-Asiatic family, which occupies the northern part of the continent, has been extensively studied. The five main branches of Afro-Asiatic are Semitic, Egyptian, Berber, Cushitic, and Chad. The Semitic group includes such languages of antiquity as Hebrew, Akkadian, Aramaic, and Phoenician, as well as Arabic and the contemporary languages of Ethiopia. Ancient Egyptian, which is known from as far back as

4000 B.C., survived until the seventh century A.D., when it was replaced by Arabic through the Arab conquest of North Africa. However, Egyptian still survives as a liturgical language known as Coptic. The Berber languages, among them Tuareg, Zenaga, Kabyl, and Shilh, are spoken in various parts of North Africa. Somali and Galla are two of the more important Cushitic languages, which are spoken in eastern Africa, below Saudi Arabia. Of the Chad languages, spoken in and around Nigeria, Hausa is by far the most important.

Most of the southern half of Africa is occupied by the Niger-Congo family, of which the major subfamily is Bantu. The best known of the Bantu languages is probably Swahili, which is used in much of East Africa as a trade language. Others include Zulu, Nyanja, Xhosa, and Sotho. The other subfamilies of Niger-Congo are centered in the southern portion of the western horn of Africa. Some of the languages found there and to the east are Ibo, Yoruba, Ewe, Twi, Fanti, Malinke, Fulani, Wolof, and Sango.

Bushman and Hottentot constitute the Khoisan family; it extends from the southern tip of Africa northward, surrounded by Bantu. Sandwiched between the Afro-Asiatic family to the north and the Niger-Congo family to the south are the languages of three other families, Chari-Nile, Songhai, and Central Saharan.

the new world

We have now covered everything except the native languages of the New World. Compared with those of North America, the languages and language families of Central and South America are poorly known. The situation in South America is so unclear that we can do little more than mention some linguistic groups, without speculating about how they combine in larger families. One of the best known is Quechua, located in Peru. Among the others are Chibchan, Huelche, Cariban, Pano, Jivaro, Tucano, Arawakan, and Tupi-Guaraní.

The situation in Central America is somewhat clearer. Restricting ourselves for the moment to southern Mexico and points south, we can most easily distinguish the Mayan family. It occupies the Yucatán peninsula of Mexico, as well as parts of Guatemala, Honduras, and El Salvador. To the east and south of this region are languages of the Chibchan and other families. To the north and west are found various languages and language groups that are tentatively believed to be related; Otomanguian is the name used to designate this putative family, which is thought to include Mixteco, Zapoteco, Trique, Amusgo, Zoque, Popoloca, Otomi, and others.

Relatively speaking, a great deal of work has been done on the indigenous languages of North America. The major families have been established quite firmly; disagreement stems mainly from attempts to combine these into more inclusive families. It is customary to discuss the geographical arrangement of the American Indian languages in terms of their location when Europeans first came into contact with them. Since then, of course, the picture we will sketch has changed considerably.

The Eskimo-Aleut family rims the continent on the north. It extends from the Aleutian islands, along the Alaskan coast, across northern Canada, to the coast of Greenland. Its two neighbors to the south are the Athabaskan and Algonkian families. The Athabaskan family occupies Alaska and northwestern Canada. It includes Chipewyan, Sarsi, Carrier, Hare, and quite a few others. (Tlingit and Haida, found along the coast, are related to Athabaskan in a larger family called Nadene.) Enclaves of Athabaskan are also found farther south, in California and Oregon. In addition, Navaho and the Apache languages, found in New Mexico and Texas, are Athabaskan. The Algonkian family is spread over central and eastern Canada, taking in parts of the United States as well, particularly the Great Lakes region and the upper Atlantic coast. Among the languages of this family are Blackfoot, Cree, Ojibwa, Illinois, Shawnee, Miami, Potawatomi, Kickapoo, Sauk, Fox, Menomini, Micmac, Abnaki, Delaware, Cheyenne, and Arapaho.

Located around Lake Erie and Lake Ontario is the Iroquoian family, which includes such languages as Mohawk, Wyandot, Oneida, Onondaga, Cayuga, Seneca, and Cherokee. The Natchez-Muskogean family is situated in the southeastern corner of the United States. The more familiar names among these languages are Natchez, Choctaw, Chickasaw, Creek, and Alabama. Continuing west along the Gulf of Mexico, we encounter a small family known as Tunican. Farther west, on the Gulf coast of Texas and northeastern Mexico, we find the Coahuiltecan family, which is entirely extinct.

Several families are represented in the Great Plains and farther west. A major one is the Siouan family, including Crow, Hidatsa, Mandan, Omaha, Iowa, Missouri, Osage, Winnebago, and a number of others. Other families found in this area are Caddoan (Wichita, Caddo, Arikara, Pawnee) and Kiowa-Tanoan (Kiowa, Jemez, Tewa, Taos, Tano, and some others). The Uto-Aztecan family occupies much of the western United States and northwestern Mexico. To the far south lies Aztec, or Nahuatl, which survives in various modern dialects in the area of Mexico City. Others, extending north from Mexico, include Cora, Huichol, Yaqui, Papago, Cahuilla, Luiseño, Northern Paiute, Southern Paiute, Ute, Shoshoni, Hopi, and Comanche.

By far the greatest diversity of American Indian languages is found along the Pacific coast. Among the Hokan languages, found in Baja California, California, and Arizona, are Diegueño, Maricopa, Walapai, Havasupai, Yavapai, Washo, Achomawi, Shasta, and Karok. The California Penutian family (including Yokuts, Miwok, Maidu, Costanoan, Wintu, and Patwin) occupies much of the central and northern part of California. Continuing north, we find Takelman (Takelma, Coos, Siuslaw, and others), Chinookan, and Plateau Penutian (including Klamath, Modoc, Nez Percé, Cayuse, and Yakima). In the northern part of Washington and adjoining portions of Canada, we find the Salish family (Squamish, Spokane, Bella-Coola, Clallam, and various others) and Wakashan (Kwakiutl, Bella-Bella, Nootka-Nitinat). Directly to the north of these lies the small Tsimshian family, beyond which are found Athabaskan and Eskimo-Aleut, with which we started.

suggestions for study and discussion

1. Reexamine the data from dialect 3 of Papago given in question 7 of the preceding chapter, page 203. Probable earlier phonetic shapes for these words can be determined by internal reconstruction. What are these earlier phonetic forms? How do they compare to the underlying phonological representations?

2. The non-third-person pronoun forms of Shoshone, a Uto-Aztecan language, are listed below. First-person forms are those designating a group that includes the speaker, and second-person forms designate a group that includes the hearer. A singular form refers to one person, a dual form to two, and a plural form to more than two. A first-person inclusive form is one that includes the hearer as well as the speaker; an exclusive form is one that does not.

From this data, five morphemes can be isolated from which the pronouns are constructed. The formation of these pronouns from the basic morphemes is fully regular, with the exception of the second-person plural form, which is unexpected given the rest of the data. Isolate the five morphemes and give the meaning of each. Show how the regular pronouns are constructed from them. Assume that the current second-person plural form is a modification of a historically earlier form that was fully regular; posit this earlier second-person plural pronoun by internal reconstruction. Can you suggest any factors that might have led to its modification?

nɨ	First-person singular
tawɨh	First-person dual inclusive
nɨwɨh	First-person dual exclusive
tammɨn	First-person plural inclusive
nɨmmɨn	First-person plural exclusive

ʔɨn   Second-person singular
mɨmmɨn   Second-person plural

3. Cahuilla, Cupeño, and Luiseño, three Uto-Aztecan languages spoken in southern California, constitute a subfamily called Cupan. Proto Cupan *[l] is reflected in the daughter languages by two different sound correspondences, the choice depending on the phonological environment. On the basis of the cognate sets that follow (data from William Bright and Jane Hill, 'The Linguistic History of the Cupeño,' in Dell Hymes, ed., *Studies in Southwestern Ethnolinguistics* [The Hague: Mouton, 1967, pp. 351–71]), list the two correspondences that derive from proto *[l] and state the principle that determines which one will occur in the reflexes of a particular proto form. ([lʸ] stands for a palatalized [l].)

Cahuilla	Cupeño	Luiseño	
haal	hal	hal	'look for'
silʸi	silʸi	şiili	'pour'
qasilʸ	qəsilʸ	qaaşil	'sagebrush'
puul	puul	puula	'doctor'
mukilʸ	mukʔilʸ	muukil	'sore'
laʔlaʔ	ləʔəl	laʔla	'goose'

4. Cognate sets from six languages of the Lolo-Burmese family are listed below (data from Robbins Burling, *Proto Lolo-Burmese*, Bloomington, Indiana University Research Center in Anthropology, Folklore, and Linguistics, Publication 43, 1967, supplement to *International Journal of American Linguistics* 33:2). Consider only the initial consonant of each form (exclusive of parenthesized material). Six correspondences involving labial and dental consonants are represented in the data. List these correspondences. ([ü] stands for a high front rounded vowel, [ö] for a mid front rounded vowel, and [z̧] for a voiced alveolar affricate. The superscript [ʰ] indicates aspiration of the preceding segment, and [ʔ] after a consonant indicates glottalization. Tones have been omitted.)

Burmese	Atsi	Maru	Lisu	Lahu	Akha	
teʔ	toʔ	toʔ	dæ	taʔ	daʔ	'ascend'
tʰa	——	tʔoyeʔ	tu	tuhu	tu	'stand'
tʰeʔ	tʰoʔ	——	tʰæ	——	taʔ	'sharp'
pou	pau	patʰoŋ	büi	pɨ	bö	'insect'
pʰeʔyweʔ	pʰoʔ	——	——	(sɨʔ)pʰaʔ	(a)paʔ	'leaf'
toun	tum	tam	dule	——	(yɔ)dm	'blunt'
tʰa	tʔo	tʔo	——	tɛta	(yu)ta	'put'
tʰu	tʰu	tʰau	tʰu	tʰu	tu	'thick'
pʰa	pʔo	pʔo	(wu)pa	pa	(xa)pa	'frog'
pʰwenu	pʰuic̆ʔap	(woʔ)pʰoi	(z̧a)pʰɨ	(vaʔ)pʰɨ	——	'chaff'

5. Reconstruct a Proto Lolo-Burmese sound to underlie each correspondence established in question 4. State the sound changes that have affected each of the proto sounds during the evolution of each daughter language. Assume that none of the proto segments is voiced.

6. An important aspect of comparative work is determining whether or not any of the daughter languages can be grouped in subfamilies. The chief criterion for establishing subfamilies is shared innovations. If two or more daughters have undergone a number of shared changes during their evolution from the proto language, changes that have affected no other daughters, it is likely that the daughters sharing these changes constitute a subfamily. In terms of the subfamily hypothesis, the shared changes are claimed to have occurred only once—in the intermediate proto language from which the members of the subfamily descended, before it split into separate languages. If a subfamily is not hypothesized, the changes in question are claimed to have occurred more than once, in each of the daughters individually. While this latter development is certainly not impossible, it is less likely, particularly when the number of shared innovations is relatively large.

Evaluate the evidence for positing subfamilies within Lolo-Burmese, as illustrated in questions 4 and 5.

7. Data from seven Uto-Aztecan languages is given below (from Wick R. Miller, *Uto-Aztecan Cognate Sets*, Berkeley, University of California Publications in Linguistics 48, 1967, and C. F. Voegelin, F. M. Voegelin, and Kenneth L. Hale, *Typological and Comparative Grammar of Uto-Aztecan: I [Phonology]*, Bloomington, Indiana University Publications in Anthropology and Linguistics, Memoir 17, 1962, supplement to *International Journal of American Linguistics* 28:1). Consider only the initial consonant (if any) and vowel of each form (exclusive of parenthesized material). List the systematic sound correspondences represented in the data. Reconstruct the Proto Uto-Aztecan sounds needed to account for these correspondences, as well as the initial consonant and vowel of the proto form that underlies each cognate set. State the sound changes that have characterized the evolution of each daughter language, and evaluate whatever evidence there may be for establishing subfamilies. ([q] is similar to [k] except that it is articulated farther back in the mouth; [ɬ] stands for a voiceless lateral affricate; and the superscript [ʷ] indicates that the preceding segment is labialized. Ignore vowel length.)

Comanche	Tübatulabal	Hopi	Papago	
tama	tamant	tama	taatam	'tooth'
pui	punẕil	poosi	wuhi	'eye'
kʷita	wiilaat	kʷita	biit	'excrement'
——	poht	pöhɨ	woog	'road'
kooi	——	qööya	koʔi	'kill'
kʷɨhɨ	wɨkɨt	kʷɨsɨ	——	'carry'
——	ha	qa	——	'not'
kɨh	kɨɨʔ	kɨɨka	kɨʔi	'bite'
——	tahambiš	taaqa	——	'man'
tɨkɨ	——	——	čɨɨk	'put down'
tuhu	tuugu	toko	čuk	'black'
kʷasi	——	kʷasi	bahi	'tail'
——	——	kiihɨ	kii	'house'
——	kuuŋan	kooŋʸa	kun	'husband'
karɨ	hal	qatɨ	kaač	'sit'

Cora	*Huichol*	*Aztec*	
tame	taame	ƛanƛi	'tooth'
hiʔɨsi	hɨši	iisƛi	'eye'
čʷita	kʷita	kʷiƛaƛ	'excrement'
huye	huye	ohƛi	'road'
——	——	——	'kill'
(raʔa)čʷeni	(pɨ)kʷeʔe	——	'carry'
kapu	ka	——	'not'
čeʔe	ke	kecoma	'bite'
——	——	ƛaakaƛ	'man'
——	——	teeka	'put down'
——	tɨɨ	——	'black'
kʷasi	kʷaaši	——	'tail'
čiʔi	kii	——	'house'
kɨɨn	kɨna	——	'husband'
——	——	——	'sit'

CHAPTER 9
the universality of language design

on the nature of language acquisition

what the child accomplishes

Every human child, provided he is given a fighting chance by heredity and environment, acquires a native language during the first few years of his life. Language acquisition can take place despite very severe mental or physical handicaps, and it requires no special tutoring; sufficient exposure to the use of a language seems to be all that is needed. By about the age of six, the child has mastered the essentials of his native language. He is in possession of a linguistic system that specifies an unbounded class of sentences that he can draw upon in speaking and understanding. He has the ability to create and comprehend, effortlessly and spontaneously, sentences that are completely novel to his experience.

When you stop to think about it, this is quite a remarkable achievement. The magnitude of the accomplishment should be apparent to anyone past adolescence who has ever tried to gain near-native fluency in a foreign language; it is not something that can be taken lightly or for-granted. Native language acquisition is one of the major events in the psychological development of the human child. As such, it is something that deserves explanation. If we can understand it, we will have learned something important about ourselves.

In some respects, the child learning to talk is in the same situation as a linguist investigating a language. The child must, in a manner of speaking, deduce the structure of the language spoken around him. Like the linguist, he is unable to observe this structure directly. He can only base his deduc-tions on the linguistic performance that he monitors, which is determined in part by the abstract linguistic system but which reflects it at best indi-rectly and imperfectly.

The linguistic system that a child constructs for himself thus consti-tutes a hypothesis about the structure of the language that the people around him use. By testing the consequences of this hypothesis against his further linguistic experience, the child continually refines it, until it is for all practical purposes equivalent to the system of his models. Since the systems are never compared directly, however, the possibility of restruc-turing or imperfect learning is always present.

Unlike the linguist, the child is not trying to render the structural principles of a language explicit and accessible to conscious inspection; he is simply learning to talk. He is trying, for the most part subconsciously, to make an abstract linguistic system part of his psychological organization. Only in a metaphorical sense does the child formulate a theory of linguistic structure and look for empirical evidence to verify or falsify it, but the metaphor is an instructive one. The child must somehow discover the structure of his native language; no one hands it to him ready to use.

When the child has learned to talk, when he has mastered his native tongue, he is in possession of a system of rules that specify an unbounded class of well-formed sentences. He is not conscious that he possesses such a system of rules; nor can he determine their character by introspection. He possesses this system in the sense that its structural patterns have been imposed on or integrated with his psychological processes, so that these patterns are a factor in determining the course of his verbal activity. Learning to talk, like learning to ride a bicycle, involves the mastery of a set of principles; it involves the addition of structure to the body of psy-chological skill or competence that shapes our mentally directed behavior. These rules are thus no more accessible to conscious inspection than the rules for keeping one's balance while riding a bike. We talk, and we keep our balance on bicycles, but in neither case do we know, at the level of consciousness, precisely what the guiding principles are. By way of analogy, the activity of a computer is directed by a program, but the program is not the object of the computer's activity; the computer carries out calculations related to other things, not to the program that guides it.

empiricism and rationalism

The problem of understanding language acquisition is that of finding out precisely how the child comes to possess the abstract linguistic system that is largely responsible for shaping his verbal activity. For the most part, the nature of this process is not known. We have no adequate theory to explain, stage by stage, the child's discovery of the structure of his language, although considerable progress in this domain is starting to be made.

Consequently, we will focus our attention on a more restricted question, but one that is of primary importance for a full understanding of language acquisition: How much of linguistic structure is innately specified? To put it another way, how much of the linguistic system that he ultimately commands is the child born with, and how much must he discover on the basis of his linguistic experience?

At one extreme, it could be claimed that no linguistic structure is innately specified, that language is learned entirely through experience. This is the empiricist view, mentioned briefly in Chapter One. It holds that we have no special, inborn capacity to acquire language. The fact that we acquire language and the structure of the language we learn are both due to the training we receive as children. From the linguistic point of view, we start out as blank slates. The linguistic system that is ultimately written on these slates is somehow built up from scratch, its structure being determined by experience alone. Language is thus viewed as a culturally transmitted entity, like stamp collecting or the use of forks.

At the opposite extreme, we find the rationalist view that language is innately specified almost in its entirety. Children learn to talk because the capacity for language, as well as most of the structure of language, is built into them. The function of linguistic experience, according to the rationalist view, is not so much to shape language as to activate the linguistic competence with which we are born. The blueprints for any possible linguistic system are provided as part of the innate neural equipment with which every human child is born. The role of learning is thus minimal. The child has only to learn those details of structure that differentiate the language spoken around him from other possible human languages. He has only to put flesh on the skeletal linguistic system he already possesses. In this view, then, the bulk of language is genetically transmitted. Only the peripheral structural details that make languages superficially different from one another are acquired on the basis of environmental influence.

The empiricist and rationalist views are thus in disagreement as to how much of linguistic structure is learned, but they do not conflict completely. Even adherents of the empiricist position would concede that the structure of the human organism places certain restrictions on the kind of linguistic system that it can master. Any such system must be finite, for example; no one could learn an infinite number of rules. Moreover, it must be assumed that children are born with some innate ability to learn, with some genetically transmitted capacity for combining simple psychological structures to form more complex ones. Otherwise, if the child had no in-born capacity to learn, he never would. This primitive ability to learn is usually conceived as being a relatively simple one, like the ability to form associations (for example, candy and sweetness are associated because they occur together so often in our experience; each one calls the other to mind).

The empiricist position, therefore, admits that innate properties of the organism are in some measure responsible for determining the organiza-tion of language. By the same token, the rationalist position does not deny that learning plays a significant role in language acquisition. What the child inherits genetically is not a specific language, but only the capacity for language. When he is born, the organizational and structural prop-erties that all languages share are built into him, but these properties are not exhaustive of the structure of any particular language. Using the in-born, skeletal linguistic system as a base, the child must proceed to discover those structural details that translate this base into the fully specified system that is used around him. It is here that learning is involved. In learning which language, of all possible human languages, is spoken around him, the child formulates structural hypotheses (in a manner of speaking) and tests them against further linguistic experience, continually refining them until he possesses a linguistic system equivalent to that of his models. But this process of discovery takes place within limits that are narrowly prescribed by genetic endowment, and the role of learning is thus highly restricted.

The empiricist and rationalist positions therefore differ in two im-portant respects. The empiricist holds that very little of psychological structure is innately specified, while the rationalist claims that a great deal of it is. This difference is one of degree, but the other difference is absolute. In the empiricist view, the human child is born with no special capacity for language, only a general ability to learn. A linguistic system is built up through experience by means of the same basic intellectual ability (association, for example) that is responsible for shaping all other aspects of cognitive structure. In the rationalist view, on the other hand, there is, in addition to general intelligence, a special inborn capacity for language. Above and beyond our natural ability to form and manipulate concepts, we are endowed with an innately specified predisposition to acquire a linguistic system having certain properties as opposed to all other conceivable ones.

the evidence for innate specification

The evidence for the rationalist claim is very strong. Consider first the uniformity of language acquisition throughout the human race. We have seen that every human child learns a language unless he is the victim of extreme mental deficiency or isolation from language use. There are all sorts of physical and intellectual skills that children can fail to master despite a considerable amount of instruction, but talking is not among them. This is precisely what one would expect on the basis of the assumption that language is innately specified almost fully, with linguistic experience serving mainly to activate the genetically specified system.

While the species uniformity of language acquisition fits in perfectly with the rationalist position, it conflicts with what we would expect on the basis of the empiricist viewpoint. If the acquisition of language depended mainly on the training the child receives, we would expect differences in training to correlate directly with differences in language acquisition (if general intelligence is held constant). In fact, however, this expectation turns out to be false. A child learns to talk regardless of whether or not his parents constantly pursue him, correct him, and put him through linguistic drills. Some parents do this, others do not, and some children don't even have parents—but they all learn to talk. Despite wide variations in the amount of speech they are exposed to, all children acquire a full-blown linguistic system. There are no cases on record of children who have learned only half a language, who have failed to master any syntactic rules, who lack underlying phonological representations, or who have not picked up any complex lexical items. The vicissitudes of early linguistic experience are not matched by any comparable variations in linguistic structure.

A second argument in favor of the rationalist position is provided by the fact that mastery of a language is restricted to the human species. Since the empiricist position holds that language is a function of general intelligence, not of any special linguistic capacity, it predicts that other animals should, given proper training, succeed in acquiring language to a degree proportional to their intelligence. Some caution is required here, given the difficulty of comparing the intelligence of different species, but present evidence would seem to indicate that this prediction is false. Higher apes such as chimpanzees are the most likely candidates for mastering language, since they can learn to use tools and solve simple problems; the difference in intelligence between chimpanzees and human beings is thus not absolute, but only a matter of degree. However, the linguistic ability that chimpanzees have demonstrated so far differs from human language, not just in degree, but in its basic character. Despite some success in teaching chimps to communicate through visual signs, investigators have not yet shown them capable of mastering anything remotely comparable to the syntactic systems discussed in Chapter Five. Syntactic rules expressing systematic relations between sentence types, derivations involving the ordered application of numerous distinct rules, complex sentences with multiple embeddings and clearly defined clauses —all these and more seem to be completely lacking, not just present to a limited degree. These observations are perfectly compatible with the rationalist view, which attributes the existence of complex syntactic systems in the human species to a special, inborn linguistic capacity. Apes simply do not possess this innate structure.

The relative perfection of language acquisition is a third argument for innate specification. If language reflected general intelligence and not a special linguistic capacity, we would expect differences in intelligence to correlate directly with differences in language acquisition (if training is held constant). We would expect bright children to do better than stupid ones in mastering a linguistic system. We would also expect some children to fail miserably at acquiring language, just as many children fail to learn geography or the procedure for extracting square roots. We would expect some children to wind up with linguistic systems so deficient or so distorted as to be unrecognizable.

These expectations are not borne out, however. Bright children, average children, and stupid children all learn to talk. They are all successful at mastering a linguistic system that is virtually identical to that of their models, one that is neither distorted nor deficient. Regardless of general intelligence, a child succeeds in mastering a complex system of rules and underlying representations that specifies an infinite set of sentences. Children may vary on such points as volubility or size of vocabulary, but they do not vary with respect to the significant structural features of linguistic organization. If the role of learning is minimal, serving only to activate the innate system and to fill in some details at the structural fringes, then it is impossible for radical structural errors to arise.

The abstractness and structural complexity of languages is a fourth strong argument in favor of the rationalist view. We know a great deal about language, but despite centuries of serious investigation, we would be at a complete loss to describe exhaustively the structure of any language, even the most intensively studied. But this is essentially what the child does. He masters the entire set of lexical items and structural principles that constitutes a linguistic system. He does this on the basis of indirect and fragmentary evidence, and at an age when he is not yet capable of logical, analytical thought. This remarkable phenomenon can be explained in terms of the rationalist view, but hardly in terms of the empiricist position. If linguistic structure is genetically transmitted, its tremendous complexity does not pose a problem for the child. His learning task is the relatively simple one of narrowing down the range of innately specified possibilities until he arrives at the right one. It is not a matter of building up the entire linguistic system from scratch, but only of filling in some peripheral details.

The empiricist claim, however, is that the entire linguistic system is indeed built up from scratch on the basis of the child's general intellectual capacity. The child is purported to discover not just some structural details, but the entire scheme of linguistic organization as well. Born without any linguistic expectations or predilections, he is supposed to make, at a preintellectual age, a series of linguistic discoveries that far surpass the cumulative results of the efforts of all those scholars who have ever investigated language!

This would not seem to be a reasonable claim. It is important to remember that the linguistic system that is acquired can never be directly observed. The structure of this system must be discovered on the basis of the very indirect evidence of linguistic performance. Even if the child learned to talk at an age when he was capable of analytical thought, therefore, he would still not be able to master the principles of linguistic organization if they were not part of his genetic endowment. Any number of structural hypotheses can be conceived that will account for the finite set of linguistic observations that the child has available to him as evidence; to take one example, he would have no reason not to believe that a language was just a finite list of utterances that had to be memorized. With no inborn structural principles to guide him, the child could hardly be expected to discover the nature of the linguistic system that partially underlies the verbal activity of the people around him. He would have no basis even for suspecting the existence of this system. Furthermore, its abstractness and complexity puts it well beyond the possibility of being discovered by trial and error.

language universals

We have seen that, in the rationalist view, linguistic structure is innately specified in considerable detail. The same inborn structural framework underlies all languages, and the function of the child's exposure to language is more to activate his linguistic capacity than to shape it.

If this view is correct, then all languages must be structurally very similar to one another. If the same genetically transmitted structural framework underlies all languages, then languages can differ from one another only with respect to the peripheral structural features that the child learns through experience. Despite their surface differences, all languages must be alike in most respects. They must constitute variations on the same structural theme.

To put it another way, the claim that language is innately specified implies that all human languages must fall within a fairly narrow range of structural possibilities, as illustrated in Figure 9.1. The outer circle represents the total spectrum of conceivable linguistic systems that could in principle be invented by or for an intelligent being like man. Out of this wide range of systems, only a small subset will display the structural properties of human languages; this subset is represented by the smaller circle. This narrow range of structural possibilities is imposed by the innate linguistic specifications that enable the human child to acquire language. The learning task that the child is faced with, then, is that of narrowing down this range of possibilities still further, until he has in effect discovered which particular language L, of all possible languages, is the one spoken around him. Of all conceivable linguistic systems, only those that fall within this narrow range of possibilities can be acquired by the child in a natural, spontaneous fashion.

The claim that all languages are very much alike is often met with skepticism. After all, when we compare linguistic systems—in learning a foreign language, for example—we are struck by the differences between them. No one will deny that languages differ from one another in a multitude of details. On the other hand, we must realize that surface peculiarities are much more likely to attract our attention than underlying structural principles, while it is in the latter that we would expect to find language

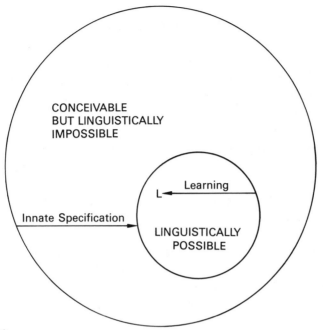

figure 9.1

universals. By now it should be clear that surface linguistic diversity often conceals underlying uniformity.

the concept of language universals

Many structural properties are so common in languages of the world that their widespread occurrence requires some special explanation. Such properties are referred to as **language universals**. Some of these structural features are shared by all human languages without exception (so far as present evidence indicates); we will call these **absolute universals**. Others are not universal in this absolute sense, but are nevertheless so ubiquitous that chance, borrowing, and genetic relationship are all insufficient to explain their prevalence; these will be called **universal tendencies**.

By and large, we may equate language universals—both absolute universals and universal tendencies—with those structural features of languages that are innately specified; if all or significantly many languages share a certain property, it is probably because this feature is part of our genetic endowment as human beings. This outlook is consistent with the rationalist hypothesis, which claims that much of language structure is determined by a special linguistic capacity that is innate in the human organism. Without positing such a capacity, we would find it difficult to explain the recurrence of highly specific structural features in languages that are scattered all over the world and that are, so far as we can determine, unrelated.

Language universals thus constitute the set of expectations with which the child is provided concerning the structural properties of any language that might be spoken in his environment. Some of these expectations are absolute, and presumably he would have difficulty mastering a language that violated them. Others (universal tendencies) are not absolute expectations but only predispositions, and the child must learn through experience which ones are in accordance with the actual linguistic system to which he is exposed. The structural features of language probably form a continuum leading from absolute universals on one end to totally language-specific properties on the other, and this continuum defines the range of possibilities within which any human language must fall.

organization

To begin our discussion of language universals in very general terms, let us observe that all languages exemplify the same basic organizational scheme. More specifically, every human language comprises an infinite set of sentences, each of which manifests, in phonetic form, a conceptual structure. A complex series of syntactic rules serves to connect conceptual structures with surface structures, which are linear strings of lexical items grouped hierarchically. A series of phonological rules connects the surface structure of each sentence with its phonetic manifestation on the basis of the underlying phonological representations of its lexical items. Each individual lexical item consists in the association of semantic, syntactic, and phonological properties, the relation between its semantic and phonological properties being arbitrary in most cases. Phonologically, a lexical item is represented as a linear sequence of segments, each segment specified with respect to distinctive phonological information.

There are simply no exceptions to this organizational scheme. No one has ever found a human language lacking syntactic rules, phonological rules, or discrete lexical items. No one has found a language in which lexical items were not composed of linear sequences of sound segments. Out of all conceivable ways in which a language could be put together, actual human languages are unanimous in using this particular way. Linguistic systems differ somewhat in structure, but they vary only within the confines of this common framework.

In outlining this common organizational scheme, we have barely begun to point out the universal characteristics of language design. Absolute universals and universal tendencies can also be observed with respect to inventories of semantic, syntactic, and phonological elements; the structures formed by combining these elements; and even the details of syntactic and phonological rules. We will examine the first two domains rather briefly and concentrate on universals pertaining to rules.

elements

We may discuss semantic and syntactic elements together, because there is no clear dividing line between the two. In every language, it is possible to pose questions and give commands, in addition to making statements; usually, these functions are served by special sentence types with distinctive properties. Every language has demonstratives of some kind, personal pronouns, words indicating quantity, and some way of expressing negation. Evidence can virtually always be found for positing two major classes of lexical items: a noun class, a large percentage of which designate objects; and a verb class, most of which designate actions, states, events, or relations. There is also a universal tendency for languages to have such categories as adjectives, articles, pro forms, adverbs of time and place, conjunctions, subordinators, and either prepositions (which precede nouns), postpositions (which follow nouns), or case inflections expressing location and direction. In terms of more specific semantic categories, it would be most surprising to find a language lacking proper names of some kind, verbs of motion, color terms, modifiers indicating relative size, kinship terms, names for body parts, lexical items describing emotional states, or nouns naming plants and animals. This list is only a sample and could easily be extended.

Languages display numerous universal tendencies in their inventories of distinctive phonological elements. All languages have at least two distinctive vowels and a considerably larger number of distinctive consonants. Among the vowels, one always expects to find a distinction in height, and the front-versus-back dimension is virtually always exploited contrastively in systems with three or more vowels. Vowel nasalization is usually predictable (hence nondistinctive), and rounding tends to be. Front vowels are normally unrounded, while back vowels (other than [a]) are normally rounded; a language will not have rounded front vowels unless it also has unrounded ones, nor will it have unrounded back vowels without having rounded ones as well. With respect to consonant inventories, the existence of stops and fricatives is an absolute universal, while nasals, liquids, glides, and affricates represent very strong universal tendencies, probably in that order. Few if any languages lack a stop and a fricative articulated in the dental-alveolar region; the prevalence of velar and labial stops is almost as great, and that of glottal stops somewhat less. Any language will have at least several stops, but it may have only one fricative and will tend to have fewer fricatives than stops. It is unusual for a language not to have both [m] and [n], but velar and palatal nasals are not quite so common as distinctive segments. Palatal affricates (such as [č]) are by far the most usual type, while [w] and [y] are the basic glides. Features such as voicing, labialization, aspiration, and glottalization are very frequently used to distinguish stops with the same place of articulation, somewhat less frequently for fricatives and affricates, occasionally for liquids, and seldom for nasals and glides. Suprasegmental phenomena also show universal tendencies. When length is contrastive, a simple distinction between long and short segments is virtually always sufficient, and a three-way distinction is certainly the maximum possible. Stress tends to be at least partially predictable, and it is unlikely that more than two degrees of distinctive stress will have to be recognized for any language. Twelve distinctive tones may be the maximum, but in most tone languages the number is far smaller; the number of distinctive tones is most commonly two, three, or four.

structures

The grammatical and phonological elements of a language combine to form structures of varying degrees of complexity, such as sentences, clauses, phrases, words, morphemes, and syllables. To a considerable extent, the composition of these structures is universal in character.

In every language, there are complex lexical items that are constructed out of simpler ones. Besides the metaphorical extension that gives rise to idioms, languages almost invariably exploit the processes of affixation and compounding in the formation of complex lexical items. Suffixes tend to be more prevalent than prefixes, especially when numerous affixes are attached to a single root, and infixes are fairly uncommon. When both derivational and inflectional affixes occur before or after a root, there is a strong universal tendency for the derivational affixes to be closer to the root than are the inflectional ones. Compounds tend very strongly to be binary in character; that is, they tend to consist in the juxtaposition of exactly two stems. (Compounds with more than two stems can usually be broken down into a series of binary compounds. For example, *birdcage bottom* is a binary compound with the two components *birdcage* and *bottom; birdcage* in turn is a binary compound consisting of the stems *bird* and *cage.*)

Every language has an unbounded set of complex sentences involving embedding, conjoining, or both. The clauses of complex sentences show extensive universal tendencies with respect to both their function and their internal structure. In almost any language, we find clauses functioning as conjuncts, relative clauses, complement clauses, and adverbial clauses of various kinds; moreover, the syntactic properties of these clause types tend to be quite similar from language to language (in terms of position, marking, and the rules they undergo).

As for internal structure, we find that the basic clause structure of a language almost invariably involves a verbal element together with a selection of adjuncts appropriate to express the desired meaning; these adjuncts include subjects, direct objects, oblique objects (marked by prepositions, postpositions, or equivalent case inflections), adverbs, and auxiliary verbs. Although these elements can be ordered in many different ways, a number of fairly strong tendencies can be observed. For example, subjects normally precede objects, and auxiliary verbs are usually found as the second element of a sentence or else suffixed to the main verb. Important universals have been observed in regard to the linear order of a verb and its objects. In many languages (Turkish and Japanese, for instance), the verb must be the final element of a clause, and the ordering oblique-object–direct-object–verb is required; in languages of this type, postpositions predominate over prepositions, conjunctions attach to the preceding conjuncts, modifiers usually precede the nouns they modify, and suffixation tends to be heavily exploited. In many other languages (such as English and Samoan), the verb must be initial rather than final, in the sense that it must precede its objects (but may follow the subject and auxiliaries). Verb-initial languages tend to be exact inverses of verb-final languages with respect to all the properties mentioned above; the order verb–direct-object–oblique-object prevails (rather than the reverse), prepositions are used in preference to postpositions, conjunctions attach to the following conjuncts, modifiers (especially complex ones) follow the noun they modify, and suffixation is exploited less heavily. From observations such as these, it should be apparent that the ways in which languages allow clauses to be put together are highly restricted relative to the total range of possibilities.

Sound segments combine with one another to form larger phonological units, the most fundamental of which is the syllable. A syllable consists of a nucleus, which normally comprises a vowel or vowel-plus-glide combination, together with the consonants on either side that cohere to it. Letting V stand for the vocalic nucleus of a syllable, and C for a consonant, we can observe that syllables of the form CV are most basic; no language lacks CV syllables, and some languages have only CV syllables. Languages vary in the complexity and kinds of consonant clusters they allow before or after the syllable nucleus, but in both respects there are severe restrictions and strong universal tendencies. For example, more complex clusters are generally allowed before the nucleus than after it; glides tend to be closer to the nucleus than are stops; fricatives usually precede stops in prenuclear clusters instead of following them; and so on.

syntactic rules

It appears to be an absolute universal that the syntax of every language has reduction rules, insertion rules, and rearrangement rules. However, the range of operations performed by such rules is highly restricted relative to the logical possibilities. Many syntactic rules are found in unrelated languages all over the world and must therefore be considered universal. On the other hand, we can conceive of indefinitely many other a priori possible rules that simply never occur.

Let us first consider reduction rules. Every language allows one of two coreferential noun phrases in a sentence to be deleted or reduced to a pronoun; a special "reflexive" form of the pronoun is often used when the two noun phrases are in the same clause. There is a strong tendency for pronominalization and reflexivization to affect the second of the two identical nominals instead of the first. We therefore find sentences like *Alice admired herself* and *I admire Alice and I like her very much,* but *Herself admired Alice* and *I admire her and I like Alice very much* are ungrammatical (when *Alice* and *her(self)* are taken as designating the same individual). Some languages permit a pronoun to precede its antecedent in certain restricted circumstances; this is generally possible in English when the pronoun is in a subordinate clause (*Before she left, Alice kissed me*). However, no language permits only the first of two coreferential nominals to reduce but never the second.

The rule deleting a complement clause subject represents a strong universal tendency. In English, for example, *I would like for me to leave* reduces to *I would like to leave* because the main and complement clause subjects are coreferential. While complement subject deletion is very common, it is doubtful that any language requires instead retention of the complement subject and deletion of the coreferential nominal in the main clause (which would lead to surface structures such as *Would like for me to leave*). Most languages, but not all, permit the deletion of repeated verbs in conjoined clauses. For instance, *Joe likes chess, and Peter likes curling* reduces to *Joe likes chess, and Peter curling* through the application of this rule. In English, as in most other verb-initial languages, the verb of the first conjunct must be retained (note the ungrammaticalness of *Joe chess, and Peter likes curling*); in verb-final languages, on the other hand, it is normally the verb of the last conjunct that must be retained. The deletion of nonemphatic pronouns, particularly subject pronouns, is another universal process. This deletion is especially likely to be found in languages in which verb agreement makes it possible to determine the person of the subject even when it fails to surface. This is the case in Spanish and Navaho, for example, and subject pronoun deletion occurs in both; it is not normally the case in French or English, and these languages do not freely permit subject pronouns to be omitted. The rule therefore represents a universal tendency, not an absolute universal.

Turning now to insertion rules, we note that it is common for a rule to insert a semantically empty form in one particular spot in a sentence as a grammatical marker. Typical examples are the insertion of markers of subordination, like *that* in *I know that he is getting bald*; the insertion of an empty pronoun in subject position, like *it* in *It is snowing*; and the marking of subjects and direct objects for case (compare *She tripped* and *I tripped her*). Agreement rules are also very prevalent, especially agreement between a verb and its subject or object and agreement between a noun and its modifiers. Rules such as these are exemplified over and over again in human languages, but it is easy to conceive of many logically possible rules that are never in fact found. For example, no language seems to have a rule that inserts a semantically empty morpheme after every word in a sentence, yielding sentences like *I that know that he that is that getting that bald that*, nor one that inserts a copy of each word directly after it, resulting in sentences such as *Tennis tennis is is a a demanding demanding sport sport*. Similarly, no actual syntactic rule has the effect of adding to a sentence a string of grammatical morphemes equal in number to the number of the words already present; such a rule would translate *I know she tripped* into *I know that that that that she tripped*, and *I know he is getting bald* into *I know that that that that that that he is getting bald*. Linguistically impossible agreement rules are also easy to invent. Thus, linguists never encounter languages in which a verb is marked to agree with any arbitrary noun phrase other than its own subject, nor do they find languages that require that an adjective agree with any arbitrary noun other than the noun it modifies. A rule that made a verb disagree with its subject with respect to person and number in the seventh conjunct of a conjoined structure would also be a linguistic impossibility.

Languages (verb-initial languages in particular) display a universal tendency for question words, relative pronouns, or both to be moved to clause-initial position. Both are preposed in English, as in *What will they ask for?* and *I pity the dog that I bit.* Subject raising, which derives *The bomb is quite likely to explode* from *For the bomb to explode is quite likely,* also represents a universal tendency. A third rearrangement rule with universal status is the extraposition of complement clauses to final position, illustrated by sentence pairs such as *That my cat has fleas is obvious* and *It is obvious that my cat has fleas.* Many other kinds of rearrangement rules are found, but the ones actually attested occupy only a narrow sector of the spectrum of those that are conceivable. Apparently no language has a rule that obligatorily transports question words to clause-final position, or that moves relative pronouns down one clause when the relative is complex. A rule that interchanged a main-clause object with a complement-clause subject (yielding *I told Mary that Bill was a fool* as an optional variant of *I told Bill that Mary was a fool*) would be linguistically impossible. It is not uncommon for questions answerable by 'yes' or 'no' to be formed by a change in word order; thus *Would he like that?* is the interrogative version of *He would like that* in English, derived by permuting the subject and auxiliary. However, questions are never formed by reversing the order of all the words in a sentence, allowing, for instance, *Night tomorrow dinner to coming are Boston from men old blind three?* as the question corresponding to the statement *Three blind old men from Boston are coming to dinner tomorrow night.* Nor are questions ever formed by reversing the members of each successive pair of words, yielding in this case *Blind three men old Boston from coming are dinner to night tomorrow?*

phonological rules

Universal tendencies are no less common in the domain of phonological rules. Phonological rules add segments, delete segments, modify or further specify the identity of segments as given in underlying phonological representations, and so on. Within these boundaries, there is a very wide range of structural possibilities, but relatively few of these possibilities are ever exploited in human languages. Let us consider just two kinds of phonological rules, those that insert segments and those that change the identity of segments.

Certain kinds of segment insertion rules are found fairly commonly in languages of the world. In starting to investigate an unfamiliar language, for instance, a linguist would be well prepared to encounter a rule that inserted a glottal stop to separate any two adjacent vowels or to begin any word that would otherwise begin with a vowel. He would not be surprised to find a rule that inserted a vowel between two identical or similar consonants (as for English *judges* [ǰʌǰəz]). Nor would he be surprised to find a rule that inserted a vowel at the beginning of a word that would otherwise begin with a consonant cluster.

On the other hand, no linguist would expect to find a rule that inserted [a] after every second segment in a sentence; such a rule would be a linguistic impossibility. Nor would a linguist be prepared to find a rule that separated any two adjacent voiced stops in a string by inserting a voiceless stop between them, or which added [čpl] to the end of any word that would otherwise end in a nasal consonant.

In the same way, phonological rules that change the identity of segments tend to be similar in languages all over the world. Many of the same phenomena turn up in language after language, while others never seem to occur at all.

For example, there is nothing out of the ordinary in a rule that changes [ɪ] to [i] in word-final position (English has such a rule—compare *pity* [pɪti] and *pitiful* [pɪtɪfʊl]), or that makes stops voiceless in this position (as in German). It would not be at all surprising to find a language in which [f] was manifested as [h] at the beginning of a word, or in which a voiced stop showed up as a voiced fricative intervocalically. Assimilation rules in particular must be given universal status. It is very common, for instance, for a vowel to be at least partially nasalized before a nasal consonant, particularly one in the same syllable. Consonants occurring adjacent to one another are frequently assimilated in voicing, so that either they are all voiced or they are all voiceless. It would be surprising to find a language in which a stop was not labialized when it occurred directly before [w] in the same syllable. And so on.

But no linguist expects to find a language in which a consonant is made voiceless if it occurs between two voiced consonants. It is fairly certain that there is no language containing a rule that changes [a] to [t] before a nasal. No language seems to have a rule that manifests a glottal stop as a nasal vowel, or that changes [č] to [m]. Out of all conceivable rules serving to change the phonological characteristics of individual segments, only a highly restricted class is found to be operative in human languages.

conclusion

People have studied language for many different reasons, but our discussion has concentrated on two that are probably the most significant. On the one hand, we have viewed the investigation of language as an attempt to explain linguistic creativity, to find out how it is possible for a speaker to create and understand a potentially unbounded class of sentences that are completely novel to his experience. On the other hand, we have looked to linguistic investigation as an avenue that will allow us ultimately to fully comprehend language acquisition.

We found that the unbounded character of language can be traced to the nature of human conceptual powers. As human beings, we are capable in principle of conceptualizations having any degree of complexity (although there are, of course, limitations on the complexity of any thought that we can form and operate with at any given moment). From any one of an infinite number of possible conceptual situations, a surface structure can be derived by the choice of appropriate lexical items and the application of syntactic rules. Phonological rules connect each of these surface structures with a phonetic manifestation. The linguistic system thus specifies an infinite set of phonetic sequences, each of which is paired with a conceptual structure.

Because he possesses a linguistic system of this type, a speaker controls an infinite number of sentences that he can draw upon in speaking and understanding. By studying the structure of these systems, we are therefore progressing toward an explanation of linguistic creativity. We will completely understand linguistic creativity when we completely understand the structure of linguistic systems, the way these abstract systems are used in actual verbal performance, and the psychological processes that produce conceptual structures.

Even if we accept the hypothesis of innate specification, we are left with many interesting questions that must be answered before our understanding of language acquisition is complete. For example, precisely which aspects of linguistic structure are not innately specified but must be acquired through experience? How does this learning take place? What stages does a child go through in discovering the structure of his language and in learning to use it? On what kind of data is language acquisition crucially dependent? To what extent are language universals determined by general psychological constraints (constraints that affect other cognitive phenomena as well), and to what extent are they determined by our special inborn linguistic capacity? It should be apparent that these questions can be answered satisfactorily only in the context of an adequate theory of linguistic structure and an adequate theory of general psychological organization, neither of which is presently available.

Linguists readily admit to being far from knowing everything there is to know about language. The positive results of linguistic investigation are extensive and significant, but they are small when measured against the amount we still have to learn. Language is difficult to study because it is a psychological phenomenon, one that is intimately associated with other aspects of psychological structure. It is for precisely the same reason, however, that an understanding of language is of such great importance. If we want to understand human cognition, language is a good place to start.

suggestions for study and discussion

1. To what extent and in what ways do you believe linguistic ability to be correlated with general intelligence?

2. Examine English, or any other language you are familiar with, in regard to the language universals sketched in this chapter. Does the language show a substantial number of the universal tendencies described? Does it conflict with any of the proposed absolute universals?

3. Although limitations on present knowledge make attempts at "explanation" somewhat risky, the existence of certain language universals can perhaps ultimately be explained with some plausibility on the basis of physical or psychological constraints of a quite general character. For example, the tendency for the second of two identical constituents to be reduced, rather than the first, can probably be related to general considerations of information processing; only after a constituent has occurred once in a sentence do subsequent occurrences become in a sense redundant, hence reducible. Some phonological universals are no doubt directly connected to physiological factors. The tendency for consonant clusters to assimilate in voicing, for instance, can be attributed to the greater ease of articulation of clusters that are homogeneous in voicing, given the physical characteristics of the glottis and the neurophysiological mechanisms that control its activity.

Can you suggest plausible "explanations" for any of the universals mentioned in this chapter? Are there any universals for which it seems unlikely that such an explanation could be found? What would be the significance of language universals which could not be explained by reference to physical or psychological factors that are independent of linguistic ability?

4. A distinction is made in this chapter between, on the one hand, rules that are either possible or universal and, on the other hand, rules that are lin-

guistically impossible. To the extent that this distinction is valid, it should be reflected to some degree in learnability. You might try the following informal experiment to test this for yourself. Choose some linguistically possible syntactic or phonological rule that happens not to be used in English, and practice using this rule in English, keeping the rest of the linguistic system unchanged. For example, you might choose a rule making articles agree in number with the following nouns, yielding expressions such as *the dog, thes dogs, some girl, somes girls,* and so on. In phonology, you might choose a rule that palatalizes [t] to [č] before high front vowels, making *tea* and *tilt,* for instance, come out phonetically as [či] and [čɪlt]. Do you find that you can master the rule with practice and use it fairly spontaneously as part of your idiolect? Does it lead to any conflicts with the rest of the linguistic system? (For example, the palatalization rule described above would make *tip* and *chip* phonetically indistinguishable.)

Next make up a linguistically impossible rule, such as one that forms questions by reversing the linear order of each successive pair of words in the corresponding declarative sentence. Is there a difference in learnability and usability between this rule and a natural one? What is the significance of this difference or the lack of it?

5. In evaluating the claim that all languages are rather similar in their overall structure, it is instructive to compare equivalent expressions in diverse languages in order to see in precisely what ways they are similar and in what ways they differ. Even in surface structure, where linguistic diversity is most pronounced, extensive similarities can often be found.

For example, compare the following seven sentences, from English, French, Samoan, Turkish, Luiseño, Japanese, and Tyapukay (a language of Australia); only English and French are related. Hyphens are used to mark relevant morpheme boundaries, and the typography has been modified slightly to avoid immaterial distractions. Parenthesized elements are those which are structurally represented but cannot be identified with any particular sequence of segments; for example, English *we* is a special subject form of the first person plural pronoun, but it would be arbitrary to single out *w* or *e* as being a subject marker, hence the parentheses around **SUBJECT** in the morpheme-by-morpheme translation. For Samoan and Tyapukay, the designations **SUBJECT** and **OBJECT** are not fully appropriate, but they will serve for present purposes.

English:
   we cause-d the boy-s to panic
   we-(SUBJECT) cause-PAST the boy-PLURAL to panic
   'We caused the boys to panic.'

French:
   je fer-ai parti-r le-s femme-s
   I-(SUBJECT) make-FUTURE-(I) leave-to the-PLURAL woman-PLURAL
   'I will make the women leave.'

Samoan:
> sa fa'a-pa'ū e ioane le to'i
> **PAST let-fall SUBJECT John the axe**
> 'John dropped the axe.'

Turkish:
> ben fare-yi öl-dür-dü-m
> **I-(SUBJECT) mouse-the-(OBJECT) die-cause-PAST-I**
> 'I killed the mouse.'

Luiseño:
> noo nawitmal-um-i paa'i-ni-n
> **I-(SUBJECT) girl-PLURAL-OBJECT drink-cause-FUTURE**
> 'I will make the girls drink.'

Japanese:
> watasi-ga kodomo-o tabe-sase-ru
> **I-SUBJECT child-OBJECT eat-cause-PRESENT**
> 'I make a child eat.'

Tyapukay:
> pama-lu tyulpin wanta-ri-lna
> **man-SUBJECT tree-(OBJECT) fall-cause-FUTURE**
> 'The man will fell the tree.'

There are obvious differences among these sentences (apart from the different lexical items). For instance, there are differences in word order, and Luiseño lacks any morpheme meaning 'the.' However, there are also many similarities. For example, when 'the' is a separate word and not an affix, it consistently precedes the noun it modifies in this data.

Find as many other similarities as you can among the seven sentences. Examine the data in relation to the distinction between verb-initial and verb-final languages (English, French, and Samoan are verb-initial as the term is defined here; the others are all verb-final). Bring equivalent data from other languages into the comparison. Using a grammar of some foreign language, preferably a non–Indo-European one, compare in detail various other surface patterns with those of the corresponding English expressions.

selected readings

general introductions

Anderson, Wallace L., and Norman C. Stageberg, eds. *Introductory Readings on Language*, rev. ed. New York: Holt, Rinehart and Winston, 1966.

Bloomfield, Leonard. *Language*. New York: Holt, Rinehart and Winston, 1933.

Boas, Franz. *Introduction to the Handbook of American Indian Languages*. Washington, D.C.: Georgetown University Press, Institute of Languages and Linguistics, 1966.

Bolinger, Dwight. *Aspects of Language*. New York: Harcourt Brace Jovanovich, 1968.

Crystal, David. *Linguistics*. Harmondsworth, Middlesex: Penguin Books, 1971.

Dinneen, Francis P. *An Introduction to General Linguistics*. New York: Holt, Rinehart and Winston, 1967.

Elgin, Suzette Haden. *What Is Linguistics?* Englewood Cliffs, N. J.: Prentice-Hall, 1973.

Gleason, H. A. *An Introduction to Descriptive Linguistics*, rev. ed. New York: Holt, Rinehart and Winston, 1961.

Hockett, Charles F. *A Course in Modern Linguistics*. New York: Macmillan, 1958.

Hudspeth, Robert N., and Donald F. Sturtevant, eds. *The World of Language: A Reader in Linguistics*. New York: American Book Company, 1967.

Jespersen, Otto. *Language: Its Nature, Development and Origin.* New York: Macmillan, 1949 (available in paperback).

Laird, Charlton, and Robert M. Gorrell, eds. *Reading About Language.* New York: Harcourt Brace Jovanovich, 1971.

Lehmann, Winfred P. *Descriptive Linguistics: An Introduction.* New York: Random House, 1972.

Lyons, John. *Introduction to Theoretical Linguistics.* New York: Cambridge University Press, 1968.

Pyles, Thomas, and John Algeo. *English: An Introduction to Language.* New York: Harcourt Brace Jovanovich, 1970.

Sapir, Edward. *Language: An Introduction to the Study of Speech.* New York: Harcourt Brace Jovanovich, 1921 (available in paperback).

Saussure, Ferdinand de. *Course in General Linguistics.* New York: Philosophical Library, 1959.

Wardhaugh, Ronald. *Introduction to Linguistics.* New York: McGraw-Hill, 1972.

Wilson, Graham, ed. *A Linguistics Reader.* New York: Harper & Row, 1967.

history of linguistics

Chomsky, Noam. *Cartesian Linguistics.* New York: Harper & Row, 1966.

Pedersen, Holger. *The Discovery of Language.* Bloomington: Indiana University Press, 1931.

Robins, R. H. *A Short History of Linguistics.* Bloomington: Indiana University Press, 1967.

Salus, Peter H., ed *On Language, Plato to von Humboldt.* New York: Holt, Rinehart and Winston, 1969.

Waterman, John T. *Perspectives in Linguistics.* Chicago: University of Chicago Press, 1963.

syntax and semantics

Bach, Emmon. *An Introduction to Transformational Grammars.* New York: Holt, Rinehart and Winston, 1964.

Chafe, Wallace L. *Meaning and the Structure of Language.* Chicago: University of Chicago Press, 1970.

Chomsky, Noam. *Syntactic Structures.* The Hague: Mouton and Co., 1957.

Fillmore, Charles J., and D. Terence Langendoen, eds. *Studies in Linguistic Semantics.* New York: Holt, Rinehart and Winston, 1971.

Fodor, Jerry A., and Jerrold J. Katz, eds. *The Structure of Language: Readings in the Philosophy of Language.* Englewood Cliffs, N. J.: Prentice-Hall, 1964.

Grinder, John T., and Suzette Haden Elgin. *Guide to Transformational Grammar.* New York: Holt, Rinehart and Winston, 1973.

Jacobs, Roderick A., and Peter S. Rosenbaum. *English Transformational Grammar*. Waltham, Mass.: Blaisdell, 1968.

———, eds. *Readings in English Transformational Grammar*. Waltham, Mass.: Ginn and Co., 1970.

Langendoen, D. Terence. *The Study of Syntax*. New York: Holt, Rinehart and Winston, 1969.

———. *Essentials of English Grammar*. New York: Holt, Rinehart and Winston, 1970.

Palmer, Frank. *Grammar*. Harmondsworth, Middlesex: Penguin Books, 1971.

Reibel, David A., and Sanford A. Schane, eds. *Modern Studies in English*. Englewood Cliffs, N. J.: Prentice-Hall, 1969.

Stern, Gustaf. *Meaning and Change of Meaning*. Bloomington: Indiana University Press, 1931.

phonology and phonetics

Denes, Peter B., and Elliot N. Pinson. *The Speech Chain*. New York: Bell Telephone Laboratories, 1963.

Heffner, R-M. S. *General Phonetics*. Madison: University of Wisconsin Press, 1964.

Ladefoged, Peter. *Elements of Acoustic Phonetics*. Chicago: University of Chicago Press, 1962.

Malmberg, Bertil. *Phonetics*. New York: Dover Publications, 1963.

Schane, Sanford A. *Generative Phonology*. Englewood Cliffs, N. J.: Prentice-Hall, 1973.

Smalley, William A. *A Manual of Articulatory Phonetics*, rev. ed. Tarrytown, N. Y.: Practical Anthropology, 1963.

historical linguistics

Arlotto, Anthony. *Introduction to Historical Linguistics*. Boston: Houghton Mifflin Company, 1972.

Bloomfield, Morton W., and Leonard Newmark. *A Linguistic Introduction to the History of English*. New York: Alfred A. Knopf, 1963.

Hudson-Williams, T. *A Short Introduction to the Study of Comparative Grammar (Indo-European)*. Cardiff: University of Wales Press, 1961.

Hungerford, Harold, Jay Robinson, and James Sledd, eds. *English Linguistics: An Introductory Reader*. Glenview, Ill.: Scott, Foresman, 1970.

Jespersen, Otto. *Growth and Structure of the English Language*. Garden City, N. Y.: Doubleday, 1955.

Keiler, Allan R., ed. *A Reader in Historical and Comparative Linguistics*. New York: Holt, Rinehart and Winston, 1972.

King, Robert D. *Historical Linguistics and Generative Grammar*. Englewood Cliffs, N. J.: Prentice-Hall, 1969.

Lehmann, Winfred P. *Historical Linguistics: An Introduction*. New York: Holt, Rinehart and Winston, 1962.

Meillet, A. *The Comparative Method in Historical Linguistics*. Paris: Librairie Honoré Champion, 1967.

Sturtevant, E. H. *Linguistic Change: An Introduction to the Historical Study of Language*. Chicago: University of Chicago Press, 1917.

psycholinguistics

Bar-Adon, Aaron, and Werner F. Leopold, eds. *Child Language: A Book of Readings*. Englewood Cliffs, N. J.: Prentice-Hall, 1971.

Brown, Roger. *Words and Things*. New York: The Free Press, 1958.

Chomsky, Noam. *Language and Mind*, enlarged ed. New York: Harcourt Brace Jovanovich, 1972.

Jakobovits, Leon A., and Murray S. Miron, eds. *Readings in the Psychology of Language*. Englewood Cliffs, N. J.: Prentice-Hall, 1967.

Oldfield, R. C., and J. C. Marshall, eds. *Language: Selected Readings*. Harmondsworth, Middlesex: Penguin Books, 1968.

Osgood, Charles E., and Thomas A. Sebeok. *Psycholinguistics*. Bloomington: Indiana University Press, 1965.

Saporta, Sol, ed. *Psycholinguistics*. New York: Holt, Rinehart and Winston, 1961.

anthropological linguistics

Burling, Robbins. *Man's Many Voices: Language in Its Cultural Context*. New York: Holt, Rinehart and Winston, 1970.

Greenberg, Joseph H. *Anthropological Linguistics: An Introduction*. New York: Random House, 1968.

Hoijer, Harry, ed. *Language in Culture*. Chicago: University of Chicago Press, 1954.

Hymes, Dell, ed. *Language in Culture and Society*. New York: Harper & Row, 1964.

Landar, Herbert. *Language and Culture*. New York: Oxford University Press, 1966.

Samarin, William J. *Field Linguistics: A Guide to Linguistic Field Work*. New York: Holt, Rinehart and Winston, 1967.

Whorf, Benjamin Lee. *Language, Thought, and Reality*. Cambridge, Mass.: M.I.T. Press, 1965.

stylistics

Freeman, Donald C., ed. *Linguistics and Literary Style*. New York: Holt, Rinehart and Winston, 1970.

Jacobs, Roderick A., and Peter S. Rosenbaum. *Transformations, Style, and Meaning*. Waltham, Mass.: Xerox College Publishing, 1971.

Love, Glen A., and Michael Payne, eds. *Contemporary Essays on Style*. Glenview, Ill.: Scott, Foresman, 1969.

Sebeok, Thomas A., ed. *Style in Language*. Cambridge, Mass.: M.I.T. Press, 1960.

miscellaneous

Cherry, Colin. *On Human Communication*. New York: John Wiley & Sons, 1961.

Fishman, Joshua A., ed. *Readings in the Sociology of Language*. The Hague: Mouton and Co., 1968.

Gelb, I. J. *A Study of Writing*. Chicago: University of Chicago Press, 1952.

Greenberg, Joseph H., ed. *Universals of Language*. Cambridge, Mass.: M.I.T. Press, 1966.

Hays, David G. *Introduction to Computational Linguistics*. New York: American Elsevier, 1967.

Langacker, Ronald W. *Fundamentals of Linguistic Analysis*. New York: Harcourt Brace Jovanovich, 1972.

Lenneberg, Eric H. *Biological Foundations of Language*. New York: John Wiley & Sons, 1967.

Lester, Mark, ed. *Readings in Applied Transformational Grammar*. New York: Holt, Rinehart and Winston, 1970.

Index

clause *(Cont.)*
    types of, 118, 251
    universal tendencies of, 251
cluster, 162-63, 252
Coahuiltecan, 234
cognate, 218-23
cognate set, 218-23, 236
Comanche, 234, 237
communication: animal. *See* animal
    communication
    language as an instrument of,
      21-27, 54
comparative method, 209-11, 212-24
competence, 34-36, 74, 88, 97, 240,
    241
complement clause, 117, 119-21,
    134-36, 252-53
complex sentences, 108-22, 128, 251
    defined, 109
complexity of language, 17, 18, 20,
    22-23, 95
compounds, 42-43, 81-83, 84, 250-51
conceptual structure, 91-92, 97-98
    complex, 109-12
    limits of, 96, 256
    relationship of, to surface
      structure, 92, 94, 95, 109-12,
      122-27
conditioning, 43
conjoining, 112-16, 128-30, 253
conjunct. *See* conjoining
conjunction. *See* conjoining
consonants: articulation of, 150-54
    aspirated, 151
    glottalized, 151-52, 181
    labialized, 151
    pharyngealized, 151
    position of vocal organs for,
      150-54
    retroflex, 181
    universal tendencies of, 250
    voicing, 151, 152
constituent: defined, 104
    function, in syntactic rules, 107
    types of, 104-08
coordination. *See* conjoining
Coos, 235
Coptic, 233
Cora, 234, 237

coreference, 130-31, 140, 143, 252
Cornish, 230
correctness: in speech, 56-57
    in spelling, 60
Costanoan, 235
creativity, linguistic, 14-15, 20, 21-23,
    35, 54, 58, 61, 256
Cree, 234
Creek, 234
Crow, 234
culture and language, 6-7, 16-17
Cupan, 236
Cupeño, 236
Cushitic, 232-33
Czech, 206, 230

Dalmatian, 229
Danish, 229
daughter language, 205-06, 237
Dayak, 232
deafness, influence of, on language
    acquisition, 14
Delaware, 234
dental consonant, 151, 152
derivation, 122-23, 136-41, 160-63
descriptive linguistics, 6, 9, 10
dialect geography, 48-52, 68
dialects, 47-58, 63, 197-201, 206
    diversification of, 50-52,
      199-201, 206
    geographical boundaries of,
      48-52, 58
    underlying uniformity of, 53,
      198-99
    written, 60-61
dictionary, 11, 30, 60-61
Dieoueño, 27, 235
discreteness of linguistic units, 73-74
distinctive differences, 155-63
Dravidian, 181, 231
Dutch, 45, 229

Egyptian, 232, 233
    orthography, 65
embedding, 112, 116-22, 133
empiricism, 4, 241-46
empty morpheme, 76, 253

language acquisition (*Cont.*)
   relation of, to language change,
     192-97
language change, 9, 17, 19, 56, 58,
   179-204
   See also external change;
    internal change
language family, 9, 206-07, 228-35
language reform, 57-58
language study, history of, 6-10, 11
language universal, 246-57
Laotian, 232
Lappish, 231
larynx, 147
laterals, 153
Latin, 8, 55, 61, 78, 79, 183, 187,
   191-92, 201, 205, 206, 208,
   229
   orthography, 66
Latvian, 230
learnèd words, 183
length, 155
lexical change, 76, 185-89
lexical items
   borrowing, 20, 179-85
   change in, 185-89, 192-97
   classes of, 101, 249
   coinage of, 20, 76, 186
   combination of, 79-84
   complex, 79-84, 186-87, 201-02
   composition of, 94, 248
   extension of, 20, 187
   loss of, 185-86
   See also borrowing
lexical morpheme, 75-77
lexicon, 30, 85
   defined, 79
linear order, 251
linguistic diversity, 16, 45-58
   causes of, 52-54, 58
   checks on, 54-58
linguistics: branches of, 6
   defined, 5
liquids, 153
Lisu, 236
literary style, 17, 60-61
Lithuanian, 230
liturgical language, 7, 61-62
loan translation, 180

loan words, 181-84
logographic writing system, 63
   development of, into syllabic,
    65-66
Lolo-Burmese, 236, 237
Low German, 229
low vowels, 148
Luiseño, 17, 99, 100, 143, 174, 234,
   236, 258-59
Luwian, 228
Lydian, 228

Macassar, 232
Maduran, 232
Maidu, 235
Malagasy, 232
Malay, 232
Malayalam, 231
Malayo-Polynesian, 232
Malinke, 233
Manchu, 231
Mandan, 234
Manx, 230
Maori, 204, 232
Marathi, 230
Maricopa, 235
Maru, 236
Mayan, 233
meaning, 7, 10, 11, 24-27, 90
   of sentences, 24, 91-92
   of words, 7, 24-27
   See also morpheme
Melanesian, 232
Menomini, 234
mental retardation, influence of, on
   language acquisition, 14
mental structure, relation to
   language, 4, 18, 21, 95-97
metaphor, 83-84, 86-87, 98, 187
metathesis, 168, 202
Miami, 234
Micmac, 234
mid vowels, 148-49
Missouri, 234
Miwok, 235
Mixteco, 233
modal, 105
Modoc, 235

J